*"Restaurant patrons
looking for quality dining have Zagat.
For the recruitment industry,
the name is Weddle ...
Peter Weddle that is."*

—American Staffing Association

What people are saying about WEDDLE's books and services:

As a Resource for Everyone:

"... a wealth of useful, updated information."

—*Library Journal*

"refreshingly unassuming and hype-free.... It's all excellent stuff...."

—Porter Anderson
CNN

"This book is a great resource.... It's like a travel guide to job boards."

—J.D.
BrassRing Systems

"WEDDLE's is the gorilla of knowledge and Web-sites when it comes to getting a job, managing human resources and recruiting on the Internet."

—Stone Enterprises, Ltd

As a Resource for Recruiters & HR Professionals:

"WEDDLE's is a very useful tool that recruiters and HR professionals will find helpful."

—*Fortune Magazine*

"The WEDDLE's Seminar has been held in cities around the country to rave reviews; in fact, more than 95% have said they found the seminars to be both very informative and very helpful."

—CareerJournal.com
from *The Wall Street Journal*

"When in doubt, consult WEDDLE's . . . an industry standard."

—*HRWIRE*

"Peter Weddle's Wednesday post-conference session, "Internet Recruiting Strategy Update" was rated highest at our Staffing Industry Management Institute, as well as at last year's Staffing Industry Executive Forum. Typical was this comment, '*Gave me up-to-date, now information that I could use immediately*'."

—Staffing Industry Report
Global Staffing Industry Report

". . . your newsletter is tremendously helpful to our recruiters. Keep up the fantastic work."

—S.W.
Harrahs

As a Resource for Job Seekers & Career Activists:

"The *WEDDLE's Job Seeker's Guide to Employment Web Sites* supplies clear, completely current information about each site's services, features and fees—helping users instantly determine which site best meets their needs. If you are looking for an objective guide to employment websites, ExecuNet recommends *WEDDLE's Guide*."

—ExecuNet
The Center for Executive Careers

"Here's one of the best Web-sites to visit and refer to regarding job-hunting. Look into it first . . . It'll provide you with a great competitive edge in the job market."

—S. B.,
Washington, D.C.

"Highly recommended!"

—Richard Nelson Bolles
author, *What Color Is You Parachute?*

Also by Peter Weddle

Career Fitness
A Vital Regimen for Building a Successful Work Life

CliffsNotes: Finding a Job on the Web

CliffsNotes: Writing a Great Resume

Computer-Based Instruction in Military Environments
(with Robert J. Seidel)

Electronic Resumes for the New Job Market

Generalship: HR Leadership in a Time of War

Internet Resumes: Take the Net to Your Next Job

Postcards From Space
Being the Best in Online Recruitment & HR Management
(2001, 2003)

The Hollow Enterprise
Why Investors in America's Companies Should Fear It;
Why the Leaders of America's Companies Must Fix It

'Tis of Thee
A Son's Search for the Meaning of Patriotism

WEDDLE's InfoNotes (WIN): Writing a Great Resume

WEDDLE's Recruiter's Guide to Employment Web Sites
(annually, 1999-2004)

WEDDLE's Job Seeker's Guide to Employment Web Sites
(annually, 2000-2004)

WEDDLE's Directory of Employment-Related Internet Sites
(annually, 2002-2004)

WEDDLE's Recruiter's Guide to Association Web Sites

WEDDLE's Guide

to Association Web Sites

2005/6

for
- *Recruiters & HR Professionals*
- *Job Seekers & Career Activists*

Peter Weddle

ISBN: 1-928734-29-4

Special discounts on bulk quantities of WEDDLE's books are available for libraries, corporations, professional associations and other organizations. For details, please contact WEDDLE's at 203.964.1888.

The information that appears in this Guide was obtained directly from the Web-sites themselves. Most of the data were collected in mid-to-late 2004. Each site completed an extensive questionnaire about its services, features and fees and then certified the accuracy of its responses. The Internet changes quickly, however, and we work continuously to keep our information current. If you find a discrepancy in a site's profile, please notify WEDDLE's by telephone at 203.964.1888 or on the Internet at corporate@weddles.com. We will contact the site, obtain the correct information and publish it on our Web-site (www.weddles.com) in the Free Book Updates area.

Thanks to Brian Weiss and Tom Ernst.

WEDDLE's
www.weddles.com
2052 Shippan Avenue
Stamford, CT 06902
Where People Matter Most

CONTENTS

for
Recruiters & Job Seekers
both of whom deserve the best resources available

Welcome!

Welcome to *WEDDLE's 2005/6 Guide to Association Web Sites.* This edition, our second, profiles over 1,800 Web-sites operated by professional, technical and trade associations in the United States and around the world. It is the most comprehensive listing in print of the online employment resources available at these organizations.

The Guide serves two important communities:

• **Those looking for talent**, including Employment Managers, in-house corporate recruiters and Human Resource practitioners, executive recruiters, staffing firm and agency recruiters, contract recruiters, and independent and consulting recruiters. If that's your job, this Guide will help you find and select the right association Web-sites to reach those individuals with the right skills for each of your recruiting requirements.

• **Those looking for employment opportunities**, including those actively searching for a new or better job, those setting the course for their career in the future, and those simply taking a peek at the job market out of curiosity. Whether you're a first time job seeker or a mid-career professional, a senior executive or an hourly worker, whether you want a full time position or part time, contract, consulting or free agent work, this Guide will help you find the right association Web-sites to succeed at your employment objective.

Why do recruiters and HR professionals and job seekers and career activists need such a guide?

For recruiters and HR professionals, it can lead to:

Higher Quality Candidates. Many of the best employment candidates—"A" level performers and passive job seekers—do not visit the large, general purpose recruitment sites operating on the Web. Instead, they feel more at home at the site(s) of their professional and/or trade association(s). Why? Because on those sites, they can interact with their peers and check career advancement opportunities that are directly relevant to them.

Lower Cost. According to WEDDLE's 9+ years of surveys among employment-related Internet sites, those operated by professional and trade associations now provide their job posting and resume search services at prices that are generally equal to those of the better commercial job boards. However, the association Web-sites are normally much less expensive than the print advertising and other recruitment resources traditionally used to reach the dedicated professionals and skilled tradespeople who are the members of those associations.

Additional Sourcing Resources. Unlike job boards, association Web-sites often serve as career portals. In essence, they provide an array of information and activities that enable their visitors to acquire expertise and advance their careers. One of the most important of the activities is a listserv or discussion forum where association members and/or site visitors can communicate with their peers. Those communications, in turn, provide a window through which recruiters can network with employment prospects and assess their knowledge and experience. Many if not most of these prospects are not looking for a job, but they are committed to their field and often make a significant contribution to the organization that employs them.

Better Yield. Almost every organization now sources candidates from the large, well known employment sites, so there's no distinction in doing so. However, those corporate and staffing firm recruiters who know where to look "off the online beaten track"— among smaller and less visible association sites—set themselves apart in the minds of top talent. Their presence on association sites signals that they recognize and respect the extraordinary contribution that is made by the best and brightest in a career field or industry. As a result, more of the truly superior prospects are likely to consider and ultimately apply for their openings.

For job seekers and career activists, it can lead to:

Better Employment Opportunities. General purpose job boards post employment opportunities in a wide range of career fields and industries. While that means that some of their openings will definitely be of interest to any particular job seeker or career activist, many of them will not. Every single one of the jobs posted at a professional association or trade organization site, on the other hand, will be relevant to and potentially appropriate for its members. They will be in the members' field and/or their industry. No less important, they are also more likely to be those special or rare jobs that very seldom come open.

Additional Resources for Success. The Web-sites of professional associations and trade organizations often offer information and activities that can help job seekers and career activists acquire additional expertise in their field and advance their career. One of the most important of the activities is the site's listserv or discussion forum. This feature enables the association's members to meet new colleagues and to network with their peers without having to leave the office or home. In addition, it provides a way for them to contribute to the dialogue in their field and to be noticed by recruiters, many of whom monitor these discussions to identify potential candidates for key openings.

A Way to Stand Out. A growing number of recruiters believe that the best candidates are those who demonstrate an interest in and commitment to their occupational field and/or industry. Hence, they often focus on those individuals who actively participate in their professional association and/or trade organization. As the use of such groups' Web-sites is normally limited to their members, recruiters know that those on the site are likely to be the caliber of candidate they seek. Rather than being lost among a huge and undifferentiated population of candidates on a general purpose job board, they are one of a select group of prospects that recruiters value.

More Effective Use of Your Time. We all have limits to the time we can spend online, and therefore, to the number of job boards we can visit. By devoting at least part of their time online to the sites of their local, regional and/or national professional and trade groups, job seekers and career activists can network with peers, check employment opportunities in their field and acquire occupational expertise that will position them for future success. That's not to say that they shouldn't visit other niche employment sites and general purpose job boards—they should—but rather to point out that association sites should always be among whatever sites they do visit.

Finally, this guide also assists recruiters, HR professionals, job seekers and career activists by identifying the top employment sites currently operating on the Internet. These selections were not made by WEDDLE's or by so-called Internet experts, but rather by the people who actually use the sites. Each year, we invite recruiters and job seekers to cast their ballots on the WEDDLE's Web-site (www.weddles.com) for the best job boards and career portals on the Internet. The thirty (30) sites with the most votes are designated User's Choice Award winners, the elite of the online employment industry. You'll find the 2005 winners listed on page 25.

There are now over 40,000 job boards and career portals operating on the Internet. Knowing which sites to use and where they are located online is the key to success, whether you're a recruiter or a job seeker, an HR professional or a career activist. The *WEDDLE's 2005/6 Guide to Association Web Sites* will help you to do just that ... and take advantage of the extraordinary employment resources that are available online.

All the Best,
Peter Weddle
Stamford, CT

About This Guide

This Guide presents the name, physical location and Internet address (also called the Universal Resource Locator or URL) of **over 1,800 association Web-sites** operating in the United States and around the world. It also indicates whether each site operates a job board, resume database and/or networking service (typically a listserv, discussion forum or bulletin board) for use by its members, the general public or both.

The Guide is designed to be used just as you would a traditional restaurant or travel guide. Sites are listed alphabetically by their name in one or more of three categories of classifications:

- **Occupational field** (e.g., accounting and finance, engineering, sales and marketing)

- **Industry** (e.g., banking, construction, healthcare, insurance)

- **Specialty** (e.g., computer hardware, diversity, military personnel)

In addition and where appropriate, sites are also organized according to their geographic focus. These sites are listed by:

- state in the United States,

- nation or region outside the United States, *or*

- international (i.e., supporting recruitment on a global basis).

For a complete list of the classifications used in the Guide, please see the **Site Classifications & Index** on Page 27.

HOW CAN THIS GUIDE HELP YOU?

The Guide lists associations, societies, institutes, colleges and academies serving a particular occupational field and industry. It will make sure that you don't overlook an appropriate Web-site that can help you and quickly identify those sites that are most likely to address your specific requirement or objective. In addition, it will help you to assess the employment-related capabilities on those sites and determine where best to invest your time online.

For example, whether you're a recruiter looking for candidates to fill a senior level finance position or a senior level finance professional seeking a new or better job, you can check the Guide's listings under two classifications:

- **Accounting and Finance**, where you would find 165 association Web sites, 71 of which have a job board, resume database or networking service;

- **Executive/Management** (where you would find 55 association Web sites, 35 of which have a job board, resume database or networking service.

We list sites that don't offer a job board, resume database or networking service because they can still be worth a visit. Oftentimes, they provide other resources that can be helpful in recruiting or job search. These include:

- full or partial online member directories for identifying potentially helpful contacts;

- on-site content areas where you can identify and interact with thought leaders and organizers in a particular field or industry;

- links to the Web-sites of corporate sponsors, facilitating the timely exchange of information and communication between prospective candidates and employers; *and*

- banner, button and other forms of advertising where organizations can promote their employment brand and provide a point of contact for questions and inquiries from prospective candidates.

There's no guesswork, no slogging through thousands of unrelated listings on a search engine and no wandering around the Internet trying to find what you need by hit or miss. The Guide enables you to identify just the association sites you need quickly and put their resources to work for you effectively. That's the way you maximize your ROI . . . your return on the Internet.

KEEPING OUR INFORMATION UP-TO-DATE

WEDDLE's makes every effort to keep the information it publishes current and up-to-date. The Internet, however, is always changing, and WEDDLE's is always seeking updates and/or corrections to its listings. If you find a discrepancy, please notify us at 203.964.1888 or on the Internet at corporate@weddles.com. We appreciate your assistance and pay careful attention to what you tell us.

Whenever we become aware of a change or discrepancy, we contact the appropriate site, obtain the correct information and then publish it on our Web-site for you and others to see. So, **log onto www.weddles.com regularly** and click on the link entitled Free Book Updates on our toolbar. It's the best way to stay on top of the ever-changing universe of helpful employment resources on the Internet.

Explanation of Terms

Each Site Profile in this Guide identifies the site by the name of the association it represents, its Universal Resource Locator (URL) or address on the Internet, and the location or geographic area (U.S. state, country, or international) the association serves. Then, additional information is provided under three headings:

- **Job Postings**
- **Resume Service**
- **Networking Service**

An explanation of these terms is provided below.

Job Postings

Indicates whether the site posts full time, part time, consulting and/or contract positions. These announcements can be stored in a searchable database or on a scrolling bulletin board that is accessible either by all site visitors or by association members only. In addition, some sites permit the linking of postings to the employer's or recruiter's own Web-site.

Resume Service

Indicates whether the site offers a database in which job seekers can archive their resume and/or an employment profile. This database may be open to all employers and recruiters or only to those who pay a fee, and it may or may not provide a feature to protect the job seeker's privacy (typically by controlling access to their contact and other identifying information).

Networking Service

Indicates whether the site offers a listserv, discussion forum, bulletin board or chat area that supports e-mail messaging among participants. This feature may be accessible by all site visitors or only by those who are association members. It may be limited to a discussion of one or more specific topics or to any professional topic of interest to the participants.

What is WEDDLE's?

WEDDLE's is a research, publishing, consulting and training firm specializing in HR leadership, employment, job search and career self-management.
Since 1996, WEDDLE's has conducted groundbreaking surveys of:

- recruiters and job seekers, *and*
- Web-sites providing employment-related services.

Our research and findings have been cited in such publications as *The Wall Street Journal, The New York Times,* and in *Money, Fortune,* and *Inc.* magazines.

WEDDLE's also publishes books, guides and directories that focus on organizations' acquisition and leadership of human capital and on individuals' achievement of their employment and career goals.
For recruiters and HR professionals, its publications include:

- *WEDDLE's bi-weekly e-Newsletter for Recruiters & HR Professionals* [FREE]
- *WEDDLE's 2005/6 Guide to Employment Web Sites* [UPDATED]
- *WEDDLE's 2005/6 Directory of Employment-Related Internet Sites* [UPDATED]
- *Postcards From Space: Being the Best in Online Recruitment & HR Management*
- *WEDDLE's 2005/6 Guide to Association Web Sites* [UPDATED]
- *The Keys to Successful Recruiting and Staffing*

- *Generalship: HR Leadership in a Time of War*
- *The Hollow Enterprise: Why Investors in America's Companies Should Fear It ... Why the Leaders of America's Companies Must Fix It* [NEW]

For job seekers and career activists, its publications include:

- *WEDDLE's bi-weekly e-Newsletter for Job Seekers & Career Activists* [FREE]
- *WEDDLE's 2005/6 Guide to Employment Web Sites* [UPDATED]
- *WEDDLE's 2005/6 Directory of Employment-Related Internet Sites* [UPDATED]
- *WEDDLE's 2005/6 Guide to Association Web Sites* [UPDATED]
- *Career Fitness: A Vital Regimen for Building a Successful Work Life* [NEW]
- *WizNotes: Fast Guides to Job Boards and Career Portals* [NEW] with tailored guides for:
    Engineers,
    Sales & Marketing professionals,
    Finance & Accounting professionals,
    Human Resource professionals,
    Managers & Executives, and
    Recent College Graduates
- *WizNotes: Finding a Great Job on the Web*
- *WizNotes: Writing a Great Resume*

WEDDLE's also provides consultation to organizations in the areas of:

- HR leadership,
- Human capital formation,
- recruitment strategy development,
- employment brand positioning and communication,
- recruitment process reengineering and optimization, *and*
- Web-site design, development and implementation.

WEDDLE's delivers private seminars and workshops on the following subjects:

- Best Practices in Internet recruiting
    for in-house corporate recruiters and managers
    for staffing firm recruiters and managers
- Retention Strategies
    for managers and supervisors
- Human Resource leadership.

WHO IS PETER WEDDLE?

Peter Weddle is a former recruiter and business CEO turned author and speaker. He writes a bi-weekly column for CareerJournal.com from *The Wall Street Journal* and two newsletters that are distributed worldwide. Weddle has also authored or edited over twenty books and written numerous articles for leading magazines and journals. He has been cited in *The New York Times, The Washington Post, The Boston Globe, U.S. News & World Report, The Wall Street Journal, USA Today* and numerous other publications and has spoken to trade and professional associations and corporate meetings all over the world.

2005 User's Choice Awards

RECRUITERS & JOB SEEKERS PICK
THE TOP SITES ON THE WEB

Who has the best insight on which employment sites are most helpful? We think the answer to that question is obvious ... *it's you*, the recruiters and job seekers who have used the sites. And, that's what the annual **WEDDLE's User's Choice Awards** are all about. It's your chance to:

- recognize the Web-sites that provide the best level of service and value to their visitors, *and*
- help others make best use of the employment resources online.

This year's winners—your selections—are announced on the next page.

For more information about the Awards and to cast your vote for the 2006 winners, please visit the WEDDLE's site at www.weddles.com and click on the Online Poll button on our Home Page.

WEDDLE's 2005
User's Choice Awards

The Elite of the Online Employment Industry

A/E/C Job Bank

America's Job Bank

Best Jobs USA

The Blue Line

CareerBank.com

CareerBuilder.com

CareerJournal.com

Casino Careers Online

ccJobsOnline.com

ComputerJobs.com

ConstructionJobs.com

craigslist

DICE

eFinancialCareers.com

EmploymentGuide.com

ExecuNet

GetaGovJob.com

Jobing.com

jobsinthemoney.com

LocalCareers.com

Medzilla

Monster.com

Net-Temps

RegionalHelpWanted

TopUSAJobs.com

TrueCareers

VetJobs.com

Vets4Hire.com

Workopolis

Yahoo! HotJobs.com

Site Classifications & Index

This section contains an alphabetical listing of all of the classifications under which association Web-sites are listed in the Guide. Sites are listed alphabetically in each classification by the name of the association which they represent. Associations may be listed in more than one classification depending on their occupational, industry and/or geographic focus.

NOTES
Favorite Sites / Useful Resources

WEDDLE's
2005/6 Guide
to Association Web-Sites

All association Web-site addresses and information regarding their online employment resources were obtained from public sources. Some addresses and/or information may have changed since publication of the Guide.

WEDDLE's 2052 Shippan Avenue, Stamford, CT 06902 All Rights Reserved.

-A-

Accounting/Finance

Academy of Economics and Finance
http://www.jeandf.org/academy.htm
Location: US
Job Postings: No   *Resume Service:* No   *Networking Service:* No

Academy of Financial Services
http://www.academyfinancial.org/
Location: US
Job Postings: No   *Resume Service:* No   *Networking Service:* No

Activity Based Costing Benchmarking Association
http://www.abcbenchmarking.com
Location: US
Job Postings: No   *Resume Service:* No   *Networking Service:* No

Alliance of Merger and Acquisition Advisors
http://www.advisor-alliance.com
Location: US
Job Postings: No   *Resume Service:* No   *Networking Service:* No

American Academy of Actuaries
http://www.actuary.org
Location: US
Job Postings: Yes   *Resume Service:* No   *Networking Service:* No

American Accounting Association
http://aaahq.org
Location: US
Job Postings: No   *Resume Service:* No   *Networking Service:* No

Notes

Favorite sites, useful resources

American Association for Budget and Program Analysis
http://www.aabpa.org
Location: US
Job Postings: Yes   *Resume Service:* No   *Networking Service:* No

American Bankers Association
http://www.aba.com
Location: US
Job Postings: Yes   *Resume Service:* Yes   *Networking Service:* No

American Bankruptcy Institute
http://www.abiworld.org
Location: US
Job Postings: Yes   *Resume Service:* Yes   *Networking Service:* No

American Economic Association
http://www.aeaweb.org
Location: US
Job Postings: Yes   *Resume Service:* No   *Networking Service:* No

American Finance Association
http://www.afajof.org
Location: US
Job Postings: Yes   *Resume Service:* No   *Networking Service:* No

American Financial Services Association
http://www.americanfinsvcs.com
Location: US
Job Postings: No   *Resume Service:* No   *Networking Service:* No

American Institute of Banking
http://www.aibonline.org
Location: US
Job Postings: No   *Resume Service:* No   *Networking Service:* No

American Institute of Certified Public Accountants
http://www.aicpa.org
Location: US
Job Postings: Yes   *Resume Service:* Yes   *Networking Service:* No

American Law and Economics Association
http://www.amlecon.org
Location: US
Job Postings: No   *Resume Service:* No   *Networking Service:* No

American Real Estate and Urban Economics Association
http://www.areuea.org
Location: US
Job Postings: No   *Resume Service:* No   *Networking Service:* No

Notes

Favorite sites, useful resources

American Real Estate Society
http://www.aresnet.org
Location: US
Job Postings: Yes   *Resume Service:* Yes   *Networking Service:* No

American Rehabilitation Economics Association
http://www.a-r-e-a.org
Location: US
Job Postings: No   *Resume Service:* No   *Networking Service:* No

American Risk and Insurance Association
http://www.aria.org
Location: US
Job Postings: No   *Resume Service:* No   *Networking Service:* No

American Society of Military Comptrollers
http://www.asmconline.org
Location: US
Job Postings: Yes   *Resume Service:* No   *Networking Service:* No

American Society of Women Accountants
http://www.aswa.org
Location: US
Job Postings: No   *Resume Service:* No   *Networking Service:* No

American Woman's Society of Certified Public Accountants
http://www.awscpa.org
Location: US
Job Postings: Yes   *Resume Service:* Yes   *Networking Service:* No

America's Community Bankers
http://www.acbankers.org
Location: US
Job Postings: No   *Resume Service:* No   *Networking Service:* No

Asian Development Bank
http://www.adb.org
Location: Asia
Job Postings: Yes   *Resume Service:* No   *Networking Service:* No

Association of American Geographers, Economic Geography Specialty Group
http://geog.uconn.edu/aag-econ/
Location: US
Job Postings: No   *Resume Service:* No   *Networking Service:* No

Association of Christian Economists
http://www.gordon.edu/ace/
Location: US
Job Postings: No   *Resume Service:* No   *Networking Service:* No

Notes

Favorite sites, useful resources

Association for Comparative Economic Studies
http://www.wdi.bus.umich.edu/aces/
Location: US
Job Postings: No   *Resume Service:* No   *Networking Service:* No

Association of Environmental and Resource Economists
http://www.aere.org/
Location: US
Job Postings: Yes   *Resume Service:* No   *Networking Service:* No

Association for Evolutionary Economics
http://www.orgs.bucknell.edu/afee/
Location: US
Job Postings: No   *Resume Service:* No   *Networking Service:* No

Association for Financial Professionals
http://www.afponline.org
Location: US
Job Postings: Yes   *Resume Service:* Yes   *Networking Service:* Yes

Association of Financial Technology
http://www.fitech.org/
Location: US
Job Postings: No   *Resume Service:* No   *Networking Service:* No

Association of Government Accountants
http://www.agacgfm.org
Location: US
Job Postings: Yes   *Resume Service:* Yes   *Networking Service:* No

Association of Healthcare Internal Auditors
http://www.ahia.org
Location: US
Job Postings: Yes   *Resume Service:* No   *Networking Service:* No

Association for Heterodox Economics
http://www.hetecon.com
Location: US
Job Postings: No   *Resume Service:* No   *Networking Service:* No

Association for Institutional Thought
http://afit.cba.nau.edu/
Location: US
Job Postings: No   *Resume Service:* No   *Networking Service:* No

Association for Investment Management and Research
http://www.cfainstitute.org
Location: US
Job Postings: Yes   *Resume Service:* No   *Networking Service:* No

Notes
Favorite sites, useful resources

Association of Investment Management Sales Executives
http://www.aimse.com
Location: US
Job Postings: No   *Resume Service:* No   *Networking Service:* No

Association of Investment Trust Companies
http://www.trustnet.com
Location: Europe - UK
Job Postings: No   *Resume Service:* No   *Networking Service:* No

Association for Management Information Services
http://www.amifs.org
Location: US
Job Postings: Yes   *Resume Service:* Yes   *Networking Service:* Yes

The Association of Practicing CPAs
http://www.ap-cpa.org
Location: US
Job Postings: No   *Resume Service:* No   *Networking Service:* No

Association of Private Enterprise Education
http://www.apee.org
Location: US
Job Postings: No   *Resume Service:* No   *Networking Service:* No

Association for Public Policy
http://www.appam.org
Location: US
Job Postings: Yes   *Resume Service:* No   *Networking Service:* No

Association for Social Economics
http://www.socialeconomics.org
Location: US
Job Postings: No   *Resume Service:* No   *Networking Service:* No

Association for the Study of the Grants Economy
http://www.grantseconomics.org
Location: US
Job Postings: No   *Resume Service:* No   *Networking Service:* No

Association for University Business and Economic Research
http://www.auber.org
Location: US
Job Postings: No   *Resume Service:* No   *Networking Service:* No

Australian Society of Certified Public Accountants
http://www.cpaonline.com.au
Location: Australia
Job Postings: Yes   *Resume Service:* Yes   *Networking Service:* Yes

Notes

Favorite sites, useful resources

Bank Administration Institute
http://www.bai.org
Location: US
Job Postings: No   *Resume Service:* No   *Networking Service:* No

Bank Marketing Association
http://www.bmanet.org
Location: US
Job Postings: Yes   *Resume Service:* No   *Networking Service:* No

Broker Management Council
http://www.bmsales.com
Location: US
Job Postings: No   *Resume Service:* No   *Networking Service:* No

Canadian Bankers Association
http://www.cba.ca
Location: North America - Canada
Job Postings: Yes   *Resume Service:* No   *Networking Service:* No

Canadian Institute of Actuaries
http://www.actuaries.ca
Location: North America - Canada
Job Postings: Yes   *Resume Service:* No   *Networking Service:* No

Canadian Institute of Chartered Accountants
http://www.cica.ca
Location: North America - Canada
Job Postings: Yes   *Resume Service:* Yes   *Networking Service:* No

Certified Commercial Investment Member
https://www.ccim.com/
Location: US
Job Postings: No   *Resume Service:* No   *Networking Service:* No

Certified Financial Planner Board of Standards
http://www.CFP-Board.org
Location: US
Job Postings: No   *Resume Service:* No   *Networking Service:* No

Certified General Accountants' Association of Canada
http://www.cga-canada.org
Location: North America - Canada
Job Postings: No   *Resume Service:* No   *Networking Service:* No

CFA Institute
http://www.cfainstitute.org
Location: US
Job Postings: Yes   *Resume Service:* No   *Networking Service:* No

Notes

Favorite sites, useful resources

Chartered Institute of Management Accountants
http://www.cimaglobal.com
Location: Europe - UK
Job Postings: Yes   *Resume Service:* Yes   *Networking Service:* Yes

Cliometric Society
http://www.eh.net/Clio
Location: US
Job Postings: No   *Resume Service:* No   *Networking Service:* No

Commercial Finance Association
http://www.cfa.com
Location: US
Job Postings: No   *Resume Service:* No   *Networking Service:* No

Commercial Investment Real Estate Institute
http://www.ccim.com
Location: US
Job Postings: No   *Resume Service:* No   *Networking Service:* No

Committee on the Status of Women in the Economics Profession
http://www.cswep.org/
Location: US
Job Postings: Yes   *Resume Service:* No   *Networking Service:* No

Committee on Women in Agricultural Economics
http://www.aaea.org/cwae/
Location: US
Job Postings: No   *Resume Service:* No   *Networking Service:* No

Consumer Bankers Association
http://www.cbanet.org
Location: US
Job Postings: No   *Resume Service:* No   *Networking Service:* No

CPA Associates International
http://www.cpaai.com
Location: US
Job Postings: No   *Resume Service:* No   *Networking Service:* No

Credit Professionals International
http://www.creditprofessionals.org
Location: US
Job Postings: No   *Resume Service:* No   *Networking Service:* No

Credit Union National Association
http://www.cuna.org
Location: US
Job Postings: No   *Resume Service:* No   *Networking Service:* No

Notes
Favorite sites, useful resources

Decision Sciences Institute
http://www.decisionsciences.org
Location: US
Job Postings: Yes *Resume Service:* No *Networking Service:* No

Economic Development Association
http://www.ag.iastate.edu/journals/rde/eda.htm
Location: US
Job Postings: No *Resume Service:* No *Networking Service:* No

EDucational INnovation in Economics and Business Network
http://www.fdewb4.unimaas.nl/edineb/index.htm
Location: US
Job Postings: No *Resume Service:* No *Networking Service:* No

Equipment Leasing and Finance Foundation
http://www.elaonline.com
Location: US
Job Postings: No *Resume Service:* No *Networking Service:* No

European Accounting Association
http://www.eaa-online.org
Location: Europe
Job Postings: Yes *Resume Service:* No *Networking Service:* Yes

Finance Leaders Association
http://www.financeleaders.org
Location: US
Job Postings: Yes *Resume Service:* No *Networking Service:* No

Financial Accounting Standards Board
http://www.fasb.org
Location: US
Job Postings: Yes *Resume Service:* No *Networking Service:* No

Financial Economics Network
http://www.ssrn.com/fen/
Location: US
Job Postings: Yes *Resume Service:* No *Networking Service:* No

Financial Economists Roundtable
http://www.luc.edu/orgs/finroundtable/
Location: US
Job Postings: No *Resume Service:* No *Networking Service:* No

Financial Executives International
http://www.fei.org
Location: US
Job Postings: Yes *Resume Service:* Yes *Networking Service:* No

Notes

Favorite sites, useful resources

The Financial Executives Network Group
http://www.thefeng.org
Location: US
Job Postings: No   *Resume Service:* No   *Networking Service:* No

Financial Institutions Insurance Association
http://www.fiia.org
Location: US
Job Postings: No   *Resume Service:* No   *Networking Service:* No

Financial Management Association International
http://www.fma.org
Location: International
Job Postings: Yes   *Resume Service:* No   *Networking Service:* No

Financial Managers Society
http://www.fmsinc.org
Location: US
Job Postings: Yes   *Resume Service:* Yes   *Networking Service:* Yes

The Financial Planning Association
http://www.fpanet.org
Location: US
Job Postings: No   *Resume Service:* No   *Networking Service:* Yes

Financial Services Technology Consortium
http://www.fstc.org
Location: US
Job Postings: No   *Resume Service:* No   *Networking Service:* No

Financial Women International
http://www.fwi.org
Location: US
Job Postings: Yes   *Resume Service:* Yes   *Networking Service:* No

Financial Women's Association
http://www.fwa.org
Location: US
Job Postings: No   *Resume Service:* No   *Networking Service:* No

Government Finance Officers Association
http://www.gfoa.org
Location: US
Job Postings: Yes   *Resume Service:* No   *Networking Service:* No

---

Looking for a new or better job?   Looking for top talent?
Use WEDDLE's publications. Visit www.weddles.com today.

Notes

Favorite sites, useful resources

Governmental Accounting Standards Board
http://www.gasb.org
Location:　　US
Job Postings: No　　　　*Resume Service:* No　　　　*Networking Service:* No

Healthcare Financial Management Association
http://www.hfma.org
Location:　　US
Job Postings: Yes　　　　*Resume Service:* No　　　　*Networking Service:* Yes

Hospitality Financial and Technology Professionals
http://www.hftp.org
Location:　　US
Job Postings: Yes　　　　*Resume Service:* Yes　　　　*Networking Service:* No

IEEE Neural Networks Society, Technical Committee on Computational Finance
http://www.ieee-nns.org/cf/
Location:　　US
Job Postings: No　　　　*Resume Service:* No　　　　*Networking Service:* No

Independent Community Bankers of America
http://www.icba.org
Location:　　US
Job Postings: No　　　　*Resume Service:* No　　　　*Networking Service:* No

Industrial Organization Society
http://www.mgmt.purdue.edu/faculty/smartin/ios/ios
Location:　　US
Job Postings: No　　　　*Resume Service:* No　　　　*Networking Service:* No

Industrial Relations Research Association
http://www.irra.uiuc.edu/
Location:　　US
Job Postings: Yes　　　　*Resume Service:* No　　　　*Networking Service:* No

Institute of Certified Financial Planners
http://www.icfp.org
Location:　　US
Job Postings: Yes　　　　*Resume Service:* No　　　　*Networking Service:* No

Institute of Certified Public Accountants in Singapore
http://www.accountants.org.sg
Location:　　Asia - Singapore
Job Postings: No　　　　*Resume Service:* No　　　　*Networking Service:* No

Institute of Chartered Accountants of British Columbia
http://www.ica.bc.ca
Location:　　North America - Canada
Job Postings: Yes　　　　*Resume Service:* No　　　　*Networking Service:* No

Notes

Favorite sites, useful resources

Institute of Chartered Accountants in Ireland
http://www.icai.ie
Location: Europe - Ireland
Job Postings: Yes   *Resume Service:* No   *Networking Service:* Yes

Institute of Chartered Accountants of Ontario
http://www.icao.on.ca
Location: North America - Canada
Job Postings: Yes   *Resume Service:* No   *Networking Service:* Yes

Institute of Fiscal Studies
http://www.ifs.org.uk
Location: Europe - UK
Job Postings: No   *Resume Service:* No   *Networking Service:* No

The Institute of Internal Auditors
http://www.theiia.org
Location: US
Job Postings: Yes   *Resume Service:* No   *Networking Service:* Yes

Institute of Internal Auditors—United Kingdom
http://www.iia.org.uk
Location: Europe - UK
Job Postings: Yes   *Resume Service:* No   *Networking Service:* No

Institute for International Economics
http://www.iie.com
Location: US
Job Postings: No   *Resume Service:* No   *Networking Service:* No

Institute of Management Accountants
http://www.imanet.org
Location: US
Job Postings: Yes   *Resume Service:* Yes   *Networking Service:* No

Institute of Psychology and Markets
http://www.psychologyandmarkets.org
Location: US
Job Postings: No   *Resume Service:* No   *Networking Service:* No

Insurance Accounting and Systems Association
http://www.iasa.org
Location: US
Job Postings: No   *Resume Service:* No   *Networking Service:* No

Inter-American Development Bank
http://www.iadb.org
Location: US
Job Postings: Yes   *Resume Service:* No   *Networking Service:* No

Notes

Favorite sites, useful resources

International Association of Financial Engineers
http://www.iafe.org
Location: US
Job Postings: Yes   *Resume Service:* No   *Networking Service:* No

International Association for Financial Planning
http://www.iafp.org
Location: US
Job Postings: No   *Resume Service:* No   *Networking Service:* No

International Association of Hospitality Accountants
http://www.hftp.org
Location: US
Job Postings: Yes   *Resume Service:* Yes   *Networking Service:* No

International Federation of Accountants
http://www.ifac.org
Location: US
Job Postings: No   *Resume Service:* No   *Networking Service:* No

International Finance and Commodities Institute in Geneva
http://finance.wat.ch/ifci/
Location: Europe
Job Postings: No   *Resume Service:* No   *Networking Service:* No

Investment Management Consultants Association
http://www.imca.org
Location: US
Job Postings: No   *Resume Service:* No   *Networking Service:* Yes

IS Financial Management Association
http://www.isfma.com
Location: US
Job Postings: No   *Resume Service:* No   *Networking Service:* No

ITAudit
http://www.theiia.org/itaudit/
Location: US
Job Postings: Yes   *Resume Service:* Yes   *Networking Service:* No

Keizai Society: US-Japan Business Forum
http://www.keizai.org
Location: US - California
Job Postings: No   *Resume Service:* No   *Networking Service:* No

Mortgage Bankers Association of America
http://www.mbaa.org
Location: US
Job Postings: Yes   *Resume Service:* Yes   *Networking Service:* No

Notes

Favorite sites, useful resources

National Associated CPA Firms
http://www.nacpaf.com
Location: US
Job Postings: No   *Resume Service:* No   *Networking Service:* No

National Association of Black Accountants
http://www.nabainc.org
Location: US
Job Postings: Yes   *Resume Service:* Yes   *Networking Service:* No

National Association for Business Economics
http://www.nabe.com
Location: US
Job Postings: Yes   *Resume Service:* No   *Networking Service:* No

National Association of Consumer Bankruptcy Attorneys
http://nacba.com
Location: US
Job Postings: No   *Resume Service:* No   *Networking Service:* No

National Association of Credit Management
http://www.nacm.org
Location: US
Job Postings: Yes   *Resume Service:* Yes   *Networking Service:* No

National Association of Economic Educators
http://ecedweb.unomaha.edu/naee.htm
Location: US
Job Postings: No   *Resume Service:* No   *Networking Service:* No

National Association of Enrolled Agents
http://www.naea.org
Location: US
Job Postings: Yes   *Resume Service:* No   *Networking Service:* No

National Association of Financial and Estate Planning
http://www.nafep.com
Location: US
Job Postings: No   *Resume Service:* No   *Networking Service:* No

National Association of Forensic Economics
http://nafe.net/
Location: US
Job Postings: No   *Resume Service:* No   *Networking Service:* No

National Association of Insurance and Financial Advisors
http://www.naifa.org/
Location: US
Job Postings: No   *Resume Service:* No   *Networking Service:* No

Notes
Favorite sites, useful resources

National Association of Mortgage Planners
http://www.namp.org
Location: US
Job Postings: No   *Resume Service:* No   *Networking Service:* No

National Association of Real Estate Investment Trusts
http://www.nareit.com
Location: US
Job Postings: No   *Resume Service:* No   *Networking Service:* No

National Association of Small Business Investment Companies
http://www.nasbic.org
Location: US
Job Postings: No   *Resume Service:* No   *Networking Service:* No

National Association of State Boards of Accountancy
http://www.nasba.org
Location: US
Job Postings: No   *Resume Service:* No   *Networking Service:* No

National Association of Tax Practitioners
http://www.natptax.com
Location: US
Job Postings: Yes   *Resume Service:* No   *Networking Service:* No

National Automotive Finance Association
http://www.nafassociation.com
Location: US
Job Postings: No   *Resume Service:* No   *Networking Service:* No

National Business and Economics Society
http://www.nbesonline.com/
Location: US
Job Postings: No   *Resume Service:* No   *Networking Service:* No

National Economic Association
http://www.ncat.edu/~neconasc/
Location: US
Job Postings: Yes   *Resume Service:* No   *Networking Service:* No

National Economists Club
http://www.national-economists.org/
Location: US
Job Postings: Yes   *Resume Service:* No   *Networking Service:* No

National Futures Association
http://www.nfa.futures.org
Location: US
Job Postings: No   *Resume Service:* No   *Networking Service:* No

Notes

Favorite sites, useful resources

National Investment Banking Association
http://www.nibanet.org
Location: US
Job Postings: No   *Resume Service:* No   *Networking Service:* No

National Investor Relations Institute
http://www.niri.org
Location: US
Job Postings: Yes   *Resume Service:* Yes   *Networking Service:* No

National Society of Accountants
http://www.nsacct.org
Location: US
Job Postings: No   *Resume Service:* No   *Networking Service:* No

National Tax Association
http://ntanet.org/
Location: US
Job Postings: No   *Resume Service:* No   *Networking Service:* No

National Venture Capital Association
http://www.nvca.org/
Location: US
Job Postings: No   *Resume Service:* No   *Networking Service:* No

New York Society of Security Analysts, Inc.
http://www.nyssa.org
Location: US - New York
Job Postings: No   *Resume Service:* No   *Networking Service:* No

Oklahoma Bankers Association
http://www.oba.com
Location: US - Oklahoma
Job Postings: Yes   *Resume Service:* Yes   *Networking Service:* No

Pennsylvania Institute of Certified Public Accountants
http://www.picpa.com
Location: US - Pennsylvania
Job Postings: Yes   *Resume Service:* Yes   *Networking Service:* Yes

Progressive Economic Forum
http://www.web.net/~pef/
Location: US
Job Postings: Yes   *Resume Service:* No   *Networking Service:* No

Public Choice Society
http://www.pubchoicesoc.org/
Location: US
Job Postings: No   *Resume Service:* No   *Networking Service:* No

Notes

Favorite sites, useful resources

Securities Industry Association
http://www.sia.com
Location:　　US
Job Postings: Yes　　　　*Resume Service:* No　　　　*Networking Service:* No

Society of Actuaries
http://www.soa.org/ccm/content/
Location:　　US
Job Postings: Yes　　　　*Resume Service:* Yes　　　　*Networking Service:* No

Society for the Advancement of Socio-Economics
http://www.sase.org/
Location:　　US
Job Postings: No　　　　*Resume Service:* No　　　　*Networking Service:* No

Society of Computational Economists
http://wuecon.wustl.edu/sce/
Location:　　US
Job Postings: No　　　　*Resume Service:* No　　　　*Networking Service:* No

Society for Economic Anthropology
http://nautarch.tamu.edu/anth/sea/
Location:　　US
Job Postings: Yes　　*Resume Service:*　　　No　　*Networking Service:*　　No

Society for Economic Botany
http://www.econbot.org/
Location:　　US
Job Postings: No　　　　*Resume Service:* No　　　　*Networking Service:* No

Society for Economic Dynamics
http://www.economicdynamics.org/society.htm
Location:　　US
Job Postings: No　　　　*Resume Service:* No　　　　*Networking Service:* No

Society of Economic Geologists
http://www.segweb.org/
Location:　　US
Job Postings: No　　　　*Resume Service:* No　　　　*Networking Service:* No

Society for Environmental Economics and Policy Studies
http://www.seeps.org/
Location:　　US
Job Postings: No　　　　*Resume Service:* No　　　　*Networking Service:* No

Society for Financial Studies
http://www.sfs.org/
Location:　　US
Job Postings: No　　　　*Resume Service:* No　　　　*Networking Service:* No

Notes

Favorite sites, useful resources

Society of Government Economists
http://www.sge-econ.org/
Location: US
Job Postings: Yes   *Resume Service:* No   *Networking Service:* No

Society for Judgment and Decision Making
http://www.sjdm.org/
Location: US
Job Postings: No   *Resume Service:* No   *Networking Service:* No

Society of Labor Economists
http://www-gsb.uchicago.edu/labor/sole.htm
Location: US
Job Postings: No   *Resume Service:* No   *Networking Service:* No

Society for Nonlinear Dynamics and Econometrics
http://www.snde.rutgers.edu/SNDE/society/snde.html
Location: US
Job Postings: No   *Resume Service:* No   *Networking Service:* No

Society for Policy Modeling
http://www.journalofpolicymodels.com/society.shtml
Location: US
Job Postings: No   *Resume Service:* No   *Networking Service:* No

South Dakota Bankers Association
http://www.sdba.com
Location: US - South Dakota
Job Postings: No   *Resume Service:* No   *Networking Service:* No

United States Association for Energy Economics
http://www.usaee.org/
Location: US
Job Postings: No   *Resume Service:* No   *Networking Service:* No

United States Society for Ecological Economics
http://www.ussee.org/
Location: US
Job Postings: Yes   *Resume Service:* No   *Networking Service:* No

Utah Association of CPAs
http://www.uacpa.org
Location: US - Utah
Job Postings: Yes   *Resume Service:* No   *Networking Service:* No

World Bank
http://www.worldbank.org
Location: International
Job Postings: Yes   *Resume Service:* No   *Networking Service:* No

Notes
Favorite sites, useful resources

Administrative/Clerical

American Academy of Medical Administrators
http://www.aameda.org
Location: US
Job Postings: Yes   *Resume Service:* No   *Networking Service:* No

American Academy of Professional Coders
http://www.aapcnatl.org
Location: US
Job Postings: Yes   *Resume Service:* Yes   *Networking Service:* No

American Association of Health Care Administrative Mgmt.
http://www.aaham.org
Location: US
Job Postings: Yes   *Resume Service:* No   *Networking Service:* No

American Association of Medical Transcriptionists
http://www.aamt.org
Location: US
Job Postings: Yes   *Resume Service:* No   *Networking Service:* No

American Society of Corporate Secretaries Incorporated
http://www.ascs.org
Location: US
Job Postings: Yes   *Resume Service:* No   *Networking Service:* No

Association of Legal Administrators
http://www.alanet.org
Location: US
Job Postings: Yes   *Resume Service:* No   *Networking Service:* No

Healthcare Billing & Management Association
http://www.hbma.com
Location: US
Job Postings: Yes   *Resume Service:* No   *Networking Service:* No

Institute of Management and Administration
http://www.ioma.com
Location: US
Job Postings: No   *Resume Service:* No   *Networking Service:* No

International Association of Administrative Professionals
http://www.iaap-hq.org
Location: International
Job Postings: No   *Resume Service:* No   *Networking Service:* No

Notes

Favorite sites, useful resources

The Manufacturing, Science and Finance Union
http://www.amicustheunion.org
Location: Europe - UK
Job Postings: No   *Resume Service:* No   *Networking Service:* No

National Association of Legal Assistants
http://www.nala.org
Location: US
Job Postings: No   *Resume Service:* No   *Networking Service:* No

National Association of Legal Secretaries
http://www.nals.org
Location: US
Job Postings: Yes   *Resume Service:* Yes   *Networking Service:* No

National Association Medical Staff Services
http://www.namss.org
Location: US
Job Postings: Yes   *Resume Service:* No   *Networking Service:* No

The National Association of Personal Financial Advisors
http://www.napfa.org
Location: US
Job Postings: Yes   *Resume Service:* No   *Networking Service:* No

The National Association of Professional Mortgage Women
http://www.napmw.org
Location: US
Job Postings: No   *Resume Service:* No   *Networking Service:* No

National Federation of Paralegal Associations
http://www.paralegals.org
Location: US
Job Postings: Yes   *Resume Service:* No   *Networking Service:* No

National Paralegal Association
http://www.nationalparalegal.org
Location: US
Job Postings: Yes   *Resume Service:* Yes   *Networking Service:* No

Advertising/Public Relations

Advertising Education Forum
http://www.aeforum.org
Location: Europe - UK
Job Postings: No   *Resume Service:* No   *Networking Service:* No

Notes

Favorite sites, useful resources

Advertising Research Foundation
http://www.arfsite.org
Location: US
Job Postings: No   *Resume Service:* No   *Networking Service:* No

American Academy of Advertising
http://advertising.utexas.edu/AAA/
Location: US
Job Postings: Yes   *Resume Service:* No   *Networking Service:* No

American Advertising Federation
http://www.aaf.org
Location: US
Job Postings: Yes   *Resume Service:* Yes   *Networking Service:* No

American Association of Advertising Agencies
http://www.aaaa.org
Location: US
Job Postings: No   *Resume Service:* No   *Networking Service:* No

Association of Hispanic Advertising Agencies
http://www.ahaa.org
Location: US
Job Postings: No   *Resume Service:* No   *Networking Service:* No

Association of National Advertisers
http://www.ana.net
Location: US
Job Postings: Yes   *Resume Service:* No   *Networking Service:* No

Cabletelevision Advertising Bureau
http://www.cabletvadbureau.com
Location: US
Job Postings: No   *Resume Service:* No   *Networking Service:* No

Council of Public Relations Firms
http://www.prfirms.org
Location: US
Job Postings: Yes   *Resume Service:* Yes   *Networking Service:* No

Imperial Polk Advertising Federation
http://www.polkadfed.com
Location: US
Job Postings: Yes   *Resume Service:* No   *Networking Service:* No

Independent Film & Television Alliance
http://www.ifta-online.org
Location: US
Job Postings: No   *Resume Service:* No   *Networking Service:* No

Notes

Favorite sites, useful resources

Institute of Canadian Advertising
http://www.ica-ad.com
Location: North America - Canada
Job Postings: No   *Resume Service:* No   *Networking Service:* No

Institute of Practitioners in Advertising
http://www.ipa.co.uk
Location: Europe - UK
Job Postings: Yes   *Resume Service:* No   *Networking Service:* No

Institute for Public Relations
http://www.instituteforpr.com
Location: US
Job Postings: No   *Resume Service:* No   *Networking Service:* No

International Advertising Association
http://www.iaaglobal.org
Location: International
Job Postings: Yes   *Resume Service:* No   *Networking Service:* No

International Public Relations Association
http://www.ipranet.org
Location: International
Job Postings: No   *Resume Service:* No   *Networking Service:* No

Internet Advertising Bureau
http://www.itsma.com
Location: US
Job Postings: No   *Resume Service:* No   *Networking Service:* No

Internet Marketing and Advertising Association
http://www.imaa.org
Location: US
Job Postings: No   *Resume Service:* No   *Networking Service:* No

Mail Advertising Service Association
http://www.masa.org
Location: US
Job Postings: No   *Resume Service:* No   *Networking Service:* No

National Association for Promotional and Advertising Allowances
http://www.napaa.org
Location: US
Job Postings: Yes   *Resume Service:* No   *Networking Service:* No

Outdoor Advertising Association of America
http://www.oaaa.org
Location: US
Job Postings: No   *Resume Service:* No   *Networking Service:* No

Notes

Favorite sites, useful resources

Point-of-Purchase Advertising Institute
http://www.popai.com
Location: International
Job Postings: No   *Resume Service:* No   *Networking Service:* No

Promotion Marketing Association
http://www.pmalink.org
Location: US
Job Postings: Yes   *Resume Service:* Yes   *Networking Service:* No

Public Relations Society of America
http://www.prsa.org
Location: US
Job Postings: Yes   *Resume Service:* Yes   *Networking Service:* Yes

Radio Advertising Bureau
http://www.rab.com
Location: US
Job Postings: No   *Resume Service:* No   *Networking Service:* No

Specialty Advertising Association of Greater New York
http://www.saagny.org
Location: US - New York
Job Postings: No   *Resume Service:* No   *Networking Service:* No

Television Bureau of Advertising
http://www.tvb.org
Location: US
Job Postings: Yes   *Resume Service:* No   *Networking Service:* No

Agriculture

American Agricultural Economics Association
http://www.aaea.org
Location: US
Job Postings: Yes   *Resume Service:* Yes   *Networking Service:* No

The American Association of Cereal Chemists
http://www.scisoc.org/aacc
Location: US
Job Postings: Yes   *Resume Service:* No   *Networking Service:* No

American Crop Protection Association
http://www.acpa.org
Location: US
Job Postings: No   *Resume Service:* No   *Networking Service:* No

Notes

Favorite sites, useful resources

American Farm Bureau Federation
http://www.fb.com
Location: US
Job Postings: No   *Resume Service:* No   *Networking Service:* No

American Feed Industry Association
http://www.afia.org
Location: US
Job Postings: No   *Resume Service:* No   *Networking Service:* No

American Seed Trade Association
http://www.amseed.com
Location: US
Job Postings: No   *Resume Service:* No   *Networking Service:* No

American Society of Agronomy
http://www.agronomy.org
Location: US
Job Postings: No   *Resume Service:* No   *Networking Service:* No

Committee on Women in Agricultural Economics
http://www.aaea.org/cwae/
Location: US
Job Postings: No   *Resume Service:* No   *Networking Service:* No

Council for Agricultural Science and Technology
http://www.cast-science.org
Location: US
Job Postings: No   *Resume Service:* No   *Networking Service:* No

Farm Equipment Manufacturers Association
http://www.farmequip.org
Location: US
Job Postings: No   *Resume Service:* No   *Networking Service:* No

International Dairy, Deli, Bakery Association
http://www.iddba.org
Location: International
Job Postings: Yes   *Resume Service:* No   *Networking Service:* No

National Agri-Marketing Association
http://www.nama.org
Location: US
Job Postings: No   *Resume Service:* No   *Networking Service:* No

National Alliance of Independent Crop Consultants
http://www.naicc.org
Location: US
Job Postings: No   *Resume Service:* No   *Networking Service:* No

Notes

Favorite sites, useful resources

National Council of Farmer Cooperatives
http://www.ncfc.org
Location: US
Job Postings: No   *Resume Service:* No   *Networking Service:* No

National Farmers Union
http://www.nfu.org
Location: US
Job Postings: No   *Resume Service:* No   *Networking Service:* No

Architecture

American Architectural Manufacturers Association
http://www.aamanet.org
Location: US
Job Postings: No   *Resume Service:* No   *Networking Service:* No

American Design and Drafting Association
http://www.adda.org
Location: US
Job Postings: Yes   *Resume Service:* Yes   *Networking Service:* No

American Institute of Architects
http://www.aia.org
Location: US
Job Postings: Yes   *Resume Service:* Yes   *Networking Service:* No

American Institute of Architects/e-Architect
http://www.e-architect.com
Location: US
Job Postings: Yes   *Resume Service:* Yes   *Networking Service:* Yes

American Institute of Architecture Students
http://www.aiasnatl.org
Location: US
Job Postings: Yes   *Resume Service:* No   *Networking Service:* No

American Institute of Building Design
http://www.aibd.org
Location: US
Job Postings: No   *Resume Service:* No   *Networking Service:* No

American Society of Landscape Architects
http://www.asla.org
Location: US
Job Postings: No   *Resume Service:* No   *Networking Service:* No

Notes

Favorite sites, useful resources

Building Research Establishment
http://www.bre.co.uk
Location: Europe – UK
Job Postings: No   *Resume Service:* No   *Networking Service:* No

Design Build Institute of America
http://www.dbia.org
Location: US
Job Postings: No   *Resume Service:* No   *Networking Service:* No

Design Management Institute
http://www.designmgt.org
Location: US
Job Postings: Yes   *Resume Service:* No   *Networking Service:* No

International Enterprise Architects Consortium
http://www.eaci.org
Location: US
Job Postings: No   *Resume Service:* No   *Networking Service:* No

National Architectural Accrediting Board
http://www.naab.org
Location: US
Job Postings: No   *Resume Service:* No   *Networking Service:* No

National Council of Architectural Registration Boards
http://www.ncarb.org
Location: US
Job Postings: No   *Resume Service:* No   *Networking Service:* No

National Organization of Minority Architects
http://www.noma.net
Location: US
Job Postings: Yes   *Resume Service:* No   *Networking Service:* No

Society of Design Administration
http://www.sdadmin.org
Location: US
Job Postings: Yes   *Resume Service:* No   *Networking Service:* No

The Society of Naval Architects and Marine Engineers
http://www.sname.org
Location: US
Job Postings: Yes   *Resume Service:* Yes   *Networking Service:* No

Looking for a new or better job?   Looking for top talent?
Use WEDDLE's publications. Visit www.weddles.com today.

Notes

Favorite sites, useful resources

Arts

American Society of Interior Designers
http://www.asid.org
Location: US
Job Postings: Yes   *Resume Service:* No   *Networking Service:* No

Art Dealers Association of America
http://www.artdealers.org
Location: US
Job Postings: No   *Resume Service:* No   *Networking Service:* No

Art Libraries Society of North America
http://www.arlisna.org
Location: US
Job Postings: Yes   *Resume Service:* No   *Networking Service:* No

Association of Art Museum Directors
http://www.aamd.org
Location: US
Job Postings: No   *Resume Service:* No   *Networking Service:* No

College Art Association
http://www.collegeart.org/
Location: US
Job Postings: Yes   *Resume Service:* Yes   *Networking Service:* No

International Association of Theatrical Stage Employees
http://www.iatse491.com
Location: International
Job Postings: Yes   *Resume Service:* No   *Networking Service:* No

National Assembly of State Arts Agencies
http://www.nasaa-arts.org
Location: US
Job Postings: Yes   *Resume Service:* No   *Networking Service:* No

National Association of Independent Artists
http://www.naia-artists.org
Location: US
Job Postings: No   *Resume Service:* No   *Networking Service:* No

National Endowment for the Arts
http://www.arts.endow.gov
Location: US
Job Postings: No   *Resume Service:* No   *Networking Service:* No

Notes
Favorite sites, useful resources

National Press Photographers Association
http://www.nppa.org
Location: US
Job Postings: No   *Resume Service:* No   *Networking Service:* No

Professional Photographers Association
http://www.ppa-world.org
Location: US
Job Postings: No   *Resume Service:* No   *Networking Service:* No

Society of Decorative Painters
http://www.decorativepainters.org
Location: US
Job Postings: No   *Resume Service:* No   *Networking Service:* No

Astronomy

American Astronomical Society
http://www.aas.org
Location: US
Job Postings: Yes   *Resume Service:* No   *Networking Service:* No

American Meteor Society
http://www.amsmeteors.org
Location: US
Job Postings: No   *Resume Service:* No   *Networking Service:* No

American Society for Gravitational and Space Biology
http://asgsb.indstate.edu
Location: US
Job Postings: Yes   *Resume Service:* No   *Networking Service:* No

Canadian Astronomical Society
http://www.casca.ca
Location: North America - Canada
Job Postings: No   *Resume Service:* No   *Networking Service:* No

European Association for Astronomy Education
http://www.algonet.se/~sirius/eaae.htm
Location: Europe
Job Postings: No   *Resume Service:* No   *Networking Service:* No

International Astronomical Union
http://www.iau.org
Location: International
Job Postings: No   *Resume Service:* No   *Networking Service:* No

Notes

Favorite sites, useful resources

The Planetary Society
http://planetary.org
Location: US
Job Postings: No   *Resume Service:* No   *Networking Service:* No

Students for the Exploration and Development of Space
http://www.seds.org
Location: US
Job Postings: No   *Resume Service:* No   *Networking Service:* No

Automotive

American Association of Motor Vehicle Administrators
http://www.aamva.net
Location: US
Job Postings: No   *Resume Service:* No   *Networking Service:* No

Association for Car and Truck Rental Independent and Franchisees
http://www.actif.org
Location: US
Job Postings: Yes   *Resume Service:* No   *Networking Service:* No

Automotive Oil Change Association
http://www.aoca.org
Location: US
Job Postings: No   *Resume Service:* No   *Networking Service:* No

Automotive Parts & Accessories Association
http://www.apaa.org
Location: US
Job Postings: No   *Resume Service:* No   *Networking Service:* No

Automotive Parts Manufacturers' Association
http://www.apma.ca
Location: North America - Canada
Job Postings: No   *Resume Service:* No   *Networking Service:* No

Automotive Recyclers Association
http://www.autorecyc.org
Location: US
Job Postings: No   *Resume Service:* No   *Networking Service:* No

Automotive Service Association
http://www.asashop.org
Location: US
Job Postings: Yes   *Resume Service:* No   *Networking Service:* No

Notes

Favorite sites, useful resources

European Association of Automotive Suppliers
http://www.clepa.be
Location: Europe
Job Postings: No   *Resume Service:* No   *Networking Service:* No

Independent Automotive Damage Appraisers Association
http://www.iada.org
Location: US
Job Postings: Yes   *Resume Service:* Yes   *Networking Service:* No

International Carwash Association
http://www.carcarecentral.com
Location: US
Job Postings: No   *Resume Service:* No   *Networking Service:* No

National Association of Minority Automobile Dealers
http://www.namad.com
Location: US
Job Postings: No   *Resume Service:* No   *Networking Service:* No

National Automotive Finance Association
http://www.nafassociation.com
Location: US
Job Postings: No   *Resume Service:* No   *Networking Service:* No

National Independent Automobile Dealers Association
http://www.niada.com
Location: US
Job Postings: No   *Resume Service:* No   *Networking Service:* No

National Institute for Automotive Service Excellence
http://www.asecert.org
Location: US
Job Postings: Yes   *Resume Service:* Yes   *Networking Service:* No

Society of Automotive Engineers
http://www.sae.org
Location: US
Job Postings: Yes   *Resume Service:* No   *Networking Service:* No

United Auto Workers
http://www.uaw.org/index2.cfm
Location: US
Job Postings: No   *Resume Service:* No   *Networking Service:* No

Looking for a new or better job?   Looking for top talent?
Use WEDDLE's publications. Visit www.weddles.com today.

Notes

Favorite sites, useful resources

Aviation/Aerospace

Aerospace and Electronic Systems Society
http://www.ewh.ieee.org/soc/aes/
Location: US
Job Postings: Yes   *Resume Service:* No   *Networking Service:* No

Aerospace Education Foundation
http://www.aef.org
Location: US
Job Postings: No   *Resume Service:* No   *Networking Service:* No

Aerospace Industries Association
http://www.aia-aerospace.org
Location: US
Job Postings: No   *Resume Service:* No   *Networking Service:* No

Air & Waste Management Association
http://www.awma.org
Location: US
Job Postings: Yes   *Resume Service:* No   *Networking Service:* No

Air Force Association
http://www.afa.org
Location: US
Job Postings: No   *Resume Service:* No   *Networking Service:* No

Air Transport Association
http://www.air-transport.org
Location: US
Job Postings: No   *Resume Service:* No   *Networking Service:* No

Aircraft Locknut Manufacturers Association
http://www.almanet.org
Location: US
Job Postings: No   *Resume Service:* No   *Networking Service:* No

Aircraft Owners and Pilots Association
http://www.aopa.org
Location: US
Job Postings: Yes   *Resume Service:* Yes   *Networking Service:* No

Airline Suppliers Association
http://www.airlinesuppliers.com
Location: US
Job Postings: No   *Resume Service:* No   *Networking Service:* No

Notes

Favorite sites, useful resources

American Association of Airport Executives
http://www.airportnet.org
Location: US
Job Postings: Yes   *Resume Service:* Yes   *Networking Service:* No

American Institute of Aeronautics and Astronautics
http://www.aiaa.org
Location: US
Job Postings: No   *Resume Service:* No   *Networking Service:* No

Aviation Distributors and Manufacturers Association
http://www.adma.org
Location: US
Job Postings: No   *Resume Service:* No   *Networking Service:* No

Experimental Aircraft Association
http://www.eaa.org
Location: US
Job Postings: No   *Resume Service:* No   *Networking Service:* No

General Aviation Manufacturers Association
http://www.generalaviation.org
Location: US
Job Postings: No   *Resume Service:* No   *Networking Service:* No

Helicopter Association International
http://www.rotor.com
Location: US
Job Postings: No   *Resume Service:* No   *Networking Service:* No

International Council of Aircraft Owner and Pilot Associations
http://www.iaopa.org
Location: International
Job Postings: No   *Resume Service:* No   *Networking Service:* No

National Air Traffic Controllers Association
http://www.natca.org
Location: US
Job Postings: No   *Resume Service:* No   *Networking Service:* No

National Air Transportation Association
http://www.nata-online.org
Location: US
Job Postings: No   *Resume Service:* No   *Networking Service:* No

National Association of Air Traffic Specialists
http://www.naats.org
Location: US
Job Postings: No   *Resume Service:* No   *Networking Service:* No

Notes
Favorite sites, useful resources

National Association of State Aviation Officials
http://www.nasao.org
Location: US
Job Postings: No   *Resume Service:* No   *Networking Service:* No

National Broadcast Pilots Association
http://www.nbpa.rotor.com
Location: US
Job Postings: No   *Resume Service:* No   *Networking Service:* No

National Business Aviation Association
http://www.nbaa.org
Location: US
Job Postings: No   *Resume Service:* No   *Networking Service:* No

Professional Aviation Maintenance Association
http://www.pama.org
Location: US
Job Postings: No   *Resume Service:* No   *Networking Service:* No

Students for the Exploration and Development of Space
http://www.seds.org
Location: US
Job Postings: No   *Resume Service:* No   *Networking Service:* No

-B-

Banking

Alliance of Merger and Acquisition Advisors
http://www.advisor-alliance.com
Location: US
Job Postings: No   *Resume Service:* No   *Networking Service:* No

American Bankers Association
http://www.aba.com
Location: US
Job Postings: Yes   *Resume Service:* Yes   *Networking Service:* No

American Bankruptcy Institute
http://www.abiworld.org
Location: US
Job Postings: Yes   *Resume Service:* Yes   *Networking Service:* No

---

Looking for a new or better job?   Looking for top talent?
Use WEDDLE's publications. Visit www.weddles.com today.

Notes

Favorite sites, useful resources

American Institute of Banking
http://www.aibonline.org
Location: US
Job Postings: No   *Resume Service:* No   *Networking Service:* No

America's Community Bankers
http://www.acbankers.org
Location: US
Job Postings: No   *Resume Service:* No   *Networking Service:* No

Asian Development Bank
http://www.adb.org
Location: Asia
Job Postings: Yes   *Resume Service:* No   *Networking Service:* No

Association for Investment Management and Research
http://www.cfainstitute.org
Location: US
Job Postings: Yes   *Resume Service:* No   *Networking Service:* No

Association of Investment Management Sales Executives
http://www.aimse.com
Location: US
Job Postings: No   *Resume Service:* No   *Networking Service:* No

Association of Investment Trust Companies
http://www.trustnet.com
Location: Europe - UK
Job Postings: No   *Resume Service:* No   *Networking Service:* No

Bank Administration Institute
http://www.bai.org
Location: US
Job Postings: No   *Resume Service:* No   *Networking Service:* No

Bank Marketing Association
http://www.bmanet.org
Location: US
Job Postings: Yes   *Resume Service:* No   *Networking Service:* No

Canadian Bankers Association
http://www.cba.ca
Location: North America - Canada
Job Postings: Yes   *Resume Service:* No   *Networking Service:* No

Consumer Bankers Association
http://www.cbanet.org
Location: US
Job Postings: No   *Resume Service:* No   *Networking Service:* No

Notes

Favorite sites, useful resources

Credit Professionals International
http://www.creditprofessionals.org
Location: US
Job Postings: No   *Resume Service:* No   *Networking Service:* No

Credit Union Executives Society
http://www.cues.org
Location: US
Job Postings: Yes   *Resume Service:* No   *Networking Service:* No

Credit Union National Association
http://www.cuna.org
Location: US
Job Postings: No   *Resume Service:* No   *Networking Service:* No

Gold Institute
http://www.goldinstitute.org
Location: US
Job Postings: Yes   *Resume Service:* No   *Networking Service:* No

Independent Community Bankers of America
http://www.icba.org
Location: US
Job Postings: No   *Resume Service:* No   *Networking Service:* No

Institute of Fiscal Studies
http://www.ifs.org.uk
Location: Europe - UK
Job Postings: No   *Resume Service:* No   *Networking Service:* No

Inter-American Development Bank
http://www.iadb.org
Location: US
Job Postings: Yes   *Resume Service:* No   *Networking Service:* No

Investment Management Consultants Association
http://www.imca.org
Location: US
Job Postings: No   *Resume Service:* No   *Networking Service:* Yes

Mortgage Bankers Association of America
http://www.mbaa.org
Location: US
Job Postings: Yes   *Resume Service:* Yes   *Networking Service:* No

National Association of Credit Management
http://www.nacm.org
Location: US
Job Postings: Yes   *Resume Service:* Yes   *Networking Service:* No

Notes

Favorite sites, useful resources

National Association of Mortgage Planners
http://www.namp.org
Location: US
Job Postings: No   *Resume Service:* No   *Networking Service:* No

The National Association of Professional Mortgage Women
http://www.napmw.org
Location: US
Job Postings: No   *Resume Service:* No   *Networking Service:* No

National Investment Banking Association
http://www.nibanet.org
Location: US
Job Postings: No   *Resume Service:* No   *Networking Service:* No

National Investor Relations Institute
http://www.niri.org
Location: US
Job Postings: Yes   *Resume Service:* Yes   *Networking Service:* No

Oklahoma Bankers Association
http://www.oba.com
Location: US - Oklahoma
Job Postings: Yes   *Resume Service:* Yes   *Networking Service:* No

Securities Industry Association
http://www.sia.com
Location: US
Job Postings: Yes   *Resume Service:* No   *Networking Service:* No

South Dakota Bankers Association
http://www.sdba.com
Location: US - South Dakota
Job Postings: No   *Resume Service:* No   *Networking Service:* No

World Bank
http://www.worldbank.org
Location: International
Job Postings: Yes   *Resume Service:* No   *Networking Service:* No

Biology/Biotechnology

American Institute of Biological Sciences
http://www.aibs.org
Location: US
Job Postings: Yes   *Resume Service:* No   *Networking Service:* No

Notes

Favorite sites, useful resources

American Society of Animal Science
http://www.asas.org
Location: US
Job Postings: Yes   *Resume Service:* Yes   *Networking Service:* No

American Society for Gravitational and Space Biology
http://asgsb.indstate.edu
Location: US
Job Postings: Yes   *Resume Service:* No   *Networking Service:* No

American Society for Microbiology
http://www.asm.org
Location: US
Job Postings: Yes   *Resume Service:* Yes   *Networking Service:* No

American Society of Plant Physiologists
http://www.aspb.org
Location: US
Job Postings: Yes   *Resume Service:* No   *Networking Service:* No

Analytical and Life Science Systems Association
http://www.alssa.org
Location: US
Job Postings: No   *Resume Service:* No   *Networking Service:* No

Biotechnology Industry Organization
http://www.bio.org
Location: US
Job Postings: No   *Resume Service:* No   *Networking Service:* No

Federation of American Societies for Experimental Biology
http://www.faseb.org
Location: US
Job Postings: Yes   *Resume Service:* No   *Networking Service:* No

International Society for Genetic and Evolutionary Computation
http://www.isgec.org
Location: US
Job Postings: No   *Resume Service:* No   *Networking Service:* No

National Association of Biology Teachers
http://www.nabt.org
Location: US
Job Postings: No   *Resume Service:* No   *Networking Service:* No

Society for Economic Botany
http://www.econbot.org/
Location: US
Job Postings: No   *Resume Service:* No   *Networking Service:* No

Notes

Favorite sites, useful resources

Society for Experimental Biology and Medicine
http://www.sebm.org
Location: US
Job Postings: No   *Resume Service:* No   *Networking Service:* No

Washington Biotechnology Biomedical Association
http://www.wabio.com
Location: US - Washington
Job Postings: No   *Resume Service:* No   *Networking Service:* No

Building/Real Estate Management

American Industrial Real Estate Association
http://www.airea.com
Location: US
Job Postings: No   *Resume Service:* No   *Networking Service:* No

American Land Title Association
http://www.alta.org
Location: US
Job Postings: No   *Resume Service:* No   *Networking Service:* No

American Real Estate Society
http://www.aresnet.org
Location: US
Job Postings: Yes   *Resume Service:* No   *Networking Service:* No

American Real Estate and Urban Economics Association
http://www.areuea.org
Location: US
Job Postings: No   *Resume Service:* No   *Networking Service:* No

Associated Builders and Contractors
http://www.abc.org
Location: US
Job Postings: No   *Resume Service:* No   *Networking Service:* No

Association for Facilities Engineering
http://www.afe.org
Location: US
Job Postings: Yes   *Resume Service:* Yes   *Networking Service:* No

Building Owners and Mangers Association International
http://www.boma.org
Location: International
Job Postings: No   *Resume Service:* No   *Networking Service:* No

Notes
Favorite sites, useful resources

California Association of Realtors
http://www.car.org
Location: US - California
Job Postings: No   *Resume Service:* No   *Networking Service:* No

Commercial Investment Real Estate Institute
http://www.ccim.com
Location: US
Job Postings: No   *Resume Service:* No   *Networking Service:* No

Dallas Building Owners & Managers Association
http://www.bomadallas.org
Location: US - Texas
Job Postings: No   *Resume Service:* No   *Networking Service:* No

For Sale By Owner Association
tp://www.fsboa.com
Location: US
Job Postings: No   *Resume Service:* No   *Networking Service:* No

Greater Rochester Association of Realtors
http://www.homesteadnet.com
Location: US - New York
Job Postings: No   *Resume Service:* No   *Networking Service:* No

Institute of Real Estate Management
http://www.irem.org
Location: US
Job Postings: Yes   *Resume Service:* No   *Networking Service:* No

International Association of Corporate Real Estate Executives
http://www.nacore.com
Location: International
Job Postings: Yes   *Resume Service:* Yes   *Networking Service:* No

International Conference of Building Officials
http://www.icbo.org
Location: International
Job Postings: No   *Resume Service:* No   *Networking Service:* No

International Council of Shopping Centers
http://www.icsc.org
Location: US
Job Postings: Yes   *Resume Service:* Yes   *Networking Service:* No

International Facilities Management Association
http://www.ifma.org
Location: US
Job Postings: Yes   *Resume Service:* Yes   *Networking Service:* No

Notes

Favorite sites, useful resources

International Real Estate Institute
http://www.iami.org/irei.html
Location: International
Job Postings: No   *Resume Service:* No   *Networking Service:* No

Mortgage Bankers Association of America
http://www.mbaa.org
Location: US
Job Postings: Yes   *Resume Service:* Yes   *Networking Service:* No

National Association of Home Builders
http://www.nahb.com
Location: US
Job Postings: No   *Resume Service:* No   *Networking Service:* No

National Association of Home Inspectors
http://www.nahi.org
Location: US
Job Postings: No   *Resume Service:* No   *Networking Service:* No

National Association of Mortgage Planners
http://www.namp.org
Location: US
Job Postings: No   *Resume Service:* No   *Networking Service:* No

The National Association of Professional Mortgage Women
http://www.napmw.org
Location: US
Job Postings: No   *Resume Service:* No   *Networking Service:* No

National Association of Real Estate Appraisers
http://iami.org/narea.html
Location: US
Job Postings: Yes   *Resume Service:* No   *Networking Service:* No

National Association of Real Estate Investment Trusts
http://www.nareit.com
Location: US
Job Postings: No   *Resume Service:* No   *Networking Service:* No

National Association of Real Estate Publishers
http://www.narep.com
Location: US
Job Postings: No   *Resume Service:* No   *Networking Service:* No

National Association of Realtors
http://www.realtor.com
Location: US
Job Postings: No   *Resume Service:* No   *Networking Service:* No

Notes

Favorite sites, useful resources

National Association of Residential Property Managers
http://www.narpm.org
Location: US
Job Postings: No   *Resume Service:* No   *Networking Service:* No

National Network of Commercial Real Estate Women
http://www.nncrew.org
Location: US
Job Postings: Yes   *Resume Service:* No   *Networking Service:* No

National Property Management Association
http://www.npma.org
Location: US
Job Postings: No   *Resume Service:* No   *Networking Service:* No

Society of Industrial and Office Realtors
http://www.sior.com
Location: US
Job Postings: No   *Resume Service:* No   *Networking Service:* No

St. Augustine and St. Johns County Board of Realtors
http://www.bor.com
Location: US - Arizona
Job Postings: No   *Resume Service:* No   *Networking Service:* No

Wisconsin Realtors Association
http://www.wra.org
Location: US - Wisconsin
Job Postings: No   *Resume Service:* No   *Networking Service:* No

Women's Council of Realtors
http://www.wcr.org
Location: US
Job Postings: No   *Resume Service:* No   *Networking Service:* No

Business

American Association of Home Based Businesses
http://www.aahbb.org
Location: US
Job Postings: No   *Resume Service:* No   *Networking Service:* No

American Business Women's Association
http://www.abwahq.org
Location: US
Job Postings: Yes   *Resume Service:* Yes   *Networking Service:* No

Notes

Favorite sites, useful resources

American Corporate Counsel Association
http://www.acca.com
Location: US
Job Postings: Yes   *Resume Service:* No   *Networking Service:* No

The American E-Commerce Association
http://www.aeaus.com/
Location: US
Job Postings: No   *Resume Service:* No   *Networking Service:* No

American Evaluation Association
http://www.eval.org
Location: US
Job Postings: Yes   *Resume Service:* Yes   *Networking Service:* No

American Management Association
http://www.amanet.org
Location: US
Job Postings: No   *Resume Service:* No   *Networking Service:* No

Association for Corporate Growth
http://www.acg.org
Location: US
Job Postings: Yes   *Resume Service:* No   *Networking Service:* No

Association for International Business
http://www.aib-world.org
Location: International
Job Postings: No   *Resume Service:* No   *Networking Service:* No

Association of Management Consulting Firms
http://www.amcf.org
Location: US
Job Postings: Yes   *Resume Service:* No   *Networking Service:* No

The Association of MBAs
http://www.mba.org.uk
Location: Europe - UK
Job Postings: Yes   *Resume Service:* Yes   *Networking Service:* No

Association for University Business and Economic Research
http://www.auber.org
Location: US
Job Postings: No   *Resume Service:* No   *Networking Service:* No

Black Business Association
http://www.bbala.org
Location: US
Job Postings: No   *Resume Service:* No   *Networking Service:* No

Notes

Favorite sites, useful resources

Business Marketing Association
http://www.marketing.org
Location: US
Job Postings: Yes   *Resume Service:* Yes   *Networking Service:* No

California Association of Employers
http://www.employers.org
Location: US - California
Job Postings: No   *Resume Service:* No   *Networking Service:* No

Canadian Association for Business Economics
http://www.cabe.ca
Location: North America - Canada
Job Postings: Yes   *Resume Service:* No   *Networking Service:* No

The Conference Board
http://www.conference-board.org
Location: US
Job Postings: Yes   *Resume Service:* No   *Networking Service:* No

Corporation for Enterprise Development
http://www.cfed.org
Location: US
Job Postings: No   *Resume Service:* No   *Networking Service:* No

EDucational INnovation in Economics and Business Network
http://www.fdewb4.unimaas.nl/edineb/index.htm
Location: US
Job Postings: No   *Resume Service:* No   *Networking Service:* No

Global Arbitration Mediation Association
http://www.gama.com
Location: US
Job Postings: No   *Resume Service:* No   *Networking Service:* No

Healthcare Business Women's Association
http://www.hbanet.org/
Location: US
Job Postings: No   *Resume Service:* No   *Networking Service:* No

Healthcare Financial Management Association
http://www.hfma.org
Location: US
Job Postings: Yes   *Resume Service:* No   *Networking Service:* Yes

Home Office Association of America
http://www.hoaa.com
Location: US
Job Postings: No   *Resume Service:* No   *Networking Service:* No

Notes
Favorite sites, useful resources

Home-Based Working Moms
http://www.hbwm.com
Location: US
Job Postings: Yes   *Resume Service:* No   *Networking Service:* No

Institute for Business and Professional Ethics
http://condor.depaul.edu/ethics/
Location: US
Job Postings: No   *Resume Service:* No   *Networking Service:* No

Institute of Certified E-Commerce Consultants
http://certifiedcecommerceconsultant.com
Location: US
Job Postings: No   *Resume Service:* No   *Networking Service:* No

International Association of Business Communicators
http://www.iabc.com
Location: International
Job Postings: Yes   *Resume Service:* No   *Networking Service:* No

International Association of Conventions and Visitors Bureaus
http://www.iacvb.org
Location: International
Job Postings: No   *Resume Service:* No   *Networking Service:* No

International Council for Small Business
http://www.usasbe.org
Location: International
Job Postings: No   *Resume Service:* No   *Networking Service:* No

International Franchise Association
http://www.franchise.org
Location: International
Job Postings: Yes   *Resume Service:* No   *Networking Service:* No

International Telework Association & Council
http://www.telecommute.org
Location: International
Job Postings: No   *Resume Service:* No   *Networking Service:* No

Keizai Society: US-Japan Business Forum
http://www.keizai.org
Location: US - California
Job Postings: No   *Resume Service:* No   *Networking Service:* No

Mothers' Home Business Network
http://www.homeworkingmom.com
Location: US
Job Postings: Yes   *Resume Service:* No   *Networking Service:* No

Notes
Favorite sites, useful resources

National Association of American Business Clubs
http://www.ambucs.com
Location:　　US
Job Postings: No　　　　*Resume Service:* No　　　　*Networking Service:* No

National Association for Business Economics
http://www.nabe.com
Location:　　US
Job Postings: Yes　　　　*Resume Service:* No　　　　*Networking Service:* No

National Association of Church Business Administration
http://www.nacba.net
Location:　　US
Job Postings: Yes　　　　*Resume Service:* No　　　　*Networking Service:* No

National Association of College and University Business Officers
http://www.nacubo.org
Location:　　US
Job Postings: Yes　　　　*Resume Service:* Yes　　　　*Networking Service:* No

National Association of Computer Consultant Businesses
http://www.naccb.org
Location:　　US
Job Postings: No　　　　*Resume Service:* No　　　　*Networking Service:* No

National Association for Female Executives
http://www.nafe.com
Location:　　US
Job Postings: No　　　　*Resume Service:* No　　　　*Networking Service:* No

National Association of Home Based Businesses
http://www.usahomebusiness.com
Location:　　US
Job Postings: Yes　　　　*Resume Service:* No　　　　*Networking Service:* No

National Association of Independent Fee Appraisers
http://www.naifa.com
Location:　　US
Job Postings: No　　　　*Resume Service:* No　　　　*Networking Service:* No

National Association of Professional Organizers
http://www.napo.net
Location:　　US
Job Postings: No　　　　*Resume Service:* No　　　　*Networking Service:* No

The National Association for the Self Employed
http://www.nase.org
Location:　　US
Job Postings: No　　　　*Resume Service:* No　　　　*Networking Service:* No

Notes

Favorite sites, useful resources

National Association of Small Business Investment Companies
http://www.nasbic.org
Location: US
Job Postings: No   *Resume Service:* No   *Networking Service:* No

National Association of Women Business Owners
http://www.nawbo.org
Location: US
Job Postings: No   *Resume Service:* No   *Networking Service:* No

National Black MBA Association, Inc.
http://www.nbmbaa.org
Location: US
Job Postings: Yes   *Resume Service:* No   *Networking Service:* No

National Business and Economics Society
http://www.nbesonline.com/
Location: US
Job Postings: No   *Resume Service:* No   *Networking Service:* No

The National Business Incubation Association
http://www.nbia.org
Location: US
Job Postings: Yes   *Resume Service:* No   *Networking Service:* No

National Small Business United
http://www.nsbu.org
Location: US
Job Postings: No   *Resume Service:* No   *Networking Service:* No

National Society of Hispanic MBAs
http://www.nshmba.org
Location: US
Job Postings: Yes   *Resume Service:* Yes   *Networking Service:* No

Occupational Safety and Health Administration, OSHA
http://www.osha.gov
Location: US
Job Postings: No   *Resume Service:* No   *Networking Service:* No

Radiology Business Management Association
http://www.rbma.org
Location: US
Job Postings: Yes   *Resume Service:* No   *Networking Service:* No

Society for Industrial & Organizational Psychology
http://www.siop.org
Location: US
Job Postings: Yes   *Resume Service:* No   *Networking Service:* No

Notes

Favorite sites, useful resources

Society of Research Administrators
http://www.srainternational.org
Location: US
Job Postings: Yes   *Resume Service:* Yes   *Networking Service:* Yes

Technical Business Network
http://www.techbiz.com
Location: US
Job Postings: No   *Resume Service:* No   *Networking Service:* No

Toastmasters International
http://www.toastmasters.org
Location: US
Job Postings: No   *Resume Service:* No   *Networking Service:* No

United States Chamber of Commerce
http://www.uschamber.org
Location: US
Job Postings: Yes   *Resume Service:* No   *Networking Service:* No

US Small Business Administration
http://www.sba.gov
Location: US
Job Postings: Yes   *Resume Service:* No   *Networking Service:* No

Young Entrepreneurs Organization
http://www.yeo.org
Location: US
Job Postings: No   *Resume Service:* No   *Networking Service:* Yes

-C-

Career Counseling

Association of Career Professionals
http://www.acpinternational.org
Location: US
Job Postings: No   *Resume Service:* Yes   *Networking Service:* No

National Career Development Association
http://www.ncda.org
Location: US
Job Postings: No   *Resume Service:* No   *Networking Service:* No

Looking for a new or better job?   Looking for top talent?
Use WEDDLE's publications. Visit www.weddles.com today.

Notes
Favorite sites, useful resources

National Resume Writers Association
http://www.nrwa.com
Location: US
Job Postings: No   *Resume Service:* No   *Networking Service:* No

Professional Association of Resume Writers
http://www.parw.com
Location: US
Job Postings: No   *Resume Service:* No   *Networking Service:* No

Chemistry

Adhesion Society
http://www.adhesionsociety.org
Location: US
Job Postings: No   *Resume Service:* No   *Networking Service:* No

The American Association of Cereal Chemists
http://www.scisoc.org/aacc
Location: US
Job Postings: Yes   *Resume Service:* No   *Networking Service:* No

American Association for Clinical Chemistry
http://www.aacc.org/
Location: US
Job Postings: Yes   *Resume Service:* Yes   *Networking Service:* No

American Association of Textile Chemists and Colorists
http://www.aatcc.org/
Location: US
Job Postings: Yes   *Resume Service:* Yes   *Networking Service:* No

American Chemical Society
http://www.acs.org
Location: US
Job Postings: Yes   *Resume Service:* Yes   *Networking Service:* No

American Institute of Chemical Engineers
http://www.aiche.org
Location: US
Job Postings: Yes   *Resume Service:* Yes   *Networking Service:* No

American Institute of Chemists
http://www.theaic.org/
Location: US
Job Postings: No   *Resume Service:* No   *Networking Service:* No

Notes

Favorite sites, useful resources

The American Society of Brewing Chemists
http://www.scisoc.org/asbc/
Location: US
Job Postings: No   *Resume Service:* No   *Networking Service:* No

Analytical and Life Science Systems Association
http://www.alssa.org
Location: US
Job Postings: No   *Resume Service:* No   *Networking Service:* No

Association of Consulting Chemists and Chemical Engineers
http://www.chemconsult.org
Location: US
Job Postings: No   *Resume Service:* No   *Networking Service:* No

Association of Formulation Chemists
http://www.afc-us.org
Location: US
Job Postings: No   *Resume Service:* No   *Networking Service:* No

Association of Official Analytical Chemists
http://www.aoac.org
Location: US
Job Postings: No   *Resume Service:* No   *Networking Service:* No

Association for Women in Science
http://www.awis.org/
Location: US
Job Postings: Yes   *Resume Service:* No   *Networking Service:* No

Chemical Heritage Association
http://www.chemheritage.org
Location: US
Job Postings: No   *Resume Service:* No   *Networking Service:* No

ChemPharma
http://www.chempharma.org/
Location: US - New Jersey
Job Postings: Yes   *Resume Service:* Yes   *Networking Service:* No

Commercial Development and Marketing Association
http://cdmaonline.org/home.html
Location: US
Job Postings: Yes   *Resume Service:* No   *Networking Service:* No

Division of Organic Chemistry
http://www.organicdivision.org
Location: US
Job Postings: No   *Resume Service:* No   *Networking Service:* No

Notes
Favorite sites, useful resources

Electrochemical Society
http://www.electrochem.org
Location: US
Job Postings: Yes   *Resume Service:* No   *Networking Service:* No

Federation of American Scientists
http://www.fas.org/main/home.jsp
Location: US
Job Postings: No   *Resume Service:* No   *Networking Service:* No

Geochemical Society
http://gs.wustl.edu
Location: US
Job Postings: No   *Resume Service:* No   *Networking Service:* No

International Society of Heterocyclic Chemistry
http://euch6f.chem.emory.edu/ishc.html
Location: US
Job Postings: No   *Resume Service:* No   *Networking Service:* No

International Union of Pure and Applied Chemistry
http://www.iupac.org
Location: US
Job Postings: No   *Resume Service:* No   *Networking Service:* No

National Academy of Sciences
http://www.nas.edu/
Location: US
Job Postings: Yes   *Resume Service:* No   *Networking Service:* No

National Science Teachers Association
http://www.nsta.org/
Location: US
Job Postings: Yes   *Resume Service:* Yes   *Networking Service:* No

North American Catalysis Society
http://www.nacatsoc.org
Location: US
Job Postings: No   *Resume Service:* No   *Networking Service:* No

The Oxygen Society
http://www.oxygensociety.org
Location: US
Job Postings: No   *Resume Service:* No   *Networking Service:* No

Society of Applied Spectroscopy
http://www.s-a-s.org
Location: US
Job Postings: Yes   *Resume Service:* Yes   *Networking Service:* No

Notes

Favorite sites, useful resources

Society of Chemical Industry
http://www.soci.org
Location: US
Job Postings: Yes   *Resume Service:* Yes   *Networking Service:* No

Society for College Science Teachers
http://www.scst.suu.edu/
Location: US
Job Postings: No   *Resume Service:* No   *Networking Service:* No

Society of Environmental Toxicology and Chemistry
http://www.setac.org
Location: US
Job Postings: No   *Resume Service:* No   *Networking Service:* No

TERC
http://www.terc.edu
Location: US
Job Postings: Yes   *Resume Service:* No   *Networking Service:* No

World Chlorine Council
http://www.worldchlorine.com
Location: US
Job Postings: No   *Resume Service:* No   *Networking Service:* No

College/Faculty & Staff

American Association of Collegiate Registrars and Admissions Officers
http://www.aacrao.com
Location: US
Job Postings: Yes   *Resume Service:* No   *Networking Service:* No

American Association of School Administrators
http://www.aasa.org
Location: US
Job Postings: Yes   *Resume Service:* No   *Networking Service:* No

American College Personnel Association
http://www.myacpa.org/
Location: US
Job Postings: No   *Resume Service:* No   *Networking Service:* No

Association of College & Research Libraries
http://www.ala.org/
Location: US
Job Postings: Yes   *Resume Service:* No   *Networking Service:* No

Notes

Favorite sites, useful resources

College and University Professional Association for Human Resources
http://www.cupa.org
Location: US
Job Postings: Yes   *Resume Service:* No   *Networking Service:* No

National Association for College Admission Counseling
http://www.nacac.com
Location: US
Job Postings: Yes   *Resume Service:* No   *Networking Service:* No

National Association of College Broadcasters
http://www.hofstra.edu/nacb/
Location: US
Job Postings: No   *Resume Service:* No   *Networking Service:* No

National Association of College and University Attorneys
http://www.nacua.org
Location: US
Job Postings: No   *Resume Service:* No   *Networking Service:* No

National Association of College and University Business Officers
http://www.nacubo.org
Location: US
Job Postings: Yes   *Resume Service:* Yes   *Networking Service:* No

National Association of Colleges & Employers
http://www.naceweb.org
Location: US
Job Postings: Yes   *Resume Service:* No   *Networking Service:* No

National Association of Student Financial Aid Administrators
http://www.nasfaa.org
Location: US
Job Postings: No   *Resume Service:* No   *Networking Service:* No

National Society of Collegiate Scholars
http://www.nscs.org/
Location: US
Job Postings: Yes   *Resume Service:* Yes   *Networking Service:* No

Computer/General & High Technology

ACM Committee on Women in Computing
http://women.acm.org
Location: US
Job Postings: No   *Resume Service:* No   *Networking Service:* No

Notes

Favorite sites, useful resources

American Association for Artificial Intelligence
http://www.aaai.org
Location: US
Job Postings: No   *Resume Service:* No   *Networking Service:* No

American Society for Information Science
http://www.asis.org
Location: US
Job Postings: Yes   *Resume Service:* No   *Networking Service:* Yes

Anti-Gray Market Alliance
http://www.agmaglobal.org
Location: US
Job Postings: No   *Resume Service:* No   *Networking Service:* No

The Association for Computational Linguistics
http://www.acl.org
Location: US
Job Postings: Yes   *Resume Service:* No   *Networking Service:* No

Association for Computer Operations Management
http://www.afcom.com
Location: US
Job Postings: No   *Resume Service:* No   *Networking Service:* No

Association of Computer Support Specialists
http://www.acss.org
Location: US
Job Postings: No   *Resume Service:* No   *Networking Service:* No

The Association for Computers and the Humanities
http://www.ach.org
Location: US
Job Postings: Yes   *Resume Service:* No   *Networking Service:* No

The Association for Computing Machinery
http://www.acm.org
Location: US
Job Postings: Yes   *Resume Service:* No   *Networking Service:* Yes

Association for Educational Communications and Technology
http://www.aect.org
Location: US
Job Postings: Yes   *Resume Service:* No   *Networking Service:* No

Association of Financial Technology
http://www.fitech.org/
Location: US
Job Postings: No   *Resume Service:* No   *Networking Service:* No

Notes

Favorite sites, useful resources

Association for Information and Image Management
http://www.aiim.org
Location: US
Job Postings: Yes   *Resume Service:* Yes   *Networking Service:* No

Association for Information Systems
http://www.aisnet.org
Location: US
Job Postings: Yes   *Resume Service:* No   *Networking Service:* No

Association of Information Technology Professionals
http://www.aitp.org
Location: US
Job Postings: No   *Resume Service:* No   *Networking Service:* Yes

Association of Legal Information Systems Managers
http://www.alism.org
Location: US
Job Postings: No   *Resume Service:* No   *Networking Service:* No

Association for Multimedia Communications
http://www.amcomm.org
Location: US
Job Postings: Yes   *Resume Service:* No   *Networking Service:* No

Association for Women in Computing
http://www.awc-hq.org
Location: US
Job Postings: No   *Resume Service:* No   *Networking Service:* No

The ATM Forum
http://www.atmforum.com
Location: US
Job Postings: No   *Resume Service:* No   *Networking Service:* No

Business Forms Management Association
http://www.bfma.org
Location: US
Job Postings: No   *Resume Service:* No   *Networking Service:* Yes

Center for Democracy and Technology
http://www.cdt.org
Location: US
Job Postings: No   *Resume Service:* No   *Networking Service:* No

Center for the Application of Information Technology
http://www.cait.wustl.edu
Location: US
Job Postings: No   *Resume Service:* No   *Networking Service:* No

Notes

Favorite sites, useful resources

Center of Excellence for Document Analysis and Recognition
http://www.cedar.buffalo.edu
Location: US
Job Postings: No   *Resume Service:* No   *Networking Service:* No

The Center for Information Technology Management
http://www.omicron.edu
Location: US
Job Postings: No   *Resume Service:* No   *Networking Service:* No

Computer and Communications Industry Association
http://www.ccianet.org
Location: US
Job Postings: No   *Resume Service:* No   *Networking Service:* No

Computer Incident Advisory Capability
http://www.ciac.org/ciac
Location: US
Job Postings: No   *Resume Service:* No   *Networking Service:* Yes

Computer Measurement Group, Inc.
http://www.cmg.org
Location: US
Job Postings: No   *Resume Service:* No   *Networking Service:* No

Computer Professionals for Social Responsibility
http://www.cpsr.org
Location: US
Job Postings: No   *Resume Service:* No   *Networking Service:* No

Computer Science and Telecommunications Board
http://www.nationalacademies.org/cstb/
Location: US
Job Postings: No   *Resume Service:* No   *Networking Service:* No

Computing Research Association
http://www.cra.org
Location: US
Job Postings: Yes   *Resume Service:* No   *Networking Service:* No

Computing Technology Industry Association
http://www.comptia.org
Location: US
Job Postings: No   *Resume Service:* No   *Networking Service:* No

Concurrent Supercomputing Consortium
http://www.cacr.caltech.edu/About/cscc.html
Location: US
Job Postings: No   *Resume Service:* No   *Networking Service:* No

Notes

Favorite sites, useful resources

Council of Regional Information Technology Associations
http://www.crita.org
Location: US
Job Postings: No   *Resume Service:* No   *Networking Service:* No

CyberSkills Association
http://www.cyberskills.org
Location: US
Job Postings: No   *Resume Service:* No   *Networking Service:* No

Electronic Frontier Foundation
http://www.eff.org
Location: US
Job Postings: No   *Resume Service:* No   *Networking Service:* No

Electronic Industries Alliance
http://www.cmpcmm.com/cc/orgs.html
Location: US
Job Postings: No   *Resume Service:* No   *Networking Service:* No

Electronic Publishing Association
http://www.epaonline.com
Location: International
Job Postings: No   *Resume Service:* No   *Networking Service:* No

Financial Services Technology Consortium
http://www.fstc.org
Location: US
Job Postings: No   *Resume Service:* No   *Networking Service:* No

Geospatial Information and Technology Association
http://www.gita.org
Location: US
Job Postings: No   *Resume Service:* No   *Networking Service:* No

Healthcare Information and Management Systems
http://www.himss.org
Location: US
Job Postings: Yes   *Resume Service:* Yes   *Networking Service:* No

Help Desk 2000
http://www.stiknowledge.com/helpdesk2000/index.asp
Location: US
Job Postings: Yes   *Resume Service:* No   *Networking Service:* No

High-Tech Marketing Alliance
http://64.45.51.38/
Location: US
Job Postings: Yes   *Resume Service:* No   *Networking Service:* No

Notes

Favorite sites, useful resources

Higher Education Information Technology Alliance
http://www.heitalliance.org
Location: US
Job Postings: No   *Resume Service:* No   *Networking Service:* No

Hi-Tech Club
http://www.hitechclub.com/
Location: US
Job Postings: Yes   *Resume Service:* Yes   *Networking Service:* No

IEEE Computer Society
http://www.computer.org
Location: US
Job Postings: Yes   *Resume Service:* Yes   *Networking Service:* No

Independent Computer Consultants Association
http://www.icca.org
Location: US
Job Postings: Yes   *Resume Service:* Yes   *Networking Service:* No

Information Resources Management Association
http://www.irma-international.org/
Location: US
Job Postings: No   *Resume Service:* No   *Networking Service:* Yes

Information Systems Management Benchmarking Consortium
http://www.ismbc.org
Location: US
Job Postings: No   *Resume Service:* No   *Networking Service:* No

Information Systems Security Association
http://www.issa.org
Location: US
Job Postings: Yes   *Resume Service:* No   *Networking Service:* No

The Information Technology Association of America
http://www.itaa.org
Location: US
Job Postings: No   *Resume Service:* No   *Networking Service:* No

Information Technology Industry Council
http://www.itic.org
Location: US
Job Postings: No   *Resume Service:* No   *Networking Service:* No

The Information Technology Senior Management Forum
http://www.itsmfonline.org
Location: US
Job Postings: No   *Resume Service:* No   *Networking Service:* Yes

Notes

Favorite sites, useful resources

Information Technology Services Marketing Association
http://www.itsma.com
Location: US
Job Postings: No   *Resume Service:* No   *Networking Service:* No

Information Technology & Telecommunications Association
http://www.tca.org
Location: US
Job Postings: No   *Resume Service:* No   *Networking Service:* No

Information and TMT Non-Executives Association
http://www.itnea.net
Location: US
Job Postings: No   *Resume Service:* No   *Networking Service:* No

Institute for Certification of Computing Professionals
http://www.iccp.org
Location: US
Job Postings: No   *Resume Service:* No   *Networking Service:* No

Institute for Women and Technology
http://www.iwt.org
Location: US
Job Postings: No   *Resume Service:* No   *Networking Service:* No

International Digital Imaging Association
http://pwr.com/Idia/
Location: US
Job Postings: No   *Resume Service:* No   *Networking Service:* No

International Society for Genetic and Evolutionary Computation
http://www.isgec.org
Location: US
Job Postings: No   *Resume Service:* No   *Networking Service:* No

ITAudit
http://www.theiia.org/itaudit/
Location: US
Job Postings: Yes   *Resume Service:* Yes   *Networking Service:* No

National Association of Computer Consultant Businesses
http://www.naccb.org
Location: US
Job Postings: No   *Resume Service:* No   *Networking Service:* No

Professional and Technical Consultants Association
http://www.patca.org
Location: US
Job Postings: No   *Resume Service:* No   *Networking Service:* No

Notes
Favorite sites, useful resources

Society of Computer Professionals
http://www.comprof.com
Location: US
Job Postings: No   *Resume Service:* No   *Networking Service:* No

Society for Information Management
http://www.simnet.org
Location: US
Job Postings: No   *Resume Service:* No   *Networking Service:* No

Technical Association of the Graphic Arts
http://www.taga.org
Location: US
Job Postings: Yes   *Resume Service:* No   *Networking Service:* No

Technical Business Network
http://www.techbiz.com
Location: US
Job Postings: No   *Resume Service:* No   *Networking Service:* No

Technology Executives Club
http://www.technologyexecutivesclub.com
Location: US
Job Postings: No   *Resume Service:* No   *Networking Service:* No

Telecommunications and Technology Professionals Serving State Government
http://www.nastd.org
Location: US
Job Postings: No   *Resume Service:* No   *Networking Service:* No

Toronto CICS Association
http://www.interlog.com/~tca/
Location: North America - Canada
Job Postings: Yes   *Resume Service:* No   *Networking Service:* No

USENIX Association
http://www.usenix.org
Location: US
Job Postings: No   *Resume Service:* No   *Networking Service:* No

Wise Women
http://www.wise-women.org
Location: US
Job Postings: No   *Resume Service:* No   *Networking Service:* No

Women in Technology
http://www.womenintechnology.com
Location: US
Job Postings: Yes   *Resume Service:* No   *Networking Service:* No

Notes

Favorite sites, useful resources

Computer/Hardware

The Association for Computing Machinery
http://www.acm.org
Location: US
Job Postings: Yes   *Resume Service:* No   *Networking Service:* Yes

Association of Macintosh Trainers
http://www.mactrainers.com
Location: US
Job Postings: No   *Resume Service:* No   *Networking Service:* No

Concurrent Supercomputing Consortium
http://www.cacr.caltech.edu/About/cscc.html
Location: US
Job Postings: No   *Resume Service:* No   *Networking Service:* No

Gigabit Ethernet Alliance
http://www.10gea.org
Location: US
Job Postings: No   *Resume Service:* No   *Networking Service:* No

Independent Computer Consultants Association
http://www.icca.org
Location: US
Job Postings: No   *Resume Service:* No   *Networking Service:* No

Interex: International Association of Hewlett-Packard Computer Professionals
http://www.interex.org
Location: International
Job Postings: No   *Resume Service:* No   *Networking Service:* No

Microsoft Alumni Network
http://www.msanet.org
Location: US
Job Postings: Yes   *Resume Service:* No   *Networking Service:* No

National Association of Communication Systems Engineers
http://www.nacse.com
Location: US
Job Postings: No   *Resume Service:* No   *Networking Service:* No

The Network Professional Association
http://www.npa.org
Location: US
Job Postings: Yes   *Resume Service:* No   *Networking Service:* No

Notes

Favorite sites, useful resources

Network and Systems Professionals Association
http://www.naspa.com
Location: US
Job Postings: Yes   *Resume Service:* Yes   *Networking Service:* Yes

Storage Networking Industry Association
http://www.snia.org
Location: US
Job Postings: No   *Resume Service:* No   *Networking Service:* No

System Administration, Networking, and Security Institute
http://www.sans.org
Location: US
Job Postings: No   *Resume Service:* No   *Networking Service:* No

Computer/Internet

ACM SIGCOMM Special Interest Group on Data Communications
http://www.acm.org/sigs/sigcomm/
Location: US
Job Postings: No   *Resume Service:* No   *Networking Service:* No

The American E-Commerce Association
http://www.aeaus.com/
Location: US
Job Postings: No   *Resume Service:* No   *Networking Service:* No

American Society for Information Science and Technology
http://www.asis.org
Location: US
Job Postings: No   *Resume Service:* No   *Networking Service:* No

Association for Interactive Media
http://www.interactivehq.org
Location: US
Job Postings: Yes   *Resume Service:* Yes   *Networking Service:* No

Association of Internet Researchers
http://www.aoir.org
Location: US
Job Postings: No   *Resume Service:* No   *Networking Service:* No

DSL Forum
http://www.dslforum.org
Location: US
Job Postings: No   *Resume Service:* No   *Networking Service:* No

Notes

Favorite sites, useful resources

eBusiness Association
http://www.ebusinessassociation.org
Location: US
Job Postings: No   *Resume Service:* No   *Networking Service:* Yes

eMarketing Association
http://www.emarketingassociation.com
Location: US
Job Postings: Yes   *Resume Service:* Yes   *Networking Service:* No

Federation of Internet Solutions Providers of America
http://www.fispa.org
Location: US
Job Postings: No   *Resume Service:* No   *Networking Service:* No

HTML Writers Guild
http://www.hwg.org
Location: US
Job Postings: No   *Resume Service:* No   *Networking Service:* No

Information Systems Security Association
http://www.issa.org
Location: US
Job Postings: Yes   *Resume Service:* No   *Networking Service:* No

Institute of Certified E-Commerce Consultants
http://certifiedcecommerceconsultant.com
Location: US
Job Postings: No   *Resume Service:* No   *Networking Service:* No

International Council of Online Professionals
http://www.i-cop.org
Location: US
Job Postings: No   *Resume Service:* No   *Networking Service:* No

International Society for Computers and their Applications
http://www.isca-hq.org
Location: International
Job Postings: No   *Resume Service:* No   *Networking Service:* No

International Webcasters Association
http://www.webcasters.org
Location: US
Job Postings: No   *Resume Service:* No   *Networking Service:* No

International Webmasters Association
http://www.irwa.org
Location: International
Job Postings: No   *Resume Service:* No   *Networking Service:* No

Notes

Favorite sites, useful resources

Internet Advertising Bureau
http://www.itsma.com
Location: US
Job Postings: No   *Resume Service:* No   *Networking Service:* No

Internet Brothers
http://internetbrothers.com
Location: US
Job Postings: No   *Resume Service:* No   *Networking Service:* No

The Internet Content Coalition
www.mit.edu/activities/safe/labeling/icc/mission.html
Location: US
Job Postings: No   *Resume Service:* No   *Networking Service:* No

Internet Developers Association
http://www.association.org
Location: US
Job Postings: No   *Resume Service:* No   *Networking Service:* No

The Internet Engineering Task Force
http://www.ietf.org
Location: US
Job Postings: No   *Resume Service:* No   *Networking Service:* No

Internet Marketing and Advertising Association
http://www.imaa.org
Location: US
Job Postings: No   *Resume Service:* No   *Networking Service:* No

Internet Marketing Association
http://www.imanetwork.org
Location: US
Job Postings: No   *Resume Service:* No   *Networking Service:* No

Internet Service Providers' Consortium
http://www.ispc.org
Location: US
Job Postings: No   *Resume Service:* No   *Networking Service:* No

Internet Society
http://www.isoc.org
Location: US
Job Postings: Yes   *Resume Service:* No   *Networking Service:* No

Internet Systems Consortium
http://www.isc.org
Location: US
Job Postings: No   *Resume Service:* No   *Networking Service:* No

Notes
Favorite sites, useful resources

National ISDN Council
http://www.nationalisdncouncil.com
Location: US
Job Postings: No   *Resume Service:* No   *Networking Service:* No

The Network Professional Association
http://www.npa.org
Location: US
Job Postings: Yes   *Resume Service:* Yes   *Networking Service:* No

Online Disk Jockey Association
http://www.odja.com
Location: US
Job Postings: No   *Resume Service:* No   *Networking Service:* No

The Open Group
http://www.opengroup.org
Location: US
Job Postings: No   *Resume Service:* No   *Networking Service:* No

PCI Special Interest Group (PCISIG)
http://www.pcisig.com/home
Location: US
Job Postings: No   *Resume Service:* No   *Networking Service:* No

United States Internet Service Provider Association
http://www.cix.org
Location: US
Job Postings: No   *Resume Service:* No   *Networking Service:* No

Usability Professionals' Association
http://www.upassoc.org
Location: US
Job Postings: Yes   *Resume Service:* No   *Networking Service:* No

Web Design and Developers Association
http://www.wdda.org
Location: US
Job Postings: No   *Resume Service:* No   *Networking Service:* No

WebGrrls
http://www.webgrrls.com
Location: US
Job Postings: No   *Resume Service:* No   *Networking Service:* No

World Organization of Webmasters
http://www.joinwow.org
Location: US
Job Postings: Yes   *Resume Service:* No   *Networking Service:* No

Notes

Favorite sites, useful resources

World Wide Web Consortium
http://www.w3.org
Location: US
Job Postings: No   *Resume Service:* No   *Networking Service:* No

Computer/Programming

American Society for Information Science
http://www.asis.org
Location: US
Job Postings: Yes   *Resume Service:* No   *Networking Service:* No

Association of African American Web Developers
http://www.aaawd.net
Location: US
Job Postings: No   *Resume Service:* No   *Networking Service:* No

Association for Applied Interactive Multimedia
http://www.aaim.org
Location: US
Job Postings: No   *Resume Service:* No   *Networking Service:* No

Association for Logic Programming
http://www.cs.kuleuven.ac.be/~dtai/projects/ALP//i
Location: US
Job Postings: No   *Resume Service:* No   *Networking Service:* No

CDMA Development Group
http://www.cdg.org
Location: US
Job Postings: No   *Resume Service:* No   *Networking Service:* No

The Center for Software Development
http://www.center.org
Location: US
Job Postings: Yes   *Resume Service:* No   *Networking Service:* No

Digital Divas
http://www.digitaldivas.com
Location: US
Job Postings: No   *Resume Service:* No   *Networking Service:* No

Good News Web Designers Association
http://gnwda.org
Location: US
Job Postings: No   *Resume Service:* No   *Networking Service:* No

Notes

Favorite sites, useful resources

HTML Writers Guild
http://www.hwg.org
Location: US
Job Postings: No   *Resume Service:* No   *Networking Service:* No

Information Technology Association of America
http://www.itaa.org
Location: US
Job Postings: No   *Resume Service:* No   *Networking Service:* No

National Association of Programmers
http://napusa.org
Location: US
Job Postings: Yes   *Resume Service:* No   *Networking Service:* No

Programmers Guild
http://www.programmersguild.org
Location: US
Job Postings: No   *Resume Service:* No   *Networking Service:* No

Web Design and Developers Association
http://www.wdda.org
Location: US
Job Postings: No   *Resume Service:* No   *Networking Service:* No

Women Designer's Group
http://www.womendesignersgroup.com
Location: US
Job Postings: No   *Resume Service:* No   *Networking Service:* No

Computer/Software

American Society for Information Science
http://www.asis.org
Location: US
Job Postings: Yes   *Resume Service:* No   *Networking Service:* No

Association of Shareware Professionals
http://www.asp-shareware.org
Location: US
Job Postings: No   *Resume Service:* No   *Networking Service:* No

AppleWorks Users Group
http://www.awug.org
Location: US
Job Postings: No   *Resume Service:* No   *Networking Service:* No

Notes

Favorite sites, useful resources

Association of ex-Lotus Employees
http://www.axle.org
Location:　　US
Job Postings: Yes　　　*Resume Service:* No　　　*Networking Service:* No

Association of Shareware Professionals
http://www.asp-shareware.org
Location:　　US
Job Postings: Yes　　　*Resume Service:* No　　　*Networking Service:* No

The Center for Software Development
http://www.center.org/SDForum
Location:　　US
Job Postings: Yes　　　*Resume Service:* No　　　*Networking Service:* Yes

Chicago Software Association
http://www.csa.org/
Location:　　US - Illinois
Job Postings: Yes　　　*Resume Service:* Yes　　　*Networking Service:* No

Energy Science and Technology Software Center
http://www.osti.gov/estsc
Location:　　US
Job Postings: No　　　*Resume Service:* No　　　*Networking Service:* No

Entertainment Software Association
http://www.theesa.com
Location:　　US
Job Postings: No　　　*Resume Service:* No　　　*Networking Service:* No

Information Technology Association of America
http://www.itaa.org
Location:　　US
Job Postings: No　　　*Resume Service:* No　　　*Networking Service:* No

Java Lobby
http://www.javalobby.org
Location:　　US
Job Postings: No　　　*Resume Service:* No　　　*Networking Service:* No

The Network Professional Association
http://www.npa.org
Location:　　US
Job Postings: Yes　　　*Resume Service:* No　　　*Networking Service:* No

Oracle Fan Club and User Forum
http://www.oraclefans.com/
Location:　　US
Job Postings: No　　　*Resume Service:* No　　　*Networking Service:* No

Notes

Favorite sites, useful resources

Professional Association for SQL Server
http://www.sqlpass.org
Location: US
Job Postings: No   *Resume Service:* No   *Networking Service:* No

Society for Software Quality
http://www.ssq.org
Location: US
Job Postings: No   *Resume Service:* No   *Networking Service:* No

Software & Information Industry Association
http://www.siia.net
Location: US
Job Postings: Yes   *Resume Service:* Yes   *Networking Service:* No

Software Contractors' Guild
http://www.scguild.com
Location: US
Job Postings: Yes   *Resume Service:* Yes   *Networking Service:* No

Software Publishers Association
http://www.siia.net
Location: US
Job Postings: Yes   *Resume Service:* Yes   *Networking Service:* No

Software Support Professionals Association
http://www.sspa-online.com
Location: US
Job Postings: No   *Resume Service:* No   *Networking Service:* No

Trialware Professional Association
http://www.trialware.org
Location: US
Job Postings: No   *Resume Service:* No   *Networking Service:* No

USENIX Association
http://www.USENIX.org
Location: US
Job Postings: No   *Resume Service:* No   *Networking Service:* No

Construction

Abacus Construction Index
http://www.construction-index.com
Location: Europe - UK
Job Postings: No   *Resume Service:* No   *Networking Service:* No

Notes

Favorite sites, useful resources

American Iron and Steel Institute
http://www.steel.org
Location: US
Job Postings: No   *Resume Service:* No   *Networking Service:* No

American Road and Transportation Builders Association
http://www.artba.org
Location: US
Job Postings: Yes   *Resume Service:* Yes   *Networking Service:* No

American Society of Professional Estimators
http://www.aspenational.com/
Location: US
Job Postings: No   *Resume Service:* Yes   *Networking Service:* No

Associated Builders and Contractors
http://www.abc.org
Location: US
Job Postings: No   *Resume Service:* No   *Networking Service:* No

The Associated General Contractors of America
http://www.agc.org/index.ww
Location: US
Job Postings: No   *Resume Service:* No   *Networking Service:* No

Association of Construction Inspectors
http://www.iami.org/aci.html
Location: US
Job Postings: Yes   *Resume Service:* No   *Networking Service:* No

Association of Equipment Manufacturers
http://www.aem.org
Location: US
Job Postings: No   *Resume Service:* No   *Networking Service:* No

Construction Management Association of America
http://www.cmaanet.org
Location: US
Job Postings: Yes   *Resume Service:* No   *Networking Service:* No

Construction Marketing Research Council
http://www.cmrc.net
Location: US
Job Postings: No   *Resume Service:* No   *Networking Service:* No

Home Builders Institute (HBI)
http://www.hbi.org/
Location: US
Job Postings: Yes   *Resume Service:* Yes   *Networking Service:* No

Notes

Favorite sites, useful resources

International Code Council
http://www.iccsafe.org
Location: US
Job Postings: Yes   *Resume Service:* No   *Networking Service:* No

National Association of Women in Construction
http://www.nawic.org
Location: US
Job Postings: Yes   *Resume Service:* Yes   *Networking Service:* No

National Concrete and Masonry Association
http://www.ncma.org
Location: US
Job Postings: No   *Resume Service:* No   *Networking Service:* No

National Roofing Contractors Association
http://www.nrca.net
Location: US
Job Postings: Yes   *Resume Service:* No   *Networking Service:* No

National Tile Contractors Association
http://www.Tile-Assn.com
Location: US
Job Postings: No   *Resume Service:* No   *Networking Service:* No

National Wood Flooring Association
http://www.floorbiz.com
Location: US
Job Postings: Yes   *Resume Service:* No   *Networking Service:* No

Sheet Metal and Air Conditioning Contractor's Association
http://www.smacna.org
Location: US
Job Postings: Yes   *Resume Service:* No   *Networking Service:* No

Consultants

American Association of Dental Consultants
http://www.aadc.org
Location: US
Job Postings: No   *Resume Service:* No   *Networking Service:* No

American Association of Legal Nurse Consultants
http://www.aalnc.org
Location: US
Job Postings: No   *Resume Service:* No   *Networking Service:* No

Notes

Favorite sites, useful resources

American Consulting Engineers Council
http://www.acec.org
Location: US
Job Postings: No   *Resume Service:* No   *Networking Service:* No

American Society of Consultant Pharmacists
http://www.ascp.com
Location: US
Job Postings: No   *Resume Service:* No   *Networking Service:* No

The Association of Executive Search Consultants
http://www.aesc.org
Location: US
Job Postings: No   *Resume Service:* No   *Networking Service:* No

Association of Management Consulting Firms
http://www.amcf.org
Location: US
Job Postings: Yes   *Resume Service:* No   *Networking Service:* No

Human Resources Independent Consultants
http://www.hric.org
Location: US
Job Postings: Yes   *Resume Service:* Yes   *Networking Service:* No

Independent Computer Consultants Association
http://www.icca.org
Location: US
Job Postings: Yes   *Resume Service:* Yes   *Networking Service:* No

Institute of Management Consultants
http://www.imcusa.org
Location: US
Job Postings: No   *Resume Service:* No   *Networking Service:* No

International Human Resource Consultants Association
http://www.ihrca.com
Location: International
Job Postings: Yes   *Resume Service:* No   *Networking Service:* No

Investment Management Consultants Association
http://www.imca.org
Location: US
Job Postings: No   *Resume Service:* No   *Networking Service:* Yes

National Alliance of Independent Crop Consultants
http://www.naicc.org
Location: US
Job Postings: No   *Resume Service:* No   *Networking Service:* No

Notes

Favorite sites, useful resources

National Association of Computer Consultant Businesses
http://www.naccb.org
Location: US
Job Postings: No   *Resume Service:* No   *Networking Service:* No

The National Association of Legal Search Consultants
http://www.nalsc.org
Location: US
Job Postings: No   *Resume Service:* No   *Networking Service:* No

Professional and Technical Consultants Association
http://www.patca.org
Location: US
Job Postings: No   *Resume Service:* No   *Networking Service:* No

Qualitative Research Consultants Association
http://www.qrca.org
Location: US
Job Postings: Yes   *Resume Service:* No   *Networking Service:* No

Society of Professional Consultants
http://www.spconsultants.org
Location: US
Job Postings: No   *Resume Service:* No   *Networking Service:* No

Contractors/Freelancers

Associated Builders and Contractors
http://www.abc.org
Location: US
Job Postings: No   *Resume Service:* No   *Networking Service:* No

The Associated General Contractors of America
http://www.agc.org/index.ww
Location: US
Job Postings: No   *Resume Service:* No   *Networking Service:* No

Association of Consulting Chemists and Chemical Engineers
http://www.chemconsult.org
Location: US
Job Postings: No   *Resume Service:* No   *Networking Service:* No

Editorial Freelancers Association
http://www.the-efa.org
Location: US
Job Postings: Yes   *Resume Service:* No   *Networking Service:* No

Notes
Favorite sites, useful resources

National Association for Independent Contractors in Travel
http://www.ossn.com
Location: US
Job Postings: No   *Resume Service:* No   *Networking Service:* No

National Electrical Contractors Association
http://www.necanet.org
Location: US
Job Postings: No   *Resume Service:* No   *Networking Service:* No

Software Contractors' Guild
http://www.scguild.com
Location: US
Job Postings: Yes   *Resume Service:* Yes   *Networking Service:* No

Culinary/Food & Beverage

Airline Suppliers Association
http://www.airlinesuppliers.com
Location: US
Job Postings: No   *Resume Service:* No   *Networking Service:* No

American Frozen Food Institute
http://www.affi.com
Location: US
Job Postings: No   *Resume Service:* No   *Networking Service:* No

American Malting Barley Association
http://www.ambainc.org
Location: US
Job Postings: No   *Resume Service:* No   *Networking Service:* No

The American Society of Brewing Chemists
http://www.scisoc.org/asbc/
Location: US
Job Postings: No   *Resume Service:* No   *Networking Service:* No

Association of Brewers
http://beertown.org
Location: US
Job Postings: No   *Resume Service:* No   *Networking Service:* No

Beer Institute
http://www.beerinstitute.org
Location: US
Job Postings: No   *Resume Service:* No   *Networking Service:* No

Notes

Favorite sites, useful resources

Distilled Spirits Council of the United States
http://www.discus.health.org
Location: US
Job Postings: No   *Resume Service:* No   *Networking Service:* No

Food Distributors International
http://www.fdi.org
Location: US
Job Postings: No   *Resume Service:* No   *Networking Service:* No

Food Marketing Institute
http://www.fmi.org
Location: US
Job Postings: No   *Resume Service:* No   *Networking Service:* No

Foodservice Consultants Society International
http://www.fcsi.org
Location: International
Job Postings: Yes   *Resume Service:* No   *Networking Service:* No

Fresh Produce and Floral Council
http://www.fpfc.org
Location: US
Job Postings: No   *Resume Service:* No   *Networking Service:* No

Grocery Manufacturers of America
http://www.gmabrands.com
Location: US
Job Postings: No   *Resume Service:* No   *Networking Service:* No

Institute of Food Science & Technology
http://www.ifst.org
Location: US
Job Postings: Yes   *Resume Service:* No   *Networking Service:* No

International Dairy, Deli, Bakery Association
http://www.iddba.org
Location: International
Job Postings: Yes   *Resume Service:* No   *Networking Service:* No

International Food Information Council
http://www.ific.org
Location: US
Job Postings: No   *Resume Service:* No   *Networking Service:* No

International Food Service Executives Association
http://www.ifsea.org
Location: International
Job Postings: No   *Resume Service:* No   *Networking Service:* No

Notes

Favorite sites, useful resources

International Foodservice Manufacturers Association
http://www.foodserviceworld.com/ifma/
Location: International
Job Postings: No   *Resume Service:* No   *Networking Service:* No

International Hotel and Restaurant Association
http://www.ih-ra.com
Location: International
Job Postings: Yes   *Resume Service:* Yes   *Networking Service:* No

National Beer Wholesalers Association
http://www.nbwa.org
Location: US
Job Postings: No   *Resume Service:* No   *Networking Service:* No

National Food Processors Association
http://www.nfpa-food.org
Location: US
Job Postings: Yes   *Resume Service:* Yes   *Networking Service:* No

The National Ice Cream and Yogurt Retailers Association
http://www.nicyra.org
Location: US
Job Postings: No   *Resume Service:* No   *Networking Service:* No

National Juice Products Association
http://www.njpa.com
Location: US
Job Postings: No   *Resume Service:* No   *Networking Service:* No

National Licensed Beverage Association
http://www.nlba.org
Location: US
Job Postings: No   *Resume Service:* No   *Networking Service:* No

National Nutritional Foods Association
http://www.nnfa.org
Location: US
Job Postings: No   *Resume Service:* No   *Networking Service:* No

National Restaurant Association
http://www.restaurant.org
Location: US
Job Postings: Yes   *Resume Service:* No   *Networking Service:* No

Produce Marketing Association
http://www.pma.com
Location: US
Job Postings: Yes   *Resume Service:* No   *Networking Service:* No

Notes

Favorite sites, useful resources

Snack Food Association
http://www.sfa.org
Location: US
Job Postings: No   *Resume Service:* No   *Networking Service:* No

Specialty Coffee Association of America
http://www.scaa.com
Location: US
Job Postings: No   *Resume Service:* No   *Networking Service:* No

-D-

Data Processing

AFCOM
http://www.afcom.com
Location: US
Job Postings: No   *Resume Service:* No   *Networking Service:* No

Black Data Processing Associates
http://www.bdpa.org
Location: US
Job Postings: Yes   *Resume Service:* Yes   *Networking Service:* No

Computer Measurement Group, Inc.
http://www.cmg.org
Location: US
Job Postings: No   *Resume Service:* No   *Networking Service:* No

Diversity/Disability

American Association of People with Disabilities
http://www.aapd.com
Location: US
Job Postings: Yes   *Resume Service:* Yes   *Networking Service:* No

American Council of the Blind
http://www.acb.org
Location: US
Job Postings: Yes   *Resume Service:* No   *Networking Service:* No

American Foundation for the Blind
http://www.afb.org
Location: US
Job Postings: Yes   *Resume Service:* No   *Networking Service:* No

Notes

Favorite sites, useful resources

Association of Schools and Agencies for the Handicapped
http://www.asah.org
Location: US
Job Postings: No   *Resume Service:* No   *Networking Service:* No

The Association for Severe Handicaps
http://www.tash.org
Location: US
Job Postings: Yes   *Resume Service:* No   *Networking Service:* No

Deafness Research Foundation
http://www.drf.org
Location: US
Job Postings: No   *Resume Service:* No   *Networking Service:* No

Goodwill Industries International
http://www.goodwill.org
Location: International
Job Postings: Yes   *Resume Service:* No   *Networking Service:* No

National Association of American Business Clubs
http://www.ambucs.com
Location: US
Job Postings: No   *Resume Service:* No   *Networking Service:* No

National Association of the Deaf
http://www.nad.org
Location: US
Job Postings: No   *Resume Service:* No   *Networking Service:* No

National Federation of the Blind
http://www.nfb.org
Location: US
Job Postings: Yes   *Resume Service:* No   *Networking Service:* No

National Industries for the Blind
http://www.nib.org
Location: US
Job Postings: Yes   *Resume Service:* No   *Networking Service:* No

National Institute for People with Disabilities
http://www.yai.org
Location: US
Job Postings: No   *Resume Service:* No   *Networking Service:* No

National Organization on Disability
http://www.nod.org
Location: US
Job Postings: Yes   *Resume Service:* No   *Networking Service:* No

Notes
Favorite sites, useful resources

National Rehabilitation Association
http://www.nationalrehab.org
Location: US
Job Postings: No   *Resume Service:* No   *Networking Service:* No

United Cerebral Palsy Association
http://www.ucpa.org
Location: US
Job Postings: No   *Resume Service:* No   *Networking Service:* No

Diversity/Ethnicity

Asian American Hotel Owners Association
http://www.aahoa.org
Location: US
Job Postings: No   *Resume Service:* No   *Networking Service:* No

Asian American Journalists Association
http://www.aaja.org
Location: US
Job Postings: No   *Resume Service:* No   *Networking Service:* No

Association of African American Web Developers
http://www.aaawd.net
Location: US
Job Postings: No   *Resume Service:* No   *Networking Service:* No

Association of Black Sociologists
http://www.blacksociologists.org
Location: US
Job Postings: No   *Resume Service:* No   *Networking Service:* Yes

Association of Hispanic Advertising Agencies
http://www.ahaa.org/
Location: US
Job Postings: No   *Resume Service:* No   *Networking Service:* No

Black Business Association
http://www.bbala.org
Location: US
Job Postings: No   *Resume Service:* No   *Networking Service:* No

Black Data Processing Associates
http://www.bdpa.org
Location: US
Job Postings: Yes   *Resume Service:* Yes   *Networking Service:* No

Notes

Favorite sites, useful resources

Black Entertainment & Sports Lawyers Association
http://www.besla.org
Location: US
Job Postings: No   *Resume Service:* No   *Networking Service:* No

California Korean Pharmacists Association
http://www.kpha.com
Location: US - California
Job Postings: No   *Resume Service:* No   *Networking Service:* No

Greek American Lawyers Association
http://firms.findlaw.com/gala/
Location: US
Job Postings: No   *Resume Service:* No   *Networking Service:* No

Hispanic National Bar Association
http://www.hnba.com
Location: US
Job Postings: Yes   *Resume Service:* No   *Networking Service:* No

National Arab American Medical Association
http://www.naama.com
Location: US
Job Postings: No   *Resume Service:* No   *Networking Service:* No

National Association for the Advancement of Colored People
http://www.naacp.org
Location: US
Job Postings: Yes   *Resume Service:* Yes   *Networking Service:* No

National Association of Black Accountants
http://www.nabainc.org
Location: US
Job Postings: Yes   *Resume Service:* Yes   *Networking Service:* No

The National Association of Black Journalists
http://www.nabj.org
Location: US
Job Postings: Yes   *Resume Service:* Yes   *Networking Service:* Yes

The National Association of Black Telecommunications Professionals
http://www.nabtp.org
Location: US
Job Postings: No   *Resume Service:* No   *Networking Service:* No

The National Association of Hispanic Journalists
http://www.nahj.org
Location: US
Job Postings: Yes   *Resume Service:* Yes   *Networking Service:* No

Notes

Favorite sites, useful resources

National Association of Minority Automobile Dealers
http://www.namad.com
Location: US
Job Postings: No   *Resume Service:* No   *Networking Service:* No

National Black MBA Association, Inc.
http://www.nbmbaa.org
Location: US
Job Postings: Yes   *Resume Service:* No   *Networking Service:* No

National Black Media Coalition
www.nbmc.org
Location: US
Job Postings: No   *Resume Service:* No   *Networking Service:* No

National Hispanic Medical Association
http://home.earthlink.net/~nhma/webdoc1.htm
Location: US
Job Postings: No   *Resume Service:* No   *Networking Service:* No

National Organization of Minority Architects
http://www.noma.net
Location: US
Job Postings: Yes   *Resume Service:* No   *Networking Service:* No

National Society of Black Engineers
http://www.nsbe.org
Location: US
Job Postings: Yes   *Resume Service:* No   *Networking Service:* No

National Society of Hispanic MBAs
http://www.nshmba.org
Location: US
Job Postings: Yes   *Resume Service:* Yes   *Networking Service:* No

National Urban League
http://www.nul.org
Location: US
Job Postings: Yes   *Resume Service:* Yes   *Networking Service:* No

Puerto Rico Manufacturers Association
http://www.prma.com
Location: US - Puerto Rico
Job Postings: No   *Resume Service:* No   *Networking Service:* No

---

Looking for a new or better job?   Looking for top talent?
Use WEDDLE's publications. Visit www.weddles.com today.

Notes

Favorite sites, useful resources

Diversity/Gender

ACM Committee on Women in Computing
http://women.acm.org
Location: US
Job Postings: No   *Resume Service:* No   *Networking Service:* No

American Association of Women Dentists
http://www.womendentists.org
Location: US
Job Postings: Yes   *Resume Service:* No   *Networking Service:* No

American Business Women's Association
http://www.abwahq.org
Location: US
Job Postings: Yes   *Resume Service:* Yes   *Networking Service:* No

American Medical Women's Association
http://www.amwa-doc.org
Location: US
Job Postings: No   *Resume Service:* No   *Networking Service:* No

American Society of Women Accountants
http://www.aswa.org
Location: US
Job Postings: No   *Resume Service:* No   *Networking Service:* No

American Woman's Society of Certified Public Accountants
http://www.awscpa.org
Location: US
Job Postings: Yes   *Resume Service:* Yes   *Networking Service:* No

Association for Professional Insurance Women
http://www.apiw.org
Location: US
Job Postings: No   *Resume Service:* No   *Networking Service:* No

Association for Women in Computing
http://www.awc-hq.org
Location: US
Job Postings: No   *Resume Service:* No   *Networking Service:* No

Association for Women in Science
http://www.awis.org/
Location: US
Job Postings: Yes   *Resume Service:* No   *Networking Service:* No

Notes

Favorite sites, useful resources

ASAE
American
Society of
Association
Executives

Association of Women in the Metal Industries
http://www.awmi.com
Location: US
Job Postings: No   *Resume Service:* No   *Networking Service:* No

Association of Women Surgeons
http://www.womensurgeons.org
Location: US
Job Postings: Yes   *Resume Service:* No   *Networking Service:* No

Committee on the Status of Women in the Economics Profession
http://www.cswep.org/
Location: US
Job Postings: Yes   *Resume Service:* No   *Networking Service:* No

Committee on Women in Agricultural Economics
http://www.aaea.org/cwae/
Location: US
Job Postings: No   *Resume Service:* No   *Networking Service:* No

Computing Research Association
http://www.cra.org
Location: US
Job Postings: No   *Resume Service:* No   *Networking Service:* No

Digital Divas
http://www.digitaldivas.com
Location: US
Job Postings: No   *Resume Service:* No   *Networking Service:* No

Financial Women International
http://www.fwi.org
Location: US
Job Postings: Yes   *Resume Service:* Yes   *Networking Service:* No

Financial Women's Association
http://www.fwa.org
Location: US
Job Postings: No   *Resume Service:* No   *Networking Service:* No

Healthcare Business Women's Association
http://www.hbanet.org/
Location: US
Job Postings: No   *Resume Service:* No   *Networking Service:* No

Home-Based Working Moms
http://www.hbwm.com
Location: US
Job Postings: Yes   *Resume Service:* No   *Networking Service:* No

Notes

Favorite sites, useful resources

Institute for Women and Technology
http://www.iwt.org
Location: US
Job Postings: No *Resume Service:* No *Networking Service:* No

Mothers' Home Business Network
http://www.homeworkingmom.com
Location: US
Job Postings: Yes *Resume Service:* No *Networking Service:* No

National Association for Female Executives
http://www.nafe.com
Location: US
Job Postings: No *Resume Service:* No *Networking Service:* No

National Association of Gender Diversity Training
http://www.gendertraining.com
Location: US
Job Postings: No *Resume Service:* No *Networking Service:* No

National Association of Women Business Owners
http://www.nawbo.org
Location: US
Job Postings: No *Resume Service:* No *Networking Service:* No

National Association of Women in Construction
http://www.nawic.org
Location: US
Job Postings: Yes *Resume Service:* Yes *Networking Service:* No

The National Association of Professional Mortgage Women
http://www.napmw.org
Location: US
Job Postings: No *Resume Service:* No *Networking Service:* No

National Network of Commercial Real Estate Women
http://www.nncrew.org
Location: US
Job Postings: Yes *Resume Service:* No *Networking Service:* No

Society of Women Engineers
http://www.swe.org
Location: US
Job Postings: Yes *Resume Service:* Yes *Networking Service:* No

WebGrrls
http://www.webgrrls.com
Location: US
Job Postings: No *Resume Service:* No *Networking Service:* No

Notes

Favorite sites, useful resources

Wise Women
http://www.wise-women.org
Location: US
Job Postings: No   *Resume Service:* No   *Networking Service:* No

Women in Cable & Telecommunications
http://www.wict.org
Location: US
Job Postings: No   *Resume Service:* No   *Networking Service:* No

Women Designer's Group
http://www.womendesignersgroup.com
Location: US
Job Postings: No   *Resume Service:* No   *Networking Service:* No

Women in Packaging
http://www.womeninpackaging.org
Location: US
Job Postings: Yes   *Resume Service:* No   *Networking Service:* No

Women in Technology
http://www.womenintechnology.com
Location: US
Job Postings: Yes   *Resume Service:* No   *Networking Service:* No

Women's Council of Realtors
http://www.wcr.org
Location: US
Job Postings: No   *Resume Service:* No   *Networking Service:* No

---

Looking for a new or better job?   Looking for top talent?
Use WEDDLE's publications.
Visit www.weddles.com today.

- *WEDDLE's 2005/6 Guide* is the "consumer's report" of job boards.
We've selected 350 of the best job boards and career portals across a broad array of career fields and industries. These sites are then described with a full page of information about their features, services and fees so that you can "comparison shop" them to find the best sites for you.

- *WEDDLE's 2005/6 Directory* is the "address book" of job boards.
We list over 8,000 job boards and career portals and organize them by the career field, industry and/or location on which they focus. Each site is listed by its name and address on the Internet so that you can identify and visit the sites that are most likely to work for you.

Notes

Favorite sites, useful resources

Diversity/Religion

American Academy of Religion
http://www.aarweb.org
Location: US
Job Postings: Yes   *Resume Service:* No   *Networking Service:* No

American Jewish Press Association
http://www.ajpa.org
Location: US
Job Postings: Yes   *Resume Service:* Yes   *Networking Service:* No

Anabaptist Sociology and Anthropology Association
www.hillsdale.edu/AcademicAssociations/Sociology/a
Location: US
Job Postings: No   *Resume Service:* No   *Networking Service:* No

Association of Mormon Counselors and Psychotherapists
http://www.amcap.net
Location: US
Job Postings: No   *Resume Service:* No   *Networking Service:* No

Central Conference of American Rabbis
http://www.ccarnet.org
Location: US
Job Postings: No   *Resume Service:* No   *Networking Service:* No

Christian Brothers Services
http://www.cbservices.org
Location: US
Job Postings: No   *Resume Service:* No   *Networking Service:* No

Christian Legal Society
http://www.clsnet.org
Location: US
Job Postings: Yes   *Resume Service:* No   *Networking Service:* No

International Association of Jewish Vocational Services
http://www.jvsnj.org/iajvs.html
Location: US
Job Postings: Yes   *Resume Service:* No   *Networking Service:* No

National Association of Church Business Administration
http://www.nacba.net
Location: US
Job Postings: Yes   *Resume Service:* No   *Networking Service:* No

Notes

Favorite sites, useful resources

National Association of Church Personnel Administrators
http://www.nacpa.org
Location: US
Job Postings: No   *Resume Service:* No   *Networking Service:* No

National Association of Temple Educators
http://www.rj.org/nate/
Location: US
Job Postings: No   *Resume Service:* No   *Networking Service:* No

National Church of Goods Association
http://www.ncgaweb.com
Location: US
Job Postings: No   *Resume Service:* No   *Networking Service:* No

National Religious Broadcasters Association
http://www.nrb.org
Location: US
Job Postings: Yes   *Resume Service:* No   *Networking Service:* No

North American Association of Christian Social Workers
http://www.nacsw.org
Location: US
Job Postings: Yes   *Resume Service:* Yes   *Networking Service:* No

-E-

Economics/Economists

Academy of Economics and Finance
http://www.jeandf.org/academy.htm
Location: US
Job Postings: No   *Resume Service:* No   *Networking Service:* No

American Agricultural Economics Association
http://www.aaea.org
Location: US
Job Postings: Yes   *Resume Service:* Yes   *Networking Service:* No

American Economic Association
http://www.vanderbilt.edu/AEA/
Location: US
Job Postings: Yes   *Resume Service:* No   *Networking Service:* No

---

Looking for a new or better job?   Looking for top talent?
Use WEDDLE's publications. Visit www.weddles.com today.

Notes

Favorite sites, useful resources

American Law and Economics Association
http://www.amlecon.org
Location: US
Job Postings: No   *Resume Service:* No   *Networking Service:* No

American Real Estate and Urban Economics Association
http://www.areuea.org
Location: US
Job Postings: No   *Resume Service:* No   *Networking Service:* No

American Rehabilitation Economics Association
http://www.a-r-e-a.org
Location: US
Job Postings: No   *Resume Service:* No   *Networking Service:* No

Association of Christian Economists
http://www.gordon.edu/ace/
Location: US
Job Postings: No   *Resume Service:* No   *Networking Service:* No

Association for Comparative Economic Studies
http://www.wdi.bus.umich.edu/aces/
Location: US
Job Postings: No   *Resume Service:* No   *Networking Service:* No

Association of Environmental and Resource Economists
http://www.aere.org/
Location: US
Job Postings: Yes   *Resume Service:* No   *Networking Service:* No

Association for Evolutionary Economics
http://www.orgs.bucknell.edu/afee/
Location: US
Job Postings: No   *Resume Service:* No   *Networking Service:* No

Association for Heterodox Economics
http://www.hetecon.com
Location: US
Job Postings: No   *Resume Service:* No   *Networking Service:* No

Association for Social Economics
http://www.socialeconomics.org
Location: US
Job Postings: No   *Resume Service:* No   *Networking Service:* No

Association for the Study of the Grants Economy
http://www.gratseconomics.org
Location: US
Job Postings: No   *Resume Service:* No   *Networking Service:* No

Notes

Favorite sites, useful resources

Association for University Business and Economic Research
http://www.auber.org
Location: US
Job Postings: No   *Resume Service:* No   *Networking Service:* No

Association of American Geographers, Economic Geography Specialty Group
http://geog.uconn.edu/aag-econ/
Location: US
Job Postings: No   *Resume Service:* No   *Networking Service:* No

Canadian Association for Business Economics
http://www.cabe.ca
Location: North America - Canada
Job Postings: Yes   *Resume Service:* No   *Networking Service:* No

Center for Energy and Economic Development
http://www.ceednet.org
Location: US
Job Postings: No   *Resume Service:* No   *Networking Service:* No

Committee on the Status of Women in the Economics Profession
http://www.cswep.org/
Location: US
Job Postings: Yes   *Resume Service:* No   *Networking Service:* No

Committee on Women in Agricultural Economics
http://www.aaea.org/cwae/
Location: US
Job Postings: No   *Resume Service:* No   *Networking Service:* No

Economic Development Association
http://www.ag.iastate.edu/journals/rde/eda.htm
Location: US
Job Postings: No   *Resume Service:* No   *Networking Service:* No

EDucational INnovation in Economics and Business Network
http://www.fdewb4.unimaas.nl/edineb/index.htm
Location: US
Job Postings: No   *Resume Service:* No   *Networking Service:* No

Financial Economics Network
http://www.ssrn.com/fen/
Location: US
Job Postings: Yes   *Resume Service:* No   *Networking Service:* No

Financial Economists Roundtable
http://www.luc.edu/orgs/finroundtable/
Location: US
Job Postings: No   *Resume Service:* No   *Networking Service:* No

Notes

Favorite sites, useful resources

Institute for International Economics
http://www.iie.com
Location: US
Job Postings: No   *Resume Service:* No   *Networking Service:* No

International Association for the Economics of Participation
http://ocean.st.usm.edu/~mklndnst/index.html
Location: International
Job Postings: No   *Resume Service:* No   *Networking Service:* No

National Association for Business Economics
http://www.nabe.com
Location: US
Job Postings: Yes   *Resume Service:* No   *Networking Service:* No

National Association of Economic Educators
http://ecedweb.unomaha.edu/naee.htm
Location: US
Job Postings: No   *Resume Service:* No   *Networking Service:* No

National Association of Forensic Economics
http://nafe.net/
Location: US
Job Postings: No   *Resume Service:* No   *Networking Service:* No

National Business and Economics Society
http://www.nbesonline.com/
Location: US
Job Postings: No   *Resume Service:* No   *Networking Service:* No

National Economic Association
http://www.ncat.edu/~neconasc/
Location: US
Job Postings: Yes   *Resume Service:* No   *Networking Service:* No

National Economists Club
http://www.national-economists.org/
Location: US
Job Postings: Yes   *Resume Service:* No   *Networking Service:* No

Progressive Economic Forum
http://www.web.net/~pef/
Location: US
Job Postings: Yes   *Resume Service:* No   *Networking Service:* No

Society for the Advancement of Socio-Economics
http://www.sase.org/
Location: US
Job Postings: No   *Resume Service:* No   *Networking Service:* No

Notes

Favorite sites, useful resources

Society of Computational Economists
http://wuecon.wustl.edu/sce/
Location: US
Job Postings: No   *Resume Service:* No   *Networking Service:* No

Society for Economic Anthropology
http://nautarch.tamu.edu/anth/sea/
Location: US
Job Postings: Yes   *Resume Service:*   No   *Networking Service:*   No

Society for Economic Botany
http://www.econbot.org/
Location: US
Job Postings: No   *Resume Service:* No   *Networking Service:* No

Society for Economic Dynamics
http://www.economicdynamics.org/society.htm
Location: US
Job Postings: No   *Resume Service:* No   *Networking Service:* No

Society of Economic Geologists
http://www.segweb.org/
Location: US
Job Postings: No   *Resume Service:* No   *Networking Service:* No

Society for Environmental Economics and Policy Studies
http://www.seeps.org/
Location: US
Job Postings: No   *Resume Service:* No   *Networking Service:* No

Society of Government Economists
http://www.sge-econ.org
Location: US
Job Postings: Yes   *Resume Service:* No   *Networking Service:* No

Society of Labor Economists
http://www-gsb.uchicago.edu/labor/sole.htm
Location: US
Job Postings: No   *Resume Service:* No   *Networking Service:* No

Society for Nonlinear Dynamics and Econometrics
http://www.snde.rutgers.edu/SNDE/society/snde.html
Location: US
Job Postings: No   *Resume Service:* No   *Networking Service:* No

United States Association for Energy Economics
http://www.usaee.org/
Location: US
Job Postings: No   *Resume Service:* No   *Networking Service:* No

Notes

Favorite sites, useful resources

United States Society for Ecological Economics
http://www.ussee.org/
Location: US
Job Postings: Yes   *Resume Service:* No   *Networking Service:* No

Education/K-12

American Association of School Administrators
http://www.aasa.org
Location: US
Job Postings: Yes   *Resume Service:* No   *Networking Service:* No

American Federation of Teachers
http://www.aft.org
Location: US
Job Postings: No   *Resume Service:* No   *Networking Service:* No

American Library Association
http://www.ala.org
Location: US
Job Postings: Yes   *Resume Service:* No   *Networking Service:* No

American School Counselor Association
http://www.schoolcounselor.org
Location: US
Job Postings: No   *Resume Service:* No   *Networking Service:* No

American School Health Association
http://www.ashaweb.org
Location: US
Job Postings: No   *Resume Service:* No   *Networking Service:* No

Association for Educational Communications and Technology
http://www.aect.org
Location: US
Job Postings: Yes   *Resume Service:* No   *Networking Service:* No

Association of Schools and Agencies for the Handicapped
http://www.asah.org
Location: US
Job Postings: No   *Resume Service:* No   *Networking Service:* No

Council for Advancement & Support of Education
http://www.case.org
Location: US
Job Postings: Yes   *Resume Service:* No   *Networking Service:* No

Notes

Favorite sites, useful resources

Education Law Association
http://www.educationlaw.org
Location: US
Job Postings: No   *Resume Service:* No   *Networking Service:* No

National Association of Biology Teachers
http://www.nabt.org
Location: US
Job Postings: No   *Resume Service:* No   *Networking Service:* No

National Association of School Psychologists
http://www.nasponline.org
Location: US
Job Postings: Yes   *Resume Service:* Yes   *Networking Service:* No

National Association of Temple Educators
http://www.rj.org/nate/
Location: US
Job Postings: No   *Resume Service:* No   *Networking Service:* No

National Education Association
http://www.nea.org
Location: US
Job Postings: No   *Resume Service:* No   *Networking Service:* No

National Education Writers Association
http://www.ewa.org
Location: US
Job Postings: No   *Resume Service:* No   *Networking Service:* No

National Middle School Association
http://www.nmsa.org
Location: US
Job Postings: No   *Resume Service:* No   *Networking Service:* No

National Science Teachers Association
http://www.nsta.org
Location: US
Job Postings: Yes   *Resume Service:* Yes   *Networking Service:* No

Education/College

Aerospace Education Foundation
http://www.aef.org
Location: US
Job Postings: No   *Resume Service:* No   *Networking Service:* No

Notes

Favorite sites, useful resources

Advertising Education Forum
http://www.aeforum.org
Location: Europe - UK
Job Postings: No   *Resume Service:* No   *Networking Service:* No

American Association of Collegiate Registrars and Admissions Officers
http://www.aacrao.com
Location: US
Job Postings: Yes   *Resume Service:* No   *Networking Service:* No

American Association of Law Libraries
http://www.aallnet.org
Location: US
Job Postings: Yes   *Resume Service:* No   *Networking Service:* No

American Association of School Administrators
http://www.aasa.org
Location: US
Job Postings: Yes   *Resume Service:* No   *Networking Service:* No

American College Personnel Association
http://www.myacpa.org/
Location: US
Job Postings: No   *Resume Service:* No   *Networking Service:* No

American Federation of Teachers
http://www.aft.org
Location: US
Job Postings: No   *Resume Service:* No   *Networking Service:* No

American Institute of Architecture Students
http://www.aiasnatl.org
Location: US
Job Postings: Yes   *Resume Service:* No   *Networking Service:* No

American Library Association
http://www.ala.org
Location: US
Job Postings: Yes   *Resume Service:* No   *Networking Service:* No

The Association of American Law Schools
http://www.aals.org
Location: US
Job Postings: No   *Resume Service:* No   *Networking Service:* No

Association of College & Research Libraries
http://www.ala.org/
Location: US
Job Postings: Yes   *Resume Service:* No   *Networking Service:* No

Notes

Favorite sites, useful resources

Association for Continuing Legal Education
http://www.aclea.org
Location: US
Job Postings: No   *Resume Service:* No   *Networking Service:* No

Association for Educational Communications and Technology
http://www.aect.org
Location: US
Job Postings: Yes   *Resume Service:* No   *Networking Service:* No

Association of Private Enterprise Education
http://www.apee.org
Location: US
Job Postings: No   *Resume Service:* No   *Networking Service:* No

Association of Research Libraries
http://www.arl.org
Location: US
Job Postings: Yes   *Resume Service:* No   *Networking Service:* No

College and University Professional Association for Human Resources
http://www.cupa.org
Location: US
Job Postings: Yes   *Resume Service:* No   *Networking Service:* No

Education Law Association
http://www.educationlaw.org
Location: US
Job Postings: No   *Resume Service:* No   *Networking Service:* No

European Association for Astronomy Education
http://www.algonet.se/~sirius/eaae.htm
Location: Europe
Job Postings: No   *Resume Service:* No   *Networking Service:* No

Higher Education Information Technology Alliance
http://www.heitalliance.org
Location: US
Job Postings: No   *Resume Service:* No   *Networking Service:* No

Institute of Fiscal Studies
http://www.ifs.org.uk
Location: Europe - UK
Job Postings: No   *Resume Service:* No   *Networking Service:* No

International Association of Scholarly Publishers
http://lcweb.loc.gov/loc/cfbook/coborg/iasp.html
Location: International
Job Postings: No   *Resume Service:* No   *Networking Service:* No

Notes

Favorite sites, useful resources

International College of Dentists
http://www.icd.org
Location: International
Job Postings: No   *Resume Service:* No   *Networking Service:* No

International Graphic Arts Education Association
http://www.gatf.org
Location: International
Job Postings: No   *Resume Service:* No   *Networking Service:* No

National Association of College Admission Counseling
http://www.nacac.com
Location: US
Job Postings: Yes   *Resume Service:* No   *Networking Service:* No

National Association of College Broadcasters
http://www.hofstra.edu/nacb/
Location: US
Job Postings: No   *Resume Service:* No   *Networking Service:* No

National Association of College and University Attorneys
http://www.nacua.org
Location: US
Job Postings: No   *Resume Service:* No   *Networking Service:* No

National Association of College and University Business Officers
http://www.nacubo.org
Location: US
Job Postings: Yes   *Resume Service:* Yes   *Networking Service:* No

National Association of Colleges & Employers
http://www.naceweb.org
Location: US
Job Postings: Yes   *Resume Service:* No   *Networking Service:* No

National Association of Economic Educators
http://ecedweb.unomaha.edu/naee.htm
Location: US
Job Postings: No   *Resume Service:* No   *Networking Service:* No

National Association of Student Financial Aid Administrators
http://www.nasfaa.org
Location: US
Job Postings: No   *Resume Service:* No   *Networking Service:* No

National Education Writers Association
http://www.ewa.org
Location: US
Job Postings: No   *Resume Service:* No   *Networking Service:* No

Notes

Favorite sites, useful resources

National Society of Collegiate Scholars
http://www.nscs.org/
Location: US
Job Postings: Yes   *Resume Service:* Yes   *Networking Service:* No

Society for College Science Teachers
http://www.scst.suu.edu/
Location: US
Job Postings: No   *Resume Service:* No   *Networking Service:* No

Students for the Exploration and Development of Space
http://www.seds.org
Location: US
Job Postings: No   *Resume Service:* No   *Networking Service:* No

University Research Magazine Association
http://www.urma.org
Location: US
Job Postings: No   *Resume Service:* No   *Networking Service:* Yes

Energy/Utilities

America Public Power Association
http://www.appanet.org
Location: US
Job Postings: Yes   *Resume Service:* No   *Networking Service:* No

American Gas Association
http://www.aga.org
Location: US
Job Postings: No   *Resume Service:* No   *Networking Service:* No

American Nuclear Society
http://www.ans.org
Location: US
Job Postings: Yes   *Resume Service:* Yes   *Networking Service:* No

American Petroleum Institute
http://www.api.org
Location: US
Job Postings: No   *Resume Service:* No   *Networking Service:* No

American Water Works Association
http://www.awwa.org
Location: US
Job Postings: Yes   *Resume Service:* No   *Networking Service:* No

Notes

Favorite sites, useful resources

Association of Energy Engineers
http://www.aeecenter.org
Location: US
Job Postings: Yes   *Resume Service:* No   *Networking Service:* No

Association of Energy Services Professionals
http://www.aesp.org
Location: US
Job Postings: No   *Resume Service:* No   *Networking Service:* No

Center for Energy and Economic Development
http://www.ceednet.org
Location: US
Job Postings: No   *Resume Service:* No   *Networking Service:* No

Drilling Research Institute
http://www.drillers.com
Location: US
Job Postings: Yes   *Resume Service:* No   *Networking Service:* No

Edison Electric Institute
http://www.eei.org
Location: US
Job Postings: No   *Resume Service:* No   *Networking Service:* No

Electric Power Supply Association
http://www.epsa.org
Location: US
Job Postings: No   *Resume Service:* No   *Networking Service:* No

Energy Science and Technology Software Center
http://www.osti.gov/estsc
Location: US
Job Postings: No   *Resume Service:* No   *Networking Service:* No

Gas Processors Association
http://www.gasprocessors.com
Location: US
Job Postings: No   *Resume Service:* No   *Networking Service:* No

The International District Energy Association
http://www.districtenergy.org
Location: International
Job Postings: No   *Resume Service:* Yes   *Networking Service:* No

Interstate Natural Gas Association of America
http://www.ingaa.org
Location: US
Job Postings: Yes   *Resume Service:* No   *Networking Service:* No

Notes

Favorite sites, useful resources

National Association of Energy Service Companies
http://www.naesco.org
Location: US
Job Postings: No   *Resume Service:* No   *Networking Service:* No

National Association of Regulatory Utility Commissioners
http://www.naruc.org
Location: US
Job Postings: No   *Resume Service:* No   *Networking Service:* No

National Association of Water Companies
http://www.nawc.org
Location: US
Job Postings: No   *Resume Service:* No   *Networking Service:* No

National Energy Services Association
http://www.nesanet.org
Location: US
Job Postings: Yes   *Resume Service:* Yes   *Networking Service:* No

Nuclear Energy Institute
http://www.nei.org
Location: US
Job Postings: No   *Resume Service:* No   *Networking Service:* No

Society of Petroleum Engineers
http://www.spe.org
Location: US
Job Postings: Yes   *Resume Service:* No   *Networking Service:* No

United States Association for Energy Economics
http://www.usaee.org/
Location: US
Job Postings: No   *Resume Service:* No   *Networking Service:* No

The Utility Marketing Association
http://www.umaonline.com
Location: US
Job Postings: Yes   *Resume Service:* No   *Networking Service:* No

Water Environment Federation
http://www.wef.org
Location: US
Job Postings: Yes   *Resume Service:* No   *Networking Service:* No

---

Looking for a new or better job?   Looking for top talent?
Use WEDDLE's publications. Visit www.weddles.com today.

Notes
Favorite sites, useful resources

Engineering/Aeronautical

American Institute of Aeronautics and Astronautics
http://www.aiaa.org
Location: US
Job Postings: No   *Resume Service:* No   *Networking Service:* No

Engineering/Civil

American Society of Civil Engineers
http://www.asce.org
Location: US
Job Postings: Yes   *Resume Service:* Yes   *Networking Service:* No

Association for Facilities Engineering
http://www.afe.org
Location: . US
Job Postings: Yes   *Resume Service:* Yes   *Networking Service:* No

Canadian Society for Civil Engineers
http://www.csce.ca
Location: North America - Canada
Job Postings: No   *Resume Service:* No   *Networking Service:* No

Institute of Civil Engineers
http://www.ice.org.uk
Location: Europe - UK
Job Postings: No   *Resume Service:* No   *Networking Service:* No

Engineering/Electric & Electronics

American Electronics Association
http://www.aeanet.org
Location: US
Job Postings: Yes   *Resume Service:* No   *Networking Service:* No

American Society of Heating, Refrigerating and Air-Conditioning Engineers
http://www.ashrae.org
Location: US
Job Postings: Yes   *Resume Service:* No   *Networking Service:* Yes

Institute of Electrical and Electronics Engineers
http://www.ieee.org
Location: US
Job Postings: Yes   *Resume Service:* Yes   *Networking Service:* No

Notes
Favorite sites, useful resources

National Electrical Contractors Association
http://www.necanet.org
Location: US
Job Postings: No   *Resume Service:* No   *Networking Service:* No

Engineering/General

American Association of Engineering Societies
http://www.asee.org
Location: US
Job Postings: No   *Resume Service:* No   *Networking Service:* No

Engineering Foundation
http://www.engfnd.org
Location: US
Job Postings: No   *Resume Service:* No   *Networking Service:* No

The Engineering Society
http://www.esd.org
Location: US
Job Postings: Yes   *Resume Service:* Yes   *Networking Service:* No

National Society of Black Engineers
http://www.nsbe.org
Location: US
Job Postings: Yes   *Resume Service:* No   *Networking Service:* No

National Society of Professional Engineers
http://www.nspe.org
Location: US
Job Postings: Yes   *Resume Service:* Yes   *Networking Service:* Yes

Society of Women Engineers
http://www.swe.org
Location: US
Job Postings: Yes   *Resume Service:* Yes   *Networking Service:* No

Engineering/Industrial

American Iron and Steel Institute
http://www.steel.org
Location: US
Job Postings: No   *Resume Service:* No   *Networking Service:* No

---

Looking for a new or better job?   Looking for top talent?
Use WEDDLE's publications. Visit www.weddles.com today.

Notes
Favorite sites, useful resources

Industrial Designers Society of America
http://www.idsa.org
Location: US
Job Postings: Yes   *Resume Service:* No   *Networking Service:* No

Institute of Industrial Engineers
http://www.iienet.org
Location: US
Job Postings: Yes   *Resume Service:* Yes   *Networking Service:* No

Society for Industrial and Applied Mathematics
http://www.siam.org
Location: US
Job Postings: Yes   *Resume Service:* No   *Networking Service:* No

Society of Manufacturing Engineers
http://www.sme.org
Location: US
Job Postings: Yes   *Resume Service:* Yes   *Networking Service:* No

Engineering/Other Specialty

American Academy of Environmental Engineers
http://www.enviro-engrs.org
Location: US
Job Postings: Yes   *Resume Service:* No   *Networking Service:* No

American Consulting Engineers Council
http://www.acec.org
Location: US
Job Postings: No   *Resume Service:* No   *Networking Service:* No

American Design and Drafting Association
http://www.adda.org
Location: US
Job Postings: Yes   *Resume Service:* Yes   *Networking Service:* No

American Institute of Chemical Engineers
http://www.aiche.org
Location: US
Job Postings: Yes   *Resume Service:* Yes   *Networking Service:* No

American Nuclear Society
http://www.ans.org
Location: US
Job Postings: Yes   *Resume Service:* Yes   *Networking Service:* No

Notes

Favorite sites, useful resources

American Society of Heating, Refrigerating and Air-Conditioning Engineers
http://www.ashrae.org
Location: US
Job Postings: Yes   *Resume Service:* No   *Networking Service:* Yes

American Society of Mechanical Engineers
http://www.asme.org
Location: US
Job Postings: Yes   *Resume Service:* Yes   *Networking Service:* Yes

American Society of Naval Engineers
http://www.navalengineers.org
Location: US
Job Postings: Yes   *Resume Service:* No   *Networking Service:* No

American Society of Safety Engineers
http://www.asse.org
Location: US
Job Postings: No   *Resume Service:* No   *Networking Service:* No

Association of Consulting Chemists and Chemical Engineers
http://www.chemconsult.org
Location: US
Job Postings: No   *Resume Service:* No   *Networking Service:* No

Association of Energy Engineers
http://www.aeecenter.org
Location: US
Job Postings: Yes   *Resume Service:* No   *Networking Service:* No

Association of Energy Services Professionals
http://www.aesp.org
Location: US
Job Postings: No   *Resume Service:* No   *Networking Service:* No

Association for Facilities Engineering
http://www.afe.org
Location: US
Job Postings: Yes   *Resume Service:* Yes   *Networking Service:* No

Environmental and Engineering Geophysical Society
http://www.eegs.org
Location: US
Job Postings: Yes   *Resume Service:* No   *Networking Service:* No

The Institute of Industrial Engineers
http://www.iienet.org/
Location: US
Job Postings: Yes   *Resume Service:* Yes   *Networking Service:* No

Notes

Favorite sites, useful resources

Institute of Transportation Engineers
http://www.ite.org
Location: US
Job Postings: Yes   *Resume Service:* Yes   *Networking Service:* No

Instrument Society of America
http://www.isa.org
Location: US
Job Postings: Yes   *Resume Service:* Yes   *Networking Service:* No

International Association of Financial Engineers
http://www.iafe.org
Location: US
Job Postings: Yes   *Resume Service:* No   *Networking Service:* No

International Council on Systems Engineering
http://www.incose.org/
Location: US
Job Postings: Yes   *Resume Service:* No   *Networking Service:* No

International Society for Pharmaceutical Engineering
http://www.ispe.org
Location: US - Florida
Job Postings: Yes   *Resume Service:* No   *Networking Service:* No

The Internet Engineering Task Force
http://www.ietf.org
Location: US
Job Postings: No   *Resume Service:* No   *Networking Service:* No

National Association of Communication Systems Engineers
http://www.nacse.com
Location: US
Job Postings: No   *Resume Service:* No   *Networking Service:* No

The National Association of Radio and Telecommunications Engineers
http://www.narte.org
Location: US
Job Postings: Yes   *Resume Service:* No   *Networking Service:* No

Society for Industrial and Applied Mathematics
http://www.siam.org
Location: US
Job Postings: Yes   *Resume Service:* No   *Networking Service:* No

Society of Automotive Engineers
http://www.sae.org
Location: US
Job Postings: Yes   *Resume Service:* Yes   *Networking Service:* No

Notes
Favorite sites, useful resources

Society of Logistics Engineers
http://www.sole.org
Location: US
Job Postings: No   *Resume Service:* No   *Networking Service:* No

The Society of Naval Architects and Marine Engineers
http://www.sname.org
Location: US

Society of Petroleum Engineers
http://www.spe.org
Location: US
Job Postings: Yes   *Resume Service:* No   *Networking Service:* No

Society of Reliability Engineers
http://www.enre.umd.edu/sre.htm
Location: US
Job Postings: No   *Resume Service:* No   *Networking Service:* No

Workflow and Reengineering International Association
http://www.waria.com
Location: US
Job Postings: Yes   *Resume Service:* Yes   *Networking Service:* No

Entertainment/Acting

American Film Institute
http://www.afionline.org
Location: US
Job Postings: No   *Resume Service:* No   *Networking Service:* No

Independent Film & Television Alliance
http://www.ifta-online.org
Location: US
Job Postings: No   *Resume Service:* No   *Networking Service:* No

International Association Of Theatrical Stage Employees
http://www.iatse491.com
Location: International
Job Postings: Yes   *Resume Service:* No   *Networking Service:* No

International Television Association
http://www.itva.org
Location: International
Job Postings: Yes   *Resume Service:* No   *Networking Service:* No

Notes

Favorite sites, useful resources

Motion Picture Association of America
http://www.mpaa.org
Location: US
Job Postings: No   *Resume Service:* No   *Networking Service:* No

The National Association of Television Program Executives
http://www.natpe.com
Location: US
Job Postings: No   *Resume Service:* No   *Networking Service:* No

National Black Media Coalition
www.nbmc.org
Location: US
Job Postings: No   *Resume Service:* No   *Networking Service:* No

Environment

American Academy of Environmental Engineers
http://www.enviro-engrs.org
Location: US
Job Postings: Yes   *Resume Service:* No   *Networking Service:* No

American Meteorological Society
http://www.ametsoc.org
Location: US
Job Postings: Yes   *Resume Service:* No   *Networking Service:* No

Association of American State Geologists
http://www.kgs.ukans.edu/AASG/
Location: US
Job Postings: No   *Resume Service:* No   *Networking Service:* No

Association of Environmental and Resource Economists
http://www.aere.org/
Location: US
Job Postings: Yes   *Resume Service:* No   *Networking Service:* No

Emissions Marketing Association
http://www.emissions.org/
Location: US
Job Postings: No   *Resume Service:* No   *Networking Service:* No

Environmental and Engineering Geophysical Society
http://www.eegs.org
Location: US
Job Postings: Yes   *Resume Service:* No   *Networking Service:* No

Notes

Favorite sites, useful resources

Environmental Industry Association
http://www.envasns.org
Location: US
Job Postings: No   *Resume Service:* No   *Networking Service:* No

National Association of Environmental Professionals
http://www.enfo.com/naep
Location: US
Job Postings: Yes   *Resume Service:* No   *Networking Service:* No

National Weather Association
http://www.nwas.org
Location: US
Job Postings: Yes   *Resume Service:* No   *Networking Service:* No

Society for Environmental Economics and Policy Studies
http://www.seeps.org/
Location: US
Job Postings: No   *Resume Service:* No   *Networking Service:* No

Society of Environmental Journalists
http://www.sej.org
Location: US
Job Postings: No   *Resume Service:* No   *Networking Service:* No

Society of Environmental Toxicology and Chemistry
http://www.setac.org
Location: US
Job Postings: No   *Resume Service:* No   *Networking Service:* No

United States Society for Ecological Economics
http://www.ussee.org/
Location: US
Job Postings: Yes   *Resume Service:* No   *Networking Service:* No

Water Environment Federation
http://www.wef.org
Location: US
Job Postings: Yes   *Resume Service:* No   *Networking Service:* No

Equipment Leasing

Equipment Leasing Association of America
http://www.elaonline.com
Location: US
Job Postings: Yes   *Resume Service:* No   *Networking Service:* No

Notes

Favorite sites, useful resources

National Vehicle Leasing Association
http://www.nva.org
Location: US
Job Postings: No   *Resume Service:* No   *Networking Service:* No

Executive/Management

Academy of Management
http://www.aomonline.org
Location: US
Job Postings: Yes   *Resume Service:* No   *Networking Service:* No

American Association of Airport Executives
http://www.airportnet.org
Location: US
Job Postings: Yes   *Resume Service:* Yes   *Networking Service:* No

American Association of Health Care Administrative Mgmt.
http://www.aaham.org
Location: US
Job Postings: Yes   *Resume Service:* No   *Networking Service:* No

American Association of Medical Society Executives
http://www.aamse.org
Location: US
Job Postings: Yes   *Resume Service:* No   *Networking Service:* No

American College of Healthcare Executives
http://www.ache.org
Location: US
Job Postings: Yes   *Resume Service:* Yes   *Networking Service:* No

American College of Physician Executives
http://www.acpe.org
Location: US
Job Postings: Yes   *Resume Service:* Yes   *Networking Service:* No

American Management Association
http://www.amanet.org
Location: US
Job Postings: Yes   *Resume Service:* No   *Networking Service:* No

American Society of Association Executives
http://www.asaenet.org
Location: US
Job Postings: Yes   *Resume Service:* Yes   *Networking Service:* No

Notes

Favorite sites, useful resources

Association for Computer Operations Management
http://www.afcom.com
Location: US
Job Postings: No   *Resume Service:* No   *Networking Service:* No

Association of Corporate Travel Executives
http://www.acte.org
Location: US
Job Postings: No   *Resume Service:* No   *Networking Service:* No

The Association of Executive Search Consultants
http://www.aesc.org
Location: US
Job Postings: No   *Resume Service:* No   *Networking Service:* No

Association of International Product Marketing Managers
http://www.aipmm.com
Location: International
Job Postings: Yes   *Resume Service:* Yes   *Networking Service:* No

Association for Investment Management and Research
http://www.cfainstitute.org
Location: US
Job Postings: Yes   *Resume Service:* No   *Networking Service:* No

Association for Management Information Services
http://www.amifs.org
Location: US
Job Postings: Yes   *Resume Service:* Yes   *Networking Service:* Yes

Association for Public Policy Analysis and Management
http://www.appam.org
Location: US
Job Postings: Yes   *Resume Service:* No   *Networking Service:* No

The Association for Services Management International
http://www.afsmi.org
Location: US
Job Postings: Yes   *Resume Service:* Yes   *Networking Service:* Yes

California Association of Employers
http://www.employers.org
Location: US - California
Job Postings: No   *Resume Service:* No   *Networking Service:* No

Center for International Private Enterprise
http://www.cipe.org
Location: International
Job Postings: No   *Resume Service:* No   *Networking Service:* No

Notes
Favorite sites, useful resources

Council of Logistics Management
http://clm1.org/Default.asp?XX=1
Location: US
Job Postings: No   *Resume Service:* No   *Networking Service:* Yes

Credit Union Executives Society
http://www.cues.org
Location: US
Job Postings: Yes   *Resume Service:* No   *Networking Service:* No

Financial Executives International
http://www.fei.org
Location: US
Job Postings: Yes   *Resume Service:* Yes   *Networking Service:* No

Financial Managers Society
http://www.fmsinc.org
Location: US
Job Postings: Yes   *Resume Service:* Yes   *Networking Service:* Yes

Healthcare Billing & Management Association
http://www.hbma.com
Location: US
Job Postings: Yes   *Resume Service:* No   *Networking Service:* No

Healthcare Financial Management Association
http://www.hfma.org
Location: US
Job Postings: Yes   *Resume Service:* No   *Networking Service:* Yes

Hotel & Catering International Management Association
http://hcima.org.uk
Location: International
Job Postings: Yes   *Resume Service:* No   *Networking Service:* No

The Information Technology Senior Management Forum
http://www.itsmfonline.org
Location: US
Job Postings: No   *Resume Service:* No   *Networking Service:* Yes

Institute of Management and Administration
http://www.ioma.com
Location: US
Job Postings: No   *Resume Service:* No   *Networking Service:* No

Institute of Management Consultants
http://www.imcusa.org
Location: US
Job Postings: No   *Resume Service:* No   *Networking Service:* No

Notes

Favorite sites, useful resources

Institute for Operations Research and the Management Sciences (INFORMS)
http://www.informs.org
Location: US
Job Postings: Yes   *Resume Service:* No   *Networking Service:* No

Institute of Real Estate Management
http://www.irem.org
Location: US
Job Postings: Yes   *Resume Service:* No   *Networking Service:* No

Institute for Supply Management
http://www.ism.ws
Location: US
Job Postings: Yes   *Resume Service:* No   *Networking Service:* No

International Association of Corporate Real Estate Executives
http://www.nacore.com
Location: International
Job Postings: Yes   *Resume Service:* Yes   *Networking Service:* No

International Association for the Management of Technology
http://www.iamot.org
Location: International
Job Postings: Yes   *Resume Service:* No   *Networking Service:* No

International City/County Management Association
http://www.icma.org
Location: International
Job Postings: Yes   *Resume Service:* No   *Networking Service:* No

International Facilities Management Association
http://www.ifma.org
Location: US
Job Postings: Yes   *Resume Service:* Yes   *Networking Service:* No

International Food Service Executives Association
http://www.ifsea.org
Location: International
Job Postings: No   *Resume Service:* No   *Networking Service:* No

International Institute for Management Development
http://www.imd.ch
Location: Europe
Job Postings: No   *Resume Service:* No   *Networking Service:* No

Investment Management Consultants Association
http://www.imca.org
Location: US
Job Postings: No   *Resume Service:* No   *Networking Service:* Yes

Notes

Favorite sites, useful resources

Keizai Society: US-Japan Business Forum
http://www.keizai.org
Location: US - California
Job Postings: No   *Resume Service:* No   *Networking Service:* No

Marketing Management Association
http://www.mmaglobal.org
Location: US
Job Postings: No   *Resume Service:* No   *Networking Service:* No

Medical Group Management Association
http://www.mgma.com
Location: US
Job Postings: No   *Resume Service:* No   *Networking Service:* No

National Association of Executive Recruiters
http://www.naer.org
Location: US
Job Postings: No   *Resume Service:* No   *Networking Service:* No

National Association for Female Executives
http://www.nafe.com
Location: US
Job Postings: No   *Resume Service:* No   *Networking Service:* No

National Association of Professional Geriatric Care Managers
http://www.gcmwest.com
Location: US
Job Postings: No   *Resume Service:* No   *Networking Service:* No

The National Association of Television Program Executives
http://www.natpe.com
Location: US
Job Postings: No   *Resume Service:* No   *Networking Service:* No

National Contract Management Association
http://www.ncmahq.org
Location: US
Job Postings: No   *Resume Service:* No   *Networking Service:* No

National Management Association
http://www.nma1.org
Location: US
Job Postings: No   *Resume Service:* No   *Networking Service:* No

National Society of Fund Raising Executives
http://www.nsfre.org
Location: US
Job Postings: Yes   *Resume Service:* No   *Networking Service:* No

Notes

Favorite sites, useful resources

Project Management Institute
http://www.pmi.org
Location: US
Job Postings: Yes   *Resume Service:* Yes   *Networking Service:* Yes

Radiology Business Management Association
http://www.rbma.org
Location: US
Job Postings: Yes   *Resume Service:* No   *Networking Service:* No

Sales & Marketing Executives International
http://www.smei.org
Location: US
Job Postings: Yes   *Resume Service:* No   *Networking Service:* No

Technology Executives Club
http://www.technologyexecutivesclub.com
Location: US
Job Postings: No   *Resume Service:* No   *Networking Service:* No

US Small Business Administration
http://www.sba.gov
Location: US
Job Postings: Yes   *Resume Service:* No   *Networking Service:* No

Veterinary Hospital Managers Association
http://www.vhma.org
Location: US
Job Postings: No   *Resume Service:* No   *Networking Service:* No

Young Entrepreneurs Organization
http://www.yeo.org
Location: US
Job Postings: No   *Resume Service:* No   *Networking Service:* Yes

-F-

Fashion

Professional Apparel Association
http://www.proapparel.com
Location: US
Job Postings: No   *Resume Service:* No   *Networking Service:* No

---

Looking for a new or better job?   Looking for top talent?
Use WEDDLE's publications. Visit www.weddles.com today.

Notes

Favorite sites, useful resources

Funeral

Funeral Consumers Alliance
http://www.funerals.org
Location: US
Job Postings: No   *Resume Service:* No   *Networking Service:* No

National Funeral Directors Association
http://www.nfda.org
Location: US
Job Postings: Yes   *Resume Service:* No   *Networking Service:* No

-G-

Government/Public Sector

American Association of Motor Vehicle Administrators
http://www.aamva.net
Location: US
Job Postings: No   *Resume Service:* No   *Networking Service:* No

American Association of State Highway and Transportation Officials
http://www.aashto.org
Location: US
Job Postings: Yes   *Resume Service:* No   *Networking Service:* No

American Federation of Government Employees
http://www.afge.org
Location: US
Job Postings: No   *Resume Service:* No   *Networking Service:* No

American Jail Association
http://www.corrections.com/aja/
Location: US
Job Postings: Yes   *Resume Service:* No   *Networking Service:* No

American Judges Association
http://www.ncsc.dni.us/aja/
Location: US
Job Postings: No   *Resume Service:* No   *Networking Service:* No

American Public Works Association
http://www.apwa.net
Location: US
Job Postings: Yes   *Resume Service:* No   *Networking Service:* No

Notes

Favorite sites, useful resources

Association of Government Accountants
http://www.agacgfm.org
Location: US
Job Postings: Yes   *Resume Service:* Yes   *Networking Service:* No

Association for Public Policy
http://www.appam.org
Location: US
Job Postings: Yes   *Resume Service:* No   *Networking Service:* No

Association for Public Policy Analysis and Management
http://www.appam.org
Location: US
Job Postings: Yes   *Resume Service:* No   *Networking Service:* No

Emissions Marketing Association
http://www.emissions.org/
Location: US
Job Postings: No   *Resume Service:* No   *Networking Service:* No

Governmental Accounting Standards Board
http://www.gasb.org
Location: US
Job Postings: No   *Resume Service:* No   *Networking Service:* No

Georgia Department of Human Resources
http://www.dhrjobs.com
Location: US - Georgia
Job Postings: Yes   *Resume Service:* No   *Networking Service:* No

Government Finance Officers Association
http://www.gfoa.org
Location: US
Job Postings: Yes   *Resume Service:* No   *Networking Service:* No

International City/County Management Association
http://www.icma.org
Location: International
Job Postings: Yes   *Resume Service:* No   *Networking Service:* No

National Association of County and City Health Officials
http://www.naccho.org
Location: US
Job Postings: Yes   *Resume Service:* No   *Networking Service:* No

National Association of Governmental Purchasing
www.nigp.org
Location: US
Job Postings: No   *Resume Service:* No   *Networking Service:* No

Notes
Favorite sites, useful resources

National Association of State Aviation Officials
http://www.nasao.org
Location: US
Job Postings: No   *Resume Service:* No   *Networking Service:* No

National Association of State Boards of Accountancy
http://www.nasba.org
Location: US
Job Postings: No   *Resume Service:* No   *Networking Service:* No

The National Institute of Governmental Purchasing
http://www.nigp.org
Location: US
Job Postings: No   *Resume Service:* No   *Networking Service:* No

National Sheriffs' Association
http://www.sheriffs.org
Location: US
Job Postings: No   *Resume Service:* No   *Networking Service:* No

Occupational Safety and Health Administration, OSHA
http://www.osha.gov
Location: US
Job Postings: No   *Resume Service:* No   *Networking Service:* No

Oklahoma Public Employees Association
http://www.opea.org
Location: US - Oklahoma
Job Postings: No   *Resume Service:* No   *Networking Service:* No

Society for Environmental Economics and Policy Studies
http://www.seeps.org/
Location: US
Job Postings: No   *Resume Service:* No   *Networking Service:* No

Society of Government Economists
http://www.sge-econ.org
Location: US
Job Postings: Yes   *Resume Service:* No   *Networking Service:* No

Society for Policy Modeling
http://www.journalofpolicymodels.com/society.shtml
Location: US
Job Postings: No   *Resume Service:* No   *Networking Service:* No

Telecommunications and Technology Professionals Serving State Government
http://www.nastd.org
Location: US
Job Postings: No   *Resume Service:* No   *Networking Service:* No

Notes

Favorite sites, useful resources

United States Chamber of Commerce
http://www.uschamber.org
Location: US
Job Postings: Yes   *Resume Service:* No   *Networking Service:* No

US Small Business Administration
http://www.sba.gov
Location: US
Job Postings: Yes   *Resume Service:* No   *Networking Service:* No

Graphic Arts/Electronic & Print

American Institute of Graphic Arts
http://www.aiga.org
Location: US
Job Postings: Yes   *Resume Service:* Yes   *Networking Service:* No

Association of Graphic Communications
http://www.agcomm.org
Location: US
Job Postings: Yes   *Resume Service:* No   *Networking Service:* No

Association for Multimedia Communications
http://www.amcomm.org
Location: US
Job Postings: Yes   *Resume Service:* No   *Networking Service:* No

International Graphic Arts Education Association
http://www.gatf.org
Location: International
Job Postings: No   *Resume Service:* No   *Networking Service:* No

Technical Association of the Graphic Arts
http://www.taga.org
Location: US
Job Postings: Yes   *Resume Service:* No   *Networking Service:* No

-H-

Healthcare/Dental

Academy of Dentistry International
http://www.adint.org
Location: International
Job Postings: No   *Resume Service:* No   *Networking Service:* No

Notes
Favorite sites, useful resources

Academy of General Dentistry National Office
http://www.agd.org
Location: US
Job Postings: No   *Resume Service:* No   *Networking Service:* No

Academy of Laser Dentistry
http://www.laserdentistry.org
Location: US
Job Postings: No   *Resume Service:* No   *Networking Service:* No

American Academy of Cosmetic Dentistry
http://www.aacd.com
Location: US
Job Postings: No   *Resume Service:* No   *Networking Service:* No

American Academy of Implant Dentistry
http://www.aaid-implant.org
Location: US
Job Postings: No   *Resume Service:* No   *Networking Service:* No

American Academy of Pediatric Dentistry
http://www.aapd.org
Location: US
Job Postings: Yes   *Resume Service:* No   *Networking Service:* No

American Academy of Periodontology
http://www.perio.org
Location: US
Job Postings: No   *Resume Service:* No   *Networking Service:* No

American Association of Dental Consultants
http://www.aadc.org
Location: US
Job Postings: No   *Resume Service:* No   *Networking Service:* No

American Association of Endodontists
http://www.aae.org
Location: US
Job Postings: No   *Resume Service:* No   *Networking Service:* No

American Association of Oral and Maxillofacial Surgeons
http://www.aaoms.org
Location: US
Job Postings: Yes   *Resume Service:* Yes   *Networking Service:* No

American Association of Women Dentists
http://www.womendentists.org
Location: US
Job Postings: Yes   *Resume Service:* No   *Networking Service:* No

Notes

Favorite sites, useful resources

American Dental Association
http://www.ada.org
Location: US
Job Postings: No   *Resume Service:* No   *Networking Service:* No

American Student Dental Association
http://www.asdanet.org
Location: US
Job Postings: No   *Resume Service:* No   *Networking Service:* No

California Association of Orthodontists
http://www.caortho.org
Location: US - California
Job Postings: No   *Resume Service:* No   *Networking Service:* No

California Dental Association
http://www.cda.org
Location: US - California
Job Postings: No   *Resume Service:* No   *Networking Service:* No

Canadian Dental Association
http://www.cda-adc.ca
Location: North America - Canada
Job Postings: No   *Resume Service:* No   *Networking Service:* No

Colorado Dental Association
http://www.cdaonline.org
Location: US - Colorado
Job Postings: No   *Resume Service:* No   *Networking Service:* No

Dental Assisting National Board
http://www.danb.org
Location: US
Job Postings: No   *Resume Service:* No   *Networking Service:* No

Dental Lab Association of the State of New York
http://www.dlany.org
Location: US - New York
Job Postings: Yes   *Resume Service:* No   *Networking Service:* No

Dental Manufacturers of America
http://www.dmanews.org
Location: US
Job Postings: No   *Resume Service:* No   *Networking Service:* No

Federation of Special Care Organizations in Dentistry
http://www.foscod.org
Location: US
Job Postings: No   *Resume Service:* No   *Networking Service:* No

Notes
Favorite sites, useful resources

Florida Dental Association
http://www.floridadental.org
Location: US - Florida
Job Postings: No   *Resume Service:* No   *Networking Service:* No

Greater Cleveland Dental Society
http://www.gcds.org
Location: US - Ohio
Job Postings: Yes   *Resume Service:* No   *Networking Service:* No

Illinois State Dental Society
http://www.isds.org
Location: US - Illinois
Job Postings: No   *Resume Service:* No   *Networking Service:* No

International Association for Dental Research
http://www.dentalresearch.org
Location: International
Job Postings: No   *Resume Service:* No   *Networking Service:* No

International Association for Orthodontics
http://www.iaortho.org
Location: International
Job Postings: No   *Resume Service:* No   *Networking Service:* No

International College of Dentists
http://www.icd.org
Location: International
Job Postings: No   *Resume Service:* No   *Networking Service:* No

Kentucky Dental Association
http://www.kyda.org
Location: US - Kentucky
Job Postings: No   *Resume Service:* No   *Networking Service:* No

Los Angeles Dental Society
http://www.ladentalsociety.com
Location: US - California
Job Postings: No   *Resume Service:* No   *Networking Service:* No

Maryland State Dental Association
http://www.msda.com
Location: US - Maryland
Job Postings: No   *Resume Service:* No   *Networking Service:* No

Massachusetts Dental Society
http://www.massdental.org
Location: US - Massachusetts
Job Postings: Yes   *Resume Service:* No   *Networking Service:* No

Notes

Favorite sites, useful resources

Michigan Dental Association
http://www.michigandental.org
Location: US - Michigan
Job Postings: Yes   *Resume Service:* No   *Networking Service:* No

Missouri Dental Association
http://www.modental.org
Location: US - Missouri
Job Postings: Yes   *Resume Service:* No   *Networking Service:* No

National Association of Dental Plans
http://www.nadp.org
Location: US
Job Postings: No   *Resume Service:* No   *Networking Service:* No

National Board Certification Program for Dental Technicians
http://www.nadl.org
Location: US
Job Postings: No   *Resume Service:* No   *Networking Service:* No

Nevada Dental Association
http://www.nvda.org
Location: US - Nevada
Job Postings: No   *Resume Service:* No   *Networking Service:* No

New Jersey Dental Association
http://www.njda.org
Location: US - New Jersey
Job Postings: No   *Resume Service:* No   *Networking Service:* No

New York State Dental Association
http://www.nysdental.org
Location: US - New York
Job Postings: No   *Resume Service:* No   *Networking Service:* No

North Carolina Dental Society
http://www.ncdental.org
Location: US - North Carolina
Job Postings: Yes   *Resume Service:* Yes   *Networking Service:* No

North Dakota Dental Association
http://www.nddental.com
Location: US - North Dakota
Job Postings: Yes   *Resume Service:* No   *Networking Service:* No

Ohio Dental Association
http://www.oda.org
Location: US - Ohio
Job Postings: No   *Resume Service:* No   *Networking Service:* No

Notes

Favorite sites, useful resources

Oregon Dental Association
http://www.oregondental.org
Location: US - Oregon
Job Postings: No   *Resume Service:* No   *Networking Service:* No

Pennsylvania Dental Association
http://www.padental.org
Location: US - Pennsylvania
Job Postings: Yes   *Resume Service:* No   *Networking Service:* No

Rhode Island Dental Association
http://www.ridental.com
Location: US - Rhode Island
Job Postings: Yes   *Resume Service:* No   *Networking Service:* No

South Carolina Dental Association
http://www.scda.org
Location: US - South Carolina
Job Postings: Yes   *Resume Service:* No   *Networking Service:* No

Virginia Dental Association
http://www.vadental.org
Location: US - Virginia
Job Postings: No   *Resume Service:* No   *Networking Service:* No

Washington State Dental Association
http://www.wsda.org
Location: US - Washington
Job Postings: No   *Resume Service:* No   *Networking Service:* No

Wisconsin Dental Association
http://www.wisconsindental.com
Location: US - Wisconsin
Job Postings: No   *Resume Service:* No   *Networking Service:* No

Healthcare/General & Management

American Academy of Medical Administrators
http://www.aameda.org
Location: US
Job Postings: Yes   *Resume Service:* No   *Networking Service:* No

American Academy of Professional Coders
http://www.aapcnatl.org
Location: US
Job Postings: Yes   *Resume Service:* Yes   *Networking Service:* No

Notes

Favorite sites, useful resources

American Association of Health Care Administrative Management
http://www.aaham.org
Location: US
Job Postings: Yes   *Resume Service:* No   *Networking Service:* No

American Association of Health Plans
http://www.aahp.org
Location: US
Job Postings: No   *Resume Service:* No   *Networking Service:* No

American Association of Medical Society Executives
http://www.aamse.org
Location: US
Job Postings: Yes   *Resume Service:* No   *Networking Service:* No

American College of Healthcare Executives
http://www.ache.org
Location: US
Job Postings: Yes   *Resume Service:* Yes   *Networking Service:* No

American College of Physician Executives
http://www.acpe.org
Location: US
Job Postings: Yes   *Resume Service:* Yes   *Networking Service:* No

American College of Preventive Medicine
http://www.acpm.org
Location: US
Job Postings: Yes   *Resume Service:* Yes   *Networking Service:* No

American Health Care Association
http://www.ahca.org
Location: US
Job Postings: No   *Resume Service:* No   *Networking Service:* No

American Healthcare Radiology Administrators
http://www.ahraonline.org
Location: US
Job Postings: Yes   *Resume Service:* No   *Networking Service:* No

American Holistic Health Association
http://www.ahha.org
Location: US
Job Postings: No   *Resume Service:* No   *Networking Service:* No

American Medical Association
http://www.ama-assn.org
Location: US
Job Postings: No   *Resume Service:* No   *Networking Service:* No

Notes

Favorite sites, useful resources

American Medical Directors Association
http://www.amda.com
Location: US
Job Postings: No   *Resume Service:* No   *Networking Service:* No

American Medical Group Association
http://www.amga.org
Location: US
Job Postings: No   *Resume Service:* No   *Networking Service:* No

American Medical Society
http://www.ama-assn.org
Location: US
Job Postings: Yes   *Resume Service:* No   *Networking Service:* No

American Medical Women's Association
http://www.amwa-doc.org
Location: US
Job Postings: No   *Resume Service:* No   *Networking Service:* No

American Society on Aging
http://www.asaging.org
Location: US
Job Postings: Yes   *Resume Service:* No   *Networking Service:* No

Association of Healthcare Internal Auditors
http://www.ahia.org
Location: US
Job Postings: Yes   *Resume Service:* No   *Networking Service:* No

Canadian Medical Association
http://www.cma.org
Location: North America - Canada
Job Postings: No   *Resume Service:* No   *Networking Service:* No

Canadian Society for International Health
http://www.csih.org
Location: North America - Canada
Job Postings: Yes   *Resume Service:* No   *Networking Service:* No

The Gerontological Society of America
http://www.geron.org
Location: US - District of Columbia
Job Postings: Yes   *Resume Service:* Yes   *Networking Service:* No

Health Care Compliance Association
http://www.hcca-info.org
Location: US
Job Postings: No   *Resume Service:* No   *Networking Service:* No

Notes

Favorite sites, useful resources

Health Industry Distributors Association
http://www.hida.org
Location:　　US
Job Postings: No　　　　*Resume Service:* No　　　　*Networking Service:* No

Health Insurance Association of America
http://www.hiaa.org
Location:　　US
Job Postings: No　　　　*Resume Service:* No　　　　*Networking Service:* No

Healthcare Billing & Management Association
http://www.hbma.com
Location:　　US
Job Postings: Yes　　　　*Resume Service:* No　　　　*Networking Service:* No

Healthcare Business Women's Association
http://www.hbanet.org/
Location:　　US
Job Postings: No　　　　*Resume Service:* No　　　　*Networking Service:* No

Healthcare Financial Management Association
http://www.hfma.org
Location:　　US
Job Postings: Yes　　　　*Resume Service:* No　　　　*Networking Service:* Yes

Healthcare Information and Management Systems
http://www.hlmss.org
Location:　　US
Job Postings: Yes　　　　*Resume Service:* Yes　　　　*Networking Service:* No

Hospice Foundation of America
http://www.hospicefoundation.org
Location:　　US
Job Postings: No　　　　*Resume Service:* No　　　　*Networking Service:* No

Independent Medical Distributors Association
http://www.imda.org
Location:　　US
Job Postings: No　　　　*Resume Service:* No　　　　*Networking Service:* No

Integrated Healthcare Association
http://www.iha.org
Location:　　US
Job Postings: No　　　　*Resume Service:* No　　　　*Networking Service:* No

Medical Group Management Association
http://www.mgma.com
Location:　　US
Job Postings: No　　　　*Resume Service:* No　　　　*Networking Service:* No

Notes
Favorite sites, useful resources

National Arab American Medical Association
http://www.naama.com
Location: US
Job Postings: No   *Resume Service:* No   *Networking Service:* No

National Association for Healthcare Quality
http://www.nahq.org
Location: US
Job Postings: Yes   *Resume Service:* No   *Networking Service:* No

National Association Medical Staff Services
http://www.namss.org
Location: US
Job Postings: Yes   *Resume Service:* No   *Networking Service:* No

National Association of Community Health Centers
http://www.nachc.com
Location: US
Job Postings: No   *Resume Service:* No   *Networking Service:* No

National Association of County and City Health Officials
http://www.naccho.org
Location: US
Job Postings: Yes   *Resume Service:* No   *Networking Service:* No

National Association of Health Underwriters
http://www.nahu.org
Location: US
Job Postings: No   *Resume Service:* No   *Networking Service:* No

The National Association for Health Care Recruitment
http://www.nahcr.com
Location: US
Job Postings: No   *Resume Service:* No   *Networking Service:* No

National Association of Professional Geriatric Care Managers
http://www.gcmwest.com
Location: US
Job Postings: No   *Resume Service:* No   *Networking Service:* No

National Hispanic Medical Association
http://home.earthlink.net/~nhma/webdoc1.htm
Location: US
Job Postings: No   *Resume Service:* No   *Networking Service:* No

National Medical Association
http://www.natmed.org
Location: US
Job Postings: No   *Resume Service:* No   *Networking Service:* No

Notes

Favorite sites, useful resources

The National Mental Health Association
http://www.nmha.org
Location: US
Job Postings: No   *Resume Service:* No   *Networking Service:* No

The National Rural Health Association
http://www.nrharural.org
Location: US
Job Postings: No   *Resume Service:* No   *Networking Service:* No

National Wellness Institute
http://www.nationalwellness.org
Location: US
Job Postings: No   *Resume Service:* No   *Networking Service:* No

Occupational Safety and Health Administration, OSHA
http://www.osha.gov
Location: US
Job Postings: No   *Resume Service:* No   *Networking Service:* No

Radiology Business Management Association
http://www.rbma.org
Location: US
Job Postings: Yes   *Resume Service:* No   *Networking Service:* No

Healthcare/Hospital

American Hospital Association
http://www.aha.org
Location: US
Job Postings: No   *Resume Service:* No   *Networking Service:* No

Society of Hospital Pharmacists of Australia
http://www.shpa.org.au
Location: Australia
Job Postings: Yes   *Resume Service:* No   *Networking Service:* No

South African Association of Hospital & Institutional Pharmacists
http://www.saahip.org.za
Location: Africa
Job Postings: No   *Resume Service:* No   *Networking Service:* No

Veterinary Hospital Managers Association
http://www.vhma.org
Location: US
Job Postings: No   *Resume Service:* No   *Networking Service:* No

Notes
Favorite sites, useful resources

Healthcare/Nursing

Academy of Medical-Surgical Nurses
http://www.medsurgnurse.org
Location: US
Job Postings: Yes   *Resume Service:* Yes   *Networking Service:* Yes

American Academy of Ambulatory Care Nursing
http://www.aaacn.org
Location: US
Job Postings: Yes   *Resume Service:* Yes   *Networking Service:* Yes

American Academy of Nurse Practitioners
http://www.aanp.org
Location: US
Job Postings: Yes   *Resume Service:* No   *Networking Service:* No

American Association of Critical Care Nurses
http://www.aacn.org
Location: US
Job Postings: Yes   *Resume Service:* No   *Networking Service:* No

American Association of Legal Nurse Consultants
http://www.aalnc.org
Location: US
Job Postings: No   *Resume Service:* No   *Networking Service:* No

American Association of Nurse Anesthetists
http://www.aana.com
Location: US
Job Postings: Yes   *Resume Service:* Yes   *Networking Service:* No

American Association of Occupational Health Nurses
http://www.aaohn.org
Location: US
Job Postings: Yes   *Resume Service:* Yes   *Networking Service:* Yes

American College of Nurse-Midwives
http://www.acnm.org
Location: US
Job Postings: Yes   *Resume Service:* Yes   *Networking Service:* Yes

---

Looking for a new or better job?   Looking for top talent?
Use WEDDLE's publications. Visit www.weddles.com today.
- *WEDDLE's 2005/6 Guide* is the "consumer's report" of job boards.
- *WEDDLE's 2005/6 Directory* is the "address book" of job boards.

Notes

Favorite sites, useful resources

American College of Nurse Practitioners
http://www.nurse.org/acnp/
Location: US
Job Postings: No   *Resume Service:* No   *Networking Service:* No

American Nephrology Nurses Association
http://anna.inurse.com
Location: US
Job Postings: Yes   *Resume Service:* No   *Networking Service:* No

American Nurses Association
http://www.nursingworld.org
Location: US
Job Postings: Yes   *Resume Service:* No   *Networking Service:* No

American Psychiatric Nurses Association
http://www.apna.org
Location: US
Job Postings: Yes   *Resume Service:* No   *Networking Service:* No

American School Health Association
http://www.ashaweb.org
Location: US
Job Postings: No   *Resume Service:* No   *Networking Service:* No

American Society of PeriAnesthesia Nurses
http://www.aspan.org
Location: US
Job Postings: Yes   *Resume Service:* Yes   *Networking Service:* No

Association of Operating Room Nurses
http://www.aorn.org
Location: US
Job Postings: Yes   *Resume Service:* No   *Networking Service:* No

Association of Pediatric Oncology Nurses
http://www.apon.org
Location: US
Job Postings: Yes   *Resume Service:* No   *Networking Service:* No

Association of Preoperative Registered Nurses Online
http://www.aorn.org
Location: US
Job Postings: Yes   *Resume Service:* No   *Networking Service:* No

Canadian Nurses Association
http://www.cna-nurses.ca
Location: North America - Canada
Job Postings: Yes   *Resume Service:* No   *Networking Service:* No

Notes

Favorite sites, useful resources

Dermatology Nurses' Association
http://www.dnanurse.org/
Location: US
Job Postings: Yes   *Resume Service:* Yes   *Networking Service:* Yes

Emergency Nurses Association
http://www.ena.org
Location: US
Job Postings: No   *Resume Service:* No   *Networking Service:* No

Intravenous Nurses Society
http://www.ins1.org
Location: US
Job Postings: Yes   *Resume Service:* Yes   *Networking Service:* No

Midwifery Education Accreditation Council
http://www.meacschools.org
Location: US
Job Postings: No   *Resume Service:* No   *Networking Service:* No

Midwives' Alliance of North America
http://www.mana.org
Location: US
Job Postings: No   *Resume Service:* No   *Networking Service:* No

National Association of NeoNatal Nurses
http://www.nann.org
Location: US
Job Postings: Yes   *Resume Service:* No   *Networking Service:* No

National Association of Orthopedic Nurses
http://naon.inurse.com
Location: US
Job Postings: No   *Resume Service:* No   *Networking Service:* No

National Association of Pediatric Nurse Associates and Practitioners
http://www.napnap.org
Location: US
Job Postings: No   *Resume Service:* No   *Networking Service:* No

National Gerontological Nursing Association
http://www.nursingcenter.com
Location: US
Job Postings: Yes   *Resume Service:* No   *Networking Service:* No

National League of Nursing
http://www.nln.org
Location: US
Job Postings: Yes   *Resume Service:* No   *Networking Service:* No

Notes
Favorite sites, useful resources

Society of Gastroenterology Nurses & Associates
http://www.sgna.org
Location: US
Job Postings: Yes   *Resume Service:* Yes   *Networking Service:* Yes

Healthcare/Physicians & Surgeons

American Academy of Dermatology
http://www.aad.org
Location: US
Job Postings: No   *Resume Service:* No   *Networking Service:* No

American Academy of Family Physicians
http://www.aafp.org
Location: US
Job Postings: Yes   *Resume Service:* No   *Networking Service:* No

American Academy of Neurology
http://www.aan.com
Location: US
Job Postings: No   *Resume Service:* No   *Networking Service:* No

American Academy of Orthopedic Surgeons
http://www.aaos.org
Location: US
Job Postings: No   *Resume Service:* No   *Networking Service:* No

American Academy of Otolaryngology - Head & Neck Surgery
http://www.entnet.org
Location: US
Job Postings: No   *Resume Service:* No   *Networking Service:* No

American Academy of Pediatrics
http://www.aap.org
Location: US
Job Postings: Yes   *Resume Service:* No   *Networking Service:* No

American Academy of Physicians Assistants
http://www.aapa.org
Location: US
Job Postings: Yes   *Resume Service:* Yes   *Networking Service:* No

American Association of Clinical Endocrinologists
http://www.aace.com
Location: US
Job Postings: No   *Resume Service:* No   *Networking Service:* No

Notes

Favorite sites, useful resources

American Association of Gynecologic Laparoscopists
http://www.aagl.com
Location: US
Job Postings: Yes   *Resume Service:* Yes   *Networking Service:* No

American Association of Neurological Surgeons
http://www.neurosurgery.org
Location: US
Job Postings: No   *Resume Service:* No   *Networking Service:* No

American Association of Thoracic Surgery
http://www.aats.org
Location: US
Job Postings: No   *Resume Service:* No   *Networking Service:* No

American Board of Neurological Surgery
http://www.abns.org
Location: US
Job Postings: No   *Resume Service:* No   *Networking Service:* No

American Board of Surgery
http://www.absurgery.org
Location: US
Job Postings: No   *Resume Service:* No   *Networking Service:* No

American College of Allergy, Asthma & Immunology
http://www.acaai.org
Location: US
Job Postings: Yes   *Resume Service:* Yes   *Networking Service:* No

American College of Cardiology
http://www.acc.org
Location: US
Job Postings: Yes   *Resume Service:* Yes   *Networking Service:* No

American College of Chest Physicians
http://www.chestnet.org
Location: US
Job Postings: Yes   *Resume Service:* Yes   *Networking Service:* No

American College of Foot and Ankle Surgeons
http://www.acfas.org
Location: US
Job Postings: Yes   *Resume Service:* Yes   *Networking Service:* No

American College of Obstetricians and Gynecologists
http://www.acog.org
Location: US
Job Postings: No   *Resume Service:* No   *Networking Service:* No

Notes
Favorite sites, useful resources

American College of Occupational and Environmental Medicine
http://www.acoem.org
Location: US
Job Postings: Yes   *Resume Service:* Yes   *Networking Service:* No

American College of Preventive Medicine
http://www.acpm.org
Location: US
Job Postings: Yes   *Resume Service:* Yes   *Networking Service:* No

American College of Rheumatology
http://www.rheumatology.org
Location: US
Job Postings: Yes   *Resume Service:* Yes   *Networking Service:* No

American College of Surgeons
http://www.facs.org
Location: US
Job Postings: No   *Resume Service:* No   *Networking Service:* No

American Gastroenterological Association
http://www.gastro.org/
Location: US
Job Postings: Yes   *Resume Service:* Yes   *Networking Service:* No

American Medical Society
http://www.ama-assn.org
Location: US
Job Postings: Yes   *Resume Service:* No   *Networking Service:* No

American Society for Dermatologic Surgery
http://www.asds-net.org
Location: US
Job Postings: No   *Resume Service:* No   *Networking Service:* No

American Society of Cataract and Refractive Surgery
http://www.ascrs.org
Location: US
Job Postings: Yes   *Resume Service:* No   *Networking Service:* No

American Society of Colon and Rectal Surgeons
http://www.fascrs.org
Location: US
Job Postings: Yes   *Resume Service:* No   *Networking Service:* No

American Society of General Surgeons
http://www.theasgs.org
Location: US
Job Postings: Yes   *Resume Service:* Yes   *Networking Service:* No

Notes

Favorite sites, useful resources

Association of American Physicians and Surgeons
http://www.aapsonline.org
Location: US
Job Postings: No   *Resume Service:* No   *Networking Service:* No

Association of Women Surgeons
http://www.womensurgeons.org
Location: US
Job Postings: Yes   *Resume Service:* No   *Networking Service:* No

Chicago Medical Society
http://www.cmsdocs.org
Location: US - Illinois
Job Postings: Yes   *Resume Service:* Yes   *Networking Service:* No

National Association of EMS Physicians
http://www.naemsp.org
Location: US
Job Postings: Yes   *Resume Service:* No   *Networking Service:* No

National Commission on Certification of Physician Assistants
http://www.nccpa.net
Location: US
Job Postings: No   *Resume Service:* No   *Networking Service:* No

North American Spine Society
http://www.spine.org
Location: US
Job Postings: No   *Resume Service:* No   *Networking Service:* No

Society of Neurological Surgeons
http://www.societyns.org
Location: US
Job Postings: No   *Resume Service:* No   *Networking Service:* No

Society of Thoracic Surgeons
http://www.sts.org
Location: US
Job Postings: No   *Resume Service:* No   *Networking Service:* No

Society for Vascular Surgery
http://www.vascularweb.org
Location: US
Job Postings: Yes   *Resume Service:* No   *Networking Service:* No

---

Looking for a new or better job?   Looking for top talent?
Use WEDDLE's publications. Visit www.weddles.com today.

Notes

Favorite sites, useful resources

Wisconsin Medical Society
http://www.wisconsinmedicalsociety.org
Location: US - Wisconsin
Job Postings: Yes   *Resume Service:* Yes   *Networking Service:* No

Healthcare/Specialties & Special Issues

Academy of Counseling Psychology
http://www.aacop.net
Location: US
Job Postings: No   *Resume Service:* No   *Networking Service:* No

AIDS Action
http://www.aidsaction.org
Location: US
Job Postings: No   *Resume Service:* No   *Networking Service:* No

American Academy of Dermatology
http://www.aad.org
Location: US
Job Postings: No   *Resume Service:* No   *Networking Service:* No

American Academy of Family Physicians
http://www.aafp.org
Location: US
Job Postings: Yes   *Resume Service:* No   *Networking Service:* No

American Academy of Neurology
http://www.aan.com
Location: US
Job Postings: No   *Resume Service:* No   *Networking Service:* No

American Academy of Orthopedic Surgeons
http://www.aaos.org
Location: US
Job Postings: No   *Resume Service:* No   *Networking Service:* No

American Academy of Otolaryngology - Head & Neck Surgery
http://www.entnet.org
Location: US
Job Postings: No   *Resume Service:* No   *Networking Service:* No

American Academy of Pediatrics
http://www.aap.org
Location: US
Job Postings: No   *Resume Service:* No   *Networking Service:* No

Notes
Favorite sites, useful resources

American Academy of Pharmaceutical Physicians
http://www.aapp.org
Location: US
Job Postings: Yes   *Resume Service:* No   *Networking Service:* No

American Academy of Physician Assistants
http://www.aapa.org
Location: US
Job Postings: Yes   *Resume Service:* No   *Networking Service:* No

American Association of Clinical Endocrinologists
http://www.aace.com
Location: US
Job Postings: No   *Resume Service:* No   *Networking Service:* No

American Association of Gynecologic Laparoscopists
http://www.aagl.com
Location: US
Job Postings: Yes   *Resume Service:* Yes   *Networking Service:* No

American Association of Medical Assistants
http://aama-ntl.org
Location: US - Alaska
Job Postings: Yes   *Resume Service:* Yes   *Networking Service:* No

American Association of Medical Transcriptionists
http://www.aamt.org
Location: US
Job Postings: Yes   *Resume Service:* No   *Networking Service:* No

American Association of Neurological Surgeons
http://www.neurosurgery.org
Location: US
Job Postings: No   *Resume Service:* No   *Networking Service:* No

American Association for Respiratory Care
http://www.aarc.org
Location: US
Job Postings: Yes   *Resume Service:* No   *Networking Service:* No

American Board of Medical Specialties
http://www.abms.org
Location: US
Job Postings: No   *Resume Service:* No   *Networking Service:* No

American Board of Surgery
http://www.absurgery.org
Location: US
Job Postings: No   *Resume Service:* No   *Networking Service:* No

Notes

Favorite sites, useful resources

American College of Domiciliary Midwives
http://www.goodnewsnet.org/practice/college.htm
Location: US
Job Postings: No   *Resume Service:* No   *Networking Service:* No

American College of Preventive Medicine
http://www.acpm.org
Location: US
Job Postings: Yes   *Resume Service:* Yes   *Networking Service:* No

American Counseling Association
http://www.counseling.org
Location: US
Job Postings: Yes   *Resume Service:* No   *Networking Service:* No

American Dietetic Association
http://www.eatright.org/
Location: US
Job Postings: Yes   *Resume Service:* Yes   *Networking Service:* No

American Geriatrics Society
http://www.americangeriatrics.org
Location: US
Job Postings: Yes   *Resume Service:* No   *Networking Service:* No

American Holistic Health Association
http://www.ahha.org
Location: US
Job Postings: No   *Resume Service:* No   *Networking Service:* No

American Medical Informatics Association
http://www.amia.org
Location: US
Job Postings: Yes   *Resume Service:* Yes   *Networking Service:* No\

American Medical Women's Association
http://www.amwa-doc.org
Location: US
Job Postings: No   *Resume Service:* No   *Networking Service:* No

American Occupational Therapy Association
http://www.aota.org
Location: US
Job Postings: Yes   *Resume Service:* No   *Networking Service:* No

American Orthotic and Prosthetic Association
http://www.opoffice.org
Location: US
Job Postings: No   *Resume Service:* No   *Networking Service:* No

Notes

Favorite sites, useful resources

American Podiatric Medical Association
http://www.apma.org
Location: US
Job Postings: No   *Resume Service:* No   *Networking Service:* No

American Psychiatric Association
http://www.psych.org
Location: US
Job Postings: Yes   *Resume Service:* No   *Networking Service:* No

American Registry of Diagnostic Medical Sonographers
http://www.ardms.org/
Location: US
Job Postings: Yes   *Resume Service:* Yes   *Networking Service:* No

American Registry of Radiologic Technologists
http://www.arrt.org
Location: US
Job Postings: No   *Resume Service:* No   *Networking Service:* No

American Society on Aging
http://www.asaging.org
Location: US
Job Postings: Yes   *Resume Service:* No   *Networking Service:* No

American Society of Anesthesiologists
http://www.asahq.org
Location: US
Job Postings: No   *Resume Service:* No   *Networking Service:* No

American Society of Clinical Oncology
http://www.asco.org
Location: US
Job Postings: Yes   *Resume Service:* Yes   *Networking Service:* No

American Society for Dermatologic Surgery
http://www.asds-net.org
Location: US
Job Postings: No   *Resume Service:* No   *Networking Service:* No

American Society of Internal Medicine
http://www.acponline.org
Location: US
Job Postings: Yes   *Resume Service:* No   *Networking Service:* No

American Society of Radiologic Technologists
http://www.asrt.org
Location: US
Job Postings: Yes   *Resume Service:* Yes   *Networking Service:* No

Notes

Favorite sites, useful resources

American Urological Association, Inc.
http://auanet.org
Location: US
Job Postings: Yes   *Resume Service:* No   *Networking Service:* No

American Veterinary Medical Association
http://www.avma.org
Location: US
Job Postings: Yes   *Resume Service:* Yes   *Networking Service:* No

Association of American Physicians and Surgeons
http://www.aapsonline.org
Location: US
Job Postings: No   *Resume Service:* No   *Networking Service:* No

Emergency Medicine Residents' Association
http://www.emra.org
Location: US
Job Postings: Yes   *Resume Service:* No   *Networking Service:* No

The Gerontological Society of America
http://www.geron.org
Location: US - District of Columbia
Job Postings: Yes   *Resume Service:* Yes   *Networking Service:* No

Hospice Foundation of America
http://www.hospicefoundation.org
Location: US
Job Postings: No   *Resume Service:* No   *Networking Service:* No

International Academy of Orthopedic Medicine
http://www.iaomed.com
Location: US
Job Postings: No   *Resume Service:* No   *Networking Service:* No

International AIDS Society
http://www.ias.se
Location: US
Job Postings: No   *Resume Service:* No   *Networking Service:* No

International Association of Eating Disorders Professionals
http://www.iaedp.com
Location: US
Job Postings: Yes   *Resume Service:* Yes   *Networking Service:* No

International Society for Pharmacoepidemiology
http://www.pharmacoepi.org
Location: International
Job Postings: Yes   *Resume Service:* No   *Networking Service:* No

Notes

Favorite sites, useful resources

National Arab American Medical Association
http://www.naama.com
Location: US
Job Postings: No   *Resume Service:* No   *Networking Service:* No

National Association Medical Staff Services
http://www.namss.org
Location: US
Job Postings: Yes   *Resume Service:* No   *Networking Service:* No

National Association of Community Health Centers
http://www.nachc.com
Location: US
Job Postings: No   *Resume Service:* No   *Networking Service:* No

National Association of County and City Health Officials
http://www.naccho.org
Location: US
Job Postings: Yes   *Resume Service:* No   *Networking Service:* No

National Association of Emergency Medical Technicians
http://www.naemt.org
Location: US
Job Postings: No   *Resume Service:* No   *Networking Service:* No

National Association of Professional Geriatric Care Managers
http://www.gcmwest.com
Location: US
Job Postings: No   *Resume Service:* No   *Networking Service:* No

National Commission on Certification of Physician Assistants
http://www.nccpa.net
Location: US
Job Postings: No   *Resume Service:* No   *Networking Service:* No

National Emergency Medicine Association
http://www.nemahealth.org
Location: US
Job Postings: No   *Resume Service:* No   *Networking Service:* No

National Hispanic Medical Association
http://home.earthlink.net/~nhma/webdoc1.htm
Location: US
Job Postings: No   *Resume Service:* No   *Networking Service:* No

The National Mental Health Association
http://www.nmha.org
Location: US
Job Postings: No   *Resume Service:* No   *Networking Service:* No

Notes

Favorite sites, useful resources

The National Rural Health Association
http://www.nrharural.org
Location: US
Job Postings: No   *Resume Service:* No   *Networking Service:* No

Pediatric Pharmacy Advocacy Group
http://www.ppag.org
Location: US
Job Postings: Yes   *Resume Service:* No   *Networking Service:* No

Radiology Society of North America
http://www.rsna.org
Location: International
Job Postings: Yes   *Resume Service:* No   *Networking Service:* No

Society for Academic Emergency Medicine
http://www.saem.org
Location: US
Job Postings: Yes   *Resume Service:* No   *Networking Service:* No

Society for Adolescent Medicine
http://www.adolescenthealth.org
Location: US
Job Postings: No   *Resume Service:* No   *Networking Service:* No

Society of Critical Care Medicine
http://www.sccm.org
Location: US
Job Postings: Yes   *Resume Service:* No   *Networking Service:* No

Society for Experimental Biology and Medicine
http://www.sebm.org
Location: US
Job Postings: No   *Resume Service:* No   *Networking Service:* No

Washington Biotechnology Biomedical Association
http://www.wabio.com
Location: US - Washington
Job Postings: No   *Resume Service:* No   *Networking Service:* No

World Veterinary Association
http://www.worldvet.org
Location: International
Job Postings: Yes   *Resume Service:* No   *Networking Service:* No

---

Looking for a new or better job?   Looking for top talent?
Use WEDDLE's publications. Visit www.weddles.com today.

Notes
Favorite sites, useful resources

Healthcare/Therapy & Rehabilitation

American Academy of Physical Medicine & Rehabilitation
http://www.aapmr.org
Location: US
Job Postings: Yes   *Resume Service:* No   *Networking Service:* No

American Association of Cardiovascular and Pulmonary Rehabilitation
http://www.aacvpr.org
Location: US
Job Postings: No   *Resume Service:* No   *Networking Service:* No

American Congress of Rehabilitation Medicine
http://www.acrm.org
Location: US
Job Postings: Yes   *Resume Service:* No   *Networking Service:* No

American Occupational Therapy Association
http://www.aota.org
Location: US
Job Postings: Yes   *Resume Service:* No   *Networking Service:* No

American Physical Therapy Association
http://www.apta.org
Location: US
Job Postings: Yes   *Resume Service:* No   *Networking Service:* Yes

Association of Occupational Health Professionals
http://www.aohp.org
Location: US
Job Postings: No   *Resume Service:* No   *Networking Service:* No

National Mental Health Association
http://www.nmha.org
Location: US
Job Postings: No   *Resume Service:* No   *Networking Service:* No

National Rehabilitation Association
http://www.nationalrehab.org
Location: US
Job Postings: No   *Resume Service:* No   *Networking Service:* No

Hospitality

American Hotel and Motel Association
http://www.ahma.com
Location: US
Job Postings: Yes   *Resume Service:* Yes   *Networking Service:* Yes

Notes
Favorite sites, useful resources

Asian American Hotel Owners Association
http://www.aahoa.org
Location: US
Job Postings: No   *Resume Service:* No   *Networking Service:* No

Hospitality Financial and Technology Professionals
http://www.hftp.org
Location: US
Job Postings: Yes   *Resume Service:* Yes   *Networking Service:* No

Hospitality Sales & Marketing Association International
http://www.hsmai.org
Location: International
Job Postings: No   *Resume Service:* No   *Networking Service:* No

Hotel & Catering International Management Association
http://hcima.org.uk
Location: International
Job Postings: Yes   *Resume Service:* No   *Networking Service:* No

International Association of Hospitality Accountants
http://www.hftp.org
Location: US
Job Postings: Yes   *Resume Service:* Yes   *Networking Service:* No

International Festivals and Events Association
http://www.ifea.com
Location: International
Job Postings: No   *Resume Service:* No   *Networking Service:* No

International Hotel and Restaurant Association
http://www.ih-ra.com
Location: International
Job Postings: Yes   *Resume Service:* Yes   *Networking Service:* No

Professional Association of Innkeepers International
http://www.paii.org
Location: International
Job Postings: Yes   *Resume Service:* No   *Networking Service:* No

Human Resources

Academy of Human Resource Development
http://www.ahrd.org
Location: US
Job Postings: No   *Resume Service:* No   *Networking Service:* No

Notes

Favorite sites, useful resources

American Association of Health Plans
http://www.aahp.org
Location: US
Job Postings: No   *Resume Service:* No   *Networking Service:* No

American College Personnel Association
http://www.myacpa.org
Location: US
Job Postings: No   *Resume Service:* No   *Networking Service:* No

American Psychological Association
http://www.apa.org
Location: US
Job Postings: Yes   *Resume Service:* Yes   *Networking Service:* No

Australian Human Resources Institute
http://www.ahri.com.au
Location: Australia
Job Postings: Yes   *Resume Service:* Yes   *Networking Service:* No

California Association of Employers
http://www.employers.org
Location: US - California
Job Postings: No   *Resume Service:* No   *Networking Service:* No

Chicagoland Chapter American Society of Training and Development
http://www.ccastd.org
Location: US - Illinois
Job Postings: Yes   *Resume Service:* No   *Networking Service:* No

College and University Professional Association for Human Resources
http://www.cupahr.org/
Location: US
Job Postings: Yes   *Resume Service:* No   *Networking Service:* No

Council on Employee Benefits
http://www.ceb.org
Location: US
Job Postings: Yes   *Resume Service:* No   *Networking Service:* No

Dallas Human Resource Management Association
http://www.dallashr.org
Location: US - Texas
Job Postings: Yes   *Resume Service:* Yes   *Networking Service:* No

Employee Benefit Research Institute
http://www.ebri.org
Location: US
Job Postings: No   *Resume Service:* No   *Networking Service:* No

Notes

Favorite sites, useful resources

Employers Council on Flexible Compensation
http://www.ecfc.org
Location: US
Job Postings: No   *Resume Service:* No   *Networking Service:* No

Employers Resource Association
http://www.hrxperts.org
Location: US
Job Postings: No   *Resume Service:* No   *Networking Service:* No

The ESOP Association
http://www.esopassociation.org
Location: US
Job Postings: No   *Resume Service:* No   *Networking Service:* No

Human Resource Association of the National Capital Area
http://www.hra-nca.org
Location: US - District of Columbia
Job Postings: No   *Resume Service:* No   *Networking Service:* No

Human Resource Management Association of Mid Michigan
http://www.hrmamm.com
Location: US - Michigan
Job Postings: Yes   *Resume Service:* No   *Networking Service:* No

Human Resource Planning Society
http://www.hrps.org
Location: US
Job Postings: No   *Resume Service:* No   *Networking Service:* No

Human Resources Independent Consultants
http://www.hric.org
Location: US
Job Postings: Yes   *Resume Service:* Yes   *Networking Service:* No

Human Resources Management Association of Chicago
http://www.hrmac.org
Location: US - Illinois
Job Postings: Yes   *Resume Service:* No   *Networking Service:* No

Human Resources Professionals Association of Ontario
http://www.hrpao.org
Location: North America - Canada
Job Postings: No   *Resume Service:* No   *Networking Service:* No

International Foundation of Employee Benefit Plans
http://www.ifebp.org
Location: International
Job Postings: Yes   *Resume Service:* No   *Networking Service:* No

Notes

Favorite sites, useful resources

International Human Resource Consultants Association
http://www.ihrca.com
Location: International
Job Postings: Yes   *Resume Service:* No   *Networking Service:* No

International Public Management Association for Human Resources
http://www.ipma-hr.org
Location: International
Job Postings: No   *Resume Service:* No   *Networking Service:* No

International Society of Certified Employee Benefit Specialists
http://www.ifebp.org
Location: International
Job Postings: Yes   *Resume Service:* Yes   *Networking Service:* No

Massachusetts Council of Human Service Providers
http://www.providers.org
Location: US - Massachusetts
Job Postings: Yes   *Resume Service:* No   *Networking Service:* No

Media Human Resource Association
http://www.shrm.org/mhra
Location: US
Job Postings: Yes   *Resume Service:* No   *Networking Service:* No

National Association of Church Personnel Administrators
http://www.nacpa.org
Location: US
Job Postings: No   *Resume Service:* No   *Networking Service:* No

National Association of Personnel Services
http://www.napsweb.org
Location: US
Job Postings: No   *Resume Service:* No   *Networking Service:* No

National Association of Professional Employer Organizations
http://www.napeo.org
Location: US
Job Postings: No   *Resume Service:* No   *Networking Service:* No

New England Human Resources Association
http://www.nehra.com
Location: US - Massachusetts
Job Postings: Yes   *Resume Service:* Yes   *Networking Service:* No

New Jersey Metro EMA
http://www.njmetroema.org
Location: US - New Jersey
Job Postings: No   *Resume Service:* No   *Networking Service:* No

Notes

Favorite sites, useful resources

Northern California Human Resources Association
http://www.nchra.org
Location: US - California
Job Postings: Yes   Resume Service: No   Networking Service: No

Oklahoma Public Employees Association
http://www.opea.org
Location: US - Oklahoma
Job Postings: No   Resume Service: No   Networking Service: No

Professionals in Human Resource Association
http://www.pihra.org
Location: US
Job Postings: No   Resume Service: No   Networking Service: No

Society for Human Resources Management
http://www.shrm.org
Location: US
Job Postings: Yes   Resume Service: No   Networking Service: Yes

South Carolina Association of Personnel Services
http://www.scaps.org
Location: US - South Carolina
Job Postings: No   Resume Service: No   Networking Service: No

Tulsa Area Human Resources Association
http://www.tahra.org
Location: US - Oklahoma
Job Postings: Yes   Resume Service: No   Networking Service: No

WEB Network of Benefit Professionals
http://www.webenefits.org
Location: US
Job Postings: Yes   Resume Service: No   Networking Service: No

-I-

Industrial/Manufacturing

Aerospace Industries Association
http://www.aia-aerospace.org
Location: US
Job Postings: No   Resume Service: No   Networking Service: No

---

Looking for a new or better job?   Looking for top talent?
Use WEDDLE's publications. Visit www.weddles.com today.

Notes

Favorite sites, useful resources

Aircraft Locknut Manufacturers Association
http://www.almanet.org
Location: US
Job Postings: No   *Resume Service:* No   *Networking Service:* No

Alliance for Innovative Manufacturing
http://www.stanford.edu/group/AIM/
Location: US
Job Postings: No   *Resume Service:* No   *Networking Service:* No

American Architectural Manufacturers Association
http://www.aamanet.org
Location: US
Job Postings: No   *Resume Service:* No   *Networking Service:* No

American Concrete Pavement Association
http://www.pavement.com
Location: US
Job Postings: No   *Resume Service:* No   *Networking Service:* No

American Gear Manufacturers Association
http://www.agma.org
Location: US
Job Postings: No   *Resume Service:* No   *Networking Service:* No

American Industrial Hygiene Association
http://www.aiha.org
Location: US
Job Postings: Yes   *Resume Service:* No   *Networking Service:* No

American Industrial Real Estate Association
http://www.airea.com
Location: US
Job Postings: No   *Resume Service:* No   *Networking Service:* No

American Precision Optics Manufacturers Association
http://www.apoma.org
Location: US
Job Postings: No   *Resume Service:* No   *Networking Service:* No

American Textile Manufacturers Institute
http://www.atmi.org
Location: US
Job Postings: No   *Resume Service:* No   *Networking Service:* No

Association for Computing Machinery
http://www.acm.org
Location: US
Job Postings: Yes   *Resume Service:* Yes   *Networking Service:* Yes

Notes

Favorite sites, useful resources

Association of Equipment Manufacturers
http://www.aem.org
Location: US
Job Postings: No   *Resume Service:* No   *Networking Service:* No

The Association for Manufacturing Excellence
http://www.ame.org
Location: US
Job Postings: Yes   *Resume Service:* Yes   *Networking Service:* No

Association for Manufacturing Technology
http://www.mfgtech.org
Location: US
Job Postings: No   *Resume Service:* No   *Networking Service:* No

Association of Women in the Metal Industries
http://www.awmi.com
Location: US
Job Postings: No   *Resume Service:* No   *Networking Service:* No

Automotive Parts Manufacturers' Association
http://www.apma.ca
Location: North America - Canada
Job Postings: No   *Resume Service:* No   *Networking Service:* No

Aviation Distributors and Manufacturers Association
http://www.adma.org
Location: US
Job Postings: No   *Resume Service:* No   *Networking Service:* No

Biotechnology Industry Organization
http://www.bio.org
Location: US
Job Postings: No   *Resume Service:* No   *Networking Service:* No

The Business and Institutional Furniture Manufacturer's Association
http://www.bifma.com
Location: US
Job Postings: No   *Resume Service:* No   *Networking Service:* No

Consumer Electronics Manufactures Association
http://www.cemacity.org
Location: US
Job Postings: No   *Resume Service:* No   *Networking Service:* No

---

Looking for a new or better job?   Looking for top talent?
Use WEDDLE's publications. Visit www.weddles.com today.

Notes

Favorite sites, useful resources

Dental Manufacturers of America
http://www.dmanews.org
Location: US
Job Postings: No   *Resume Service:* No   *Networking Service:* No

Electronic Industries Alliance
http://www.cmpcmm.com/cc/orgs.html
Location: US
Job Postings: No   *Resume Service:* No   *Networking Service:* No

Emissions Marketing Association
http://www.emissions.org/
Location: US
Job Postings: No   *Resume Service:* No   *Networking Service:* No

Fabricators and Manufacturers Association
http://www.fmametalfab.org
Location: US
Job Postings: Yes   *Resume Service:* Yes   *Networking Service:* No

Farm Equipment Manufacturers Association
http://www.farmequip.org
Location: US
Job Postings: No   *Resume Service:* No   *Networking Service:* No

General Aviation Manufacturers Association
http://www.generalaviation.org
Location: US
Job Postings: No   *Resume Service:* No   *Networking Service:* No

Grocery Manufacturers of America
http://www.gmabrands.com
Location: US
Job Postings: No   *Resume Service:* No   *Networking Service:* No

Health Industry Distributors Association
http://www.hida.org
Location: US
Job Postings: No   *Resume Service:* No   *Networking Service:* No

Home Furnishings International Association
http://www.hfia.com
Location: US
Job Postings: No   *Resume Service:* No   *Networking Service:* No

IEEE Components, Packaging, and Manufacturing Technology Society
http://www.cpmt.org
Location: US
Job Postings: Yes   *Resume Service:* No   *Networking Service:* No

Notes
Favorite sites, useful resources

Independent Medical Distributors Association
http://www.imda.org
Location: US
Job Postings: No   *Resume Service:* No   *Networking Service:* No

Industrial Diamond Association
http://www.superabrasives.org
Location: US
Job Postings: No   *Resume Service:* No   *Networking Service:* No

Industrial Organization Society
http://www.mgmt.purdue.edu/faculty/smartin/ios/ios
Location: US
Job Postings: No   *Resume Service:* No   *Networking Service:* No

Industrial Relations Research Association
http://www.irra.uiuc.edu/
Location: US
Job Postings: Yes   *Resume Service:* No   *Networking Service:* No

Industrial Research Institute
http://www.iriinc.org
Location: US
Job Postings: No   *Resume Service:* No   *Networking Service:* No

Industrial Safety Equipment Association
http://www.safetycentral.org/isea/
Location: US
Job Postings: No   *Resume Service:* No   *Networking Service:* No

Industrial Supply Association
http://www.ida-assoc.org
Location: US
Job Postings: No   *Resume Service:* No   *Networking Service:* No

The Institute of Industrial Engineers
http://www.iienet.org/
Location: US
Job Postings: Yes   *Resume Service:* Yes   *Networking Service:* No

International Card Manufacturers Association
http://www.icma.com
Location: US
Job Postings: Yes   *Resume Service:* Yes   *Networking Service:* Yes

International Foodservice Manufacturers Association
http://www.foodserviceworld.com/ifma/
Location: International
Job Postings: No   *Resume Service:* No   *Networking Service:* No

WEDDLE's Helping to Maximize Your ROI ... Your Return on the Internet

Notes
Favorite sites, useful resources

International Labour Organization
http://www.ilo.org
Location: International
Job Postings: No   *Resume Service:* No   *Networking Service:* No

Iron and Steel Society
http://www.issource.org
Location: US
Job Postings: No   *Resume Service:* No   *Networking Service:* No

Manufacturers' Agents National Association
http://www.manaonline.org
Location: US
Job Postings: Yes   *Resume Service:* No   *Networking Service:* No

The Manufacturing, Science and Finance Union
http://www.amicustheunion.org
Location: Europe - UK
Job Postings: Yes   *Resume Service:* No   *Networking Service:* No

Mid-America Plastics Partners, Inc.
http://www.mappinc.com
Location: US
Job Postings: Yes   *Resume Service:* No   *Networking Service:* No

Minerals, Metals and Materials Society
http://www.tms.org
Location: US
Job Postings: No   *Resume Service:* No   *Networking Service:* No

National Association of Manufacturers
http://www.nam.org
Location: US
Job Postings: No   *Resume Service:* No   *Networking Service:* No

The National Association of Store Fixture Manufacturers
http://www.nasfm.org
Location: US
Job Postings: No   *Resume Service:* No   *Networking Service:* No

National Defense Industrial Association
http://www.adpa.org
Location: US
Job Postings: No   *Resume Service:* No   *Networking Service:* No

National Coalition for Advanced Manufacturing
http://www.nacfam.org
Location: US
Job Postings: No   *Resume Service:* No   *Networking Service:* No

Notes

Favorite sites, useful resources

National Electronic Distributors Association
http://www.nedassoc.org
Location: US
Job Postings: Yes   *Resume Service:* Yes   *Networking Service:* No

National Housewares Manufacturers Association
http://www.housewares.org
Location: US
Job Postings: Yes   *Resume Service:* Yes   *Networking Service:* No

Occupational Safety and Health Administration, OSHA
http://www.osha.gov
Location: US
Job Postings: No   *Resume Service:* No   *Networking Service:* No

Precision Machined Products Association
http://www.pmpa.org
Location: US
Job Postings: Yes   *Resume Service:* No   *Networking Service:* No

Puerto Rico Manufacturers Association
http://www.prma.com
Location: US - Puerto Rico
Job Postings: No   *Resume Service:* No   *Networking Service:* No

Retail Packaging Manufacturer's Association
http://www.rpma.org
Location: US
Job Postings: No   *Resume Service:* No   *Networking Service:* No

Rubber Manufacturers Association
http://www.rma.org
Location: US
Job Postings: No   *Resume Service:* No   *Networking Service:* No

Soap and Detergent Association
http://www.sdahq.org
Location: US
Job Postings: No   *Resume Service:* No   *Networking Service:* No

Society for Industrial and Applied Mathematics
http://www.siam.org
Location: US
Job Postings: Yes   *Resume Service:* No   *Networking Service:* No

Society for Industrial & Organizational Psychology
http://www.siop.org
Location: US
Job Postings: Yes   *Resume Service:* No   *Networking Service:* No

Notes

Favorite sites, useful resources

Society of Chemical Industry
http://www.soci.org
Location: US
Job Postings: Yes   *Resume Service:* Yes   *Networking Service:* No

Society of Industrial and Office Realtors
http://www.sior.com
Location: US
Job Postings: No   *Resume Service:* No   *Networking Service:* No

Society of Manufacturing Engineers
http://www.sme.org
Location: US
Job Postings: Yes   *Resume Service:* Yes   *Networking Service:* No

Sporting Goods Manufacturers Association
http://www.sportlink.com
Location: US
Job Postings: Yes   *Resume Service:* No   *Networking Service:* No

Tool & Manufacturing Association
http://www.tmanet.com
Location: US
Job Postings: Yes   *Resume Service:* No   *Networking Service:* No

Toy Shippers Association
http://www.toysa.com
Location: US
Job Postings: No   *Resume Service:* No   *Networking Service:* No

Women in Packaging
http://www.womeninpackaging.org
Location: US
Job Postings: Yes   *Resume Service:* No   *Networking Service:* No

Insurance/Actuarial

Alliance of Claims Assistance Professionals
http://www.claims.org
Location: US
Job Postings: No   *Resume Service:* No   *Networking Service:* No

American Academy of Actuaries
http://www.actuary.org
Location: US
Job Postings: Yes   *Resume Service:* No   *Networking Service:* No

Notes

Favorite sites, useful resources

American Association of Health Plans
http://www.aahp.org
Location: US
Job Postings: No   *Resume Service:* No   *Networking Service:* No

American Insurance Association
http://www.aiadc.org
Location: US
Job Postings: No   *Resume Service:* No   *Networking Service:* No

American Mathematical Society
http://www.ams.org
Location: US
Job Postings: No   *Resume Service:* No   *Networking Service:* No

American Risk and Insurance Association
http://www.aria.org
Location: US
Job Postings: No   *Resume Service:* No   *Networking Service:* No

Association of Healthcare Internal Auditors
http://www.ahia.org
Location: US
Job Postings: Yes   *Resume Service:* No   *Networking Service:* No

Association for Professional Insurance Women
http://www.apiw.org
Location: US
Job Postings: Yes   *Resume Service:* No   *Networking Service:* No

Australian Insurance Institute
http://www.theinstitute.com.au
Location: Australia
Job Postings: Yes   *Resume Service:* No   *Networking Service:* No

Canadian Institute of Actuaries
http://www.actuaries.ca
Location: North America - Canada
Job Postings: Yes   *Resume Service:* No   *Networking Service:* No

Council of Insurance Agents and Brokers
http://www.ciab.com
Location: US
Job Postings: No   *Resume Service:* No   *Networking Service:* No

Financial Institutions Insurance Association
http://www.fiia.org
Location: US
Job Postings: No   *Resume Service:* No   *Networking Service:* No

Notes

Favorite sites, useful resources

Global Association of Risk Professionals
http://www.garp.com
Location: US
Job Postings: Yes   *Resume Service:* No   *Networking Service:* No

Health Insurance Association of America
http://www.hiaa.org
Location: US
Job Postings: No   *Resume Service:* No   *Networking Service:* No

Independent Automotive Damage Appraisers Association
http://www.iada.org
Location: US
Job Postings: Yes   *Resume Service:* Yes   *Networking Service:* No

Independent Insurance Agents of America
http://www.independentagent.com
Location: US
Job Postings: No   *Resume Service:* No   *Networking Service:* No

Insurance Accounting and Systems Association
http://www.iasa.org
Location: US
Job Postings: No   *Resume Service:* No   *Networking Service:* No

Insurance Information Institute
http://www.iii.org
Location: US
Job Postings: No   *Resume Service:* No   *Networking Service:* No

The National Academy of Social Insurance
http://www.nasi.org
Location: US
Job Postings: Yes   *Resume Service:* No   *Networking Service:* No

National Association of Dental Plans
http://www.nadp.org
Location: US
Job Postings: No   *Resume Service:* No   *Networking Service:* No

National Association of Health Underwriters
http://www.nahu.org
Location: US
Job Postings: No   *Resume Service:* No   *Networking Service:* No

National Association of Independent Insurers
http://www.naii.org
Location: US
Job Postings: No   *Resume Service:* No   *Networking Service:* No

Notes

Favorite sites, useful resources

National Association of Independent Life Brokerage Agencies
http://www.nailba.com
Location: US
Job Postings: No   *Resume Service:* No   *Networking Service:* No

National Association of Insurance and Financial Advisors
http://www.naifa.org/
Location: US
Job Postings: No   *Resume Service:* No   *Networking Service:* No

National Association of Insurance Commissioners
http://www.naic.org
Location: US
Job Postings: No   *Resume Service:* No   *Networking Service:* No

National Association of Mutual Insurance Companies
http://www.namic.org
Location: US
Job Postings: Yes   *Resume Service:* Yes   *Networking Service:* No

National Association of Professional Insurance Agents
http://www.pianet.com
Location: US
Job Postings: No   *Resume Service:* No   *Networking Service:* No

National Council on Compensation Insurance
http://www.ncci.com
Location: US
Job Postings: Yes   *Resume Service:* No   *Networking Service:* No

National Insurance Recruiters Association
http://www.nirassn.com
Location: US
Job Postings: No   *Resume Service:* No   *Networking Service:* No

Risk & Insurance Management Society
http://www.rims.org
Location: US
Job Postings: Yes   *Resume Service:* No   *Networking Service:* No

Society of Actuaries
http://www.soa.org
Location: US
Job Postings: Yes   *Resume Service:* No   *Networking Service:* Yes

Society of Risk Analysis
http://www.sra.org
Location: US
Job Postings: Yes   *Resume Service:* No   *Networking Service:* No

Notes

Favorite sites, useful resources

International

Africa

South African Association of Hospital & Institutional Pharmacists
http://www.saahip.org.za
Job Postings: No   *Resume Service:* No   *Networking Service:* No

Asia

Asian Development Bank
http://www.adb.org
Job Postings: Yes   *Resume Service:* No   *Networking Service:* No

Australia

Australasian Legal Information Institute
http://austlii.law.uts.edu.au
Job Postings: No   *Resume Service:* No   *Networking Service:* No

Australian Human Resources Institute
http://www.ahri.com.au
Job Postings: Yes   *Resume Service:* Yes   *Networking Service:* No

Australian Insurance Institute
http://www.theinstitute.com.au
Job Postings: Yes   *Resume Service:* No   *Networking Service:* No

Australian Society of Certified Public Accountants
http://www.cpaonline.com.au
Job Postings: Yes   *Resume Service:* Yes   *Networking Service:* Yes

Society of Hospital Pharmacists of Australia
http://www.shpa.org.au
Job Postings: Yes   *Resume Service:* No   *Networking Service:* No

Canada

Association of Canadian Search Employment and Staffing Services
http://www.acsess.org
Job Postings: No   *Resume Service:* No   *Networking Service:* No

Automotive Parts Manufacturers' Association
http://www.apma.ca
Job Postings: No   *Resume Service:* No   *Networking Service:* No

Notes

Favorite sites, useful resources

Canadian Association for Business Economics
http://www.cabe.ca
Job Postings: Yes   *Resume Service:* No   *Networking Service:*No

Canadian Astronomical Society
http://www.casca.ca
Job Postings: No   *Resume Service:* No   *Networking Service:*No

Canadian Bankers Association
http://www.cba.ca
Job Postings: Yes   *Resume Service:* No   *Networking Service:*No

Canadian Bar Association
http://www.cba.org
Job Postings: Yes   *Resume Service:* Yes   *Networking Service:*No

Canadian Counseling Association
http://www.ccacc.ca
Job Postings: No   *Resume Service:* No   *Networking Service:*No

Canadian Dental Association
http://www.cda-adc.ca
Job Postings: No   *Resume Service:* No   *Networking Service:*No

Canadian Institute of Actuaries
http://www.actuaries.ca
Job Postings: Yes   *Resume Service:* No   *Networking Service:*No

Canadian Institute of Chartered Accountants
http://www.cica.ca
Job Postings: Yes   *Resume Service:* Yes   *Networking Service:*No

Canadian Medical Association
http://www.cma.org
Job Postings: No   *Resume Service:* No   *Networking Service:*No

Canadian Nurses Association
http://www.cna-nurses.ca
Job Postings: Yes   *Resume Service:* No   *Networking Service:*No

Canadian Professional Sales Association
http://www.cpsa.com
Job Postings: Yes   *Resume Service:* Yes   *Networking Service:*No

Canadian Society for Civil Engineers
http://www.csce.ca
Job Postings: No   *Resume Service:* No   *Networking Service:*No

Notes

Favorite sites, useful resources

Canadian Society for International Health
http://www.csih.org
Job Postings: Yes   *Resume Service:* No   *Networking Service:* No

Canadian Society of Pharmaceutical Sciences
http://www.ualberta.ca/%7Ecsps/
Job Postings: Yes   *Resume Service:* No   *Networking Service:* No

Certified General Accountants' Association of Canada
http://www.cga-canada.org
Job Postings: No   *Resume Service:* No   *Networking Service:* No

Human Resources Professionals Association of Ontario
http://www.hrpao.org
Job Postings: No   *Resume Service:* No   *Networking Service:* No

Institute of Canadian Advertising
http://www.ica-ad.com
Job Postings: No   *Resume Service:* No   *Networking Service:* No

Institute of Chartered Accountants of British Columbia
http://www.ica.bc.ca
Job Postings: Yes   *Resume Service:* No   *Networking Service:* No

Institute of Chartered Accountants of Ontario
http://www.icao.on.ca
Job Postings: Yes   *Resume Service:* No   *Networking Service:* Yes

Toronto CICS Association
http://www.interlog.com/~tca/
Job Postings: Yes   *Resume Service:* No   *Networking Service:* No

Europe

European Accounting Association
http://www.eaa-online.org
Job Postings: Yes   *Resume Service:* No   *Networking Service:* Yes

European Association for Astronomy Education
http://www.algonet.se/~sirius/eaae.htm
Job Postings: No   *Resume Service:* No   *Networking Service:* No

European Association of Automotive Suppliers
http://www.clepa.be
Job Postings: No   *Resume Service:* No   *Networking Service:* No

Notes
Favorite sites, useful resources

European Competitive Telecommunications Association
http://www.ectaweb.org
Job Postings: No   *Resume Service:* No   *Networking Service:* No

European Society of Clinical Pharmacy
http://www.escp.nl
Job Postings: No   *Resume Service:* No   *Networking Service:* No

International Finance and Commodities Institute in Geneva
http://finance.wat.ch/ifci/
Job Postings: No   *Resume Service:* No   *Networking Service:* No

International Institute for Management Development
http://www.imd.ch
Job Postings: No   *Resume Service:* No   *Networking Service:* No

France

Association of Pharmacy Technicians
http://www.pharmacytechnician.com
Job Postings: No   *Resume Service:* No   *Networking Service:* No

French Society of Pharmacology
http://www.pharmacol-fr.org
Job Postings: No   *Resume Service:* No   *Networking Service:* No

Hong Kong

Hong Kong Institute of Marketing
http://www.hkim.org.hk
Job Postings: Yes   *Resume Service:* No   *Networking Service:* No

Ireland

Institute of Chartered Accountants in Ireland
http://www.icai.ie
Job Postings: Yes   *Resume Service:* No   *Networking Service:* Yes

Marketing Institute of Ireland
http://www.mii.ie
Job Postings: No   *Resume Service:* No   *Networking Service:* No

---

Looking for a new or better job?   Looking for top talent?
Use WEDDLE's publications. Visit www.weddles.com today.

Notes

Favorite sites, useful resources

Singapore

Institute of Certified Public Accountants in Singapore
http://www.accountants.org.sg
Job Postings: No   *Resume Service:* No   *Networking Service:* No

Law Society of Singapore
http://www.lawsoc.org.sg
Job Postings: Yes   *Resume Service:* No   *Networking Service:* No

United Kingdom

Abacus Construction Index
http://www.construction-index.com
Job Postings: No   *Resume Service:* No   *Networking Service:* No

Advertising Education Forum
http://www.aeforum.org
Job Postings: No   *Resume Service:* No   *Networking Service:* No

Association of British Travel Agents
http://www.abtanet.com
Job Postings: No   *Resume Service:* No   *Networking Service:* No

Association of Investment Trust Companies
http://www.trustnet.com
Job Postings: No   *Resume Service:* No   *Networking Service:* No

The Association of MBAs
http://www.mba.org.uk
Job Postings: Yes   *Resume Service:* Yes   *Networking Service:* No

Building Research Establishment
http://www.bre.co.uk
Job Postings: No   *Resume Service:* No   *Networking Service:* No

Chartered Institute of Management Accountants
http://www.cimaglobal.com
Job Postings: Yes   *Resume Service:* Yes   *Networking Service:* Yes

Institute of Civil Engineers
http://www.ice.org.uk
Job Postings: No   *Resume Service:* No   *Networking Service:* No

Notes
Favorite sites, useful resources

Institute of Fiscal Studies
http://www.ifs.org.uk
Job Postings: No   *Resume Service:* No   *Networking Service:*No

Institute of Internal Auditors
http://www.iia.org.uk
Job Postings: Yes   *Resume Service:* No   *Networking Service:*No

Institute of Practitioners in Advertising
http://www.ipa.co.uk
Job Postings: Yes   *Resume Service:* No   *Networking Service:*No

Law Society of England and Wales
http://www.lawsoc.org.uk
Job Postings: Yes   *Resume Service:* No   *Networking Service:*No

The Manufacturing, Science and Finance Union
http://www.amicustheunion.org
Job Postings: No   *Resume Service:* No   *Networking Service:*No

National Pharmaceutical Association
http://www.npa.co.uk
Job Postings: No   *Resume Service:* No   *Networking Service:*No

Royal Pharmaceutical Society of Great Britain
http://www.rpsgb.org.uk
Job Postings: Yes   *Resume Service:* No   *Networking Service:*No

-J-

Journalism/Creative—All Media

American Film Institute
http://www.afionline.org
Location: US
Job Postings: No   *Resume Service:* No   *Networking Service:* No

American Jewish Press Association
http://www.ajpa.org
Location: US
Job Postings: Yes   *Resume Service:* Yes   *Networking Service:* No

American Society of Journalists and Authors
http://www.asja.org
Location: US
Job Postings: No   *Resume Service:* No   *Networking Service:* No

Notes
Favorite sites, useful resources

American Society of Newspaper Editors
http://www.asne.org
Location: US

| *Job Postings:* Yes | *Resume Service:* No | *Networking Service:* No |

Asian American Journalists Association
http://www.aaja.org
Location: US

| *Job Postings:* No | *Resume Service:* No | *Networking Service:* No |

Association for Interactive Media
http://www.interactivehq.org
Location: US

| *Job Postings:* Yes | *Resume Service:* Yes | *Networking Service:* No |

Association for Multimedia Communications
http://www.amcomm.org
Location: US

| *Job Postings:* Yes | *Resume Service:* No | *Networking Service:* No |

The Association of Young Journalists and Writers
http://www.ayjw.org
Location: US

| *Job Postings:* Yes | *Resume Service:* No | *Networking Service:* No |

Cabletelevision Advertising Bureau
http://www.cabletvadbureau.com
Location: US

| *Job Postings:* No | *Resume Service:* No | *Networking Service:* No |

Council of Science Editors
http://www.amwa.org
Location: US

| *Job Postings:* Yes | *Resume Service:* No | *Networking Service:* No |

DC Science Writers Association
http://www.dcswa.org
Location: US - District of Columbia

| *Job Postings:* Yes | *Resume Service:* No | *Networking Service:* No |

Editorial Freelancers Association
http://www.the-efa.org
Location: US

| *Job Postings:* Yes | *Resume Service:* No | *Networking Service:* No |

Independent Film & Television Alliance
http://www.ifta-online.org
Location: US

| *Job Postings:* No | *Resume Service:* No | *Networking Service:* No |

Notes

Favorite sites, useful resources

Independent Press Association
http://www.indypress.org
Location: US
Job Postings: Yes   *Resume Service:* No   *Networking Service:* No

International Newspaper Marketing Association
http://www.inma.org
Location: International
Job Postings: Yes   *Resume Service:* No   *Networking Service:* No

International Television Association
http://www.itva.org
Location: International
Job Postings: Yes   *Resume Service:* No   *Networking Service:* No

Investigative Reporters and Editors, Inc.
http://www.ire.org
Location: US
Job Postings: Yes   *Resume Service:* No   *Networking Service:* Yes

Media Human Resource Association
http://www.shrm.org/mhra
Location: US
Job Postings: Yes   *Resume Service:* No   *Networking Service:* No

Motion Picture Association of America
http://www.mpaa.org
Location: US
Job Postings: No   *Resume Service:* No   *Networking Service:* No

Multi-Media Telecommunications Association
http://www.mmta.org
Location: US
Job Postings: No   *Resume Service:* No   *Networking Service:* No

The National Association of Black Journalists
http://www.nabj.org
Location: US
Job Postings: Yes   *Resume Service:* Yes   *Networking Service:* Yes

National Association of Broadcasters
http://www.nab.org
Location: US
Job Postings: Yes   *Resume Service:* Yes   *Networking Service:* No

National Association of College Broadcasters
http://www.hofstra.edu/nacb/
Location: US
Job Postings: No   *Resume Service:* No   *Networking Service:* No

Notes

Favorite sites, useful resources

The National Association of Hispanic Journalists
http://www.nahj.org
Location: US
Job Postings: Yes   *Resume Service:* Yes   *Networking Service:* No

The National Association of Radio and Telecommunications Engineers
http://www.narte.org
Location: US
Job Postings: Yes   *Resume Service:* No   *Networking Service:* No

National Association of Science Writers
http://www.nasw.org
Location: US
Job Postings: No   *Resume Service:* No   *Networking Service:* No

The National Association of Television Program Executives
http://www.natpe.com
Location: US
Job Postings: No   *Resume Service:* No   *Networking Service:* No

National Black Media Coalition
www.nbmc.org
Location: US
Job Postings: No   *Resume Service:* No   *Networking Service:* No

National Cable Television Association
http://www.ncta.com
Location: US
Job Postings: Yes   *Resume Service:* No   *Networking Service:* No

National Education Writers Association
http://www.ewa.org
Location: US
Job Postings: No   *Resume Service:* No   *Networking Service:* No

National Press Club
http://npc.press.org
Location: US
Job Postings: Yes   *Resume Service:* No   *Networking Service:* No

National Press Photographers Association
http://www.nppa.org
Location: US
Job Postings: No   *Resume Service:* No   *Networking Service:* No

National Religious Broadcasters Association
http://www.nrb.org
Location: US
Job Postings: Yes   *Resume Service:* No   *Networking Service:* No

Notes

Favorite sites, useful resources

National Writer's Union
http://www.nwu.org
Location: US
Job Postings: Yes   *Resume Service:* No   *Networking Service:* No

New York New Media Association
http://www.nynma.org
Location: US - New York
Job Postings: Yes   *Resume Service:* Yes   *Networking Service:* No

Newspaper Association of America
http://www.naa.org
Location: US
Job Postings: Yes   *Resume Service:* Yes   *Networking Service:* No

Online Disk Jockey Association
http://www.odja.com
Location: US
Job Postings: No   *Resume Service:* No   *Networking Service:* No

Professional Photographers Association
http://www.ppa-world.org
Location: US
Job Postings: No   *Resume Service:* No   *Networking Service:* No

Radio Advertising Bureau
http://www.rab.com
Location: US
Job Postings: No   *Resume Service:* No   *Networking Service:* No

Radio-Television News Directors Association
http://www.rtnda.org
Location: US
Job Postings: No   *Resume Service:* No   *Networking Service:* No

Society of Environmental Journalists
http://www.sej.org
Location: US
Job Postings: No   *Resume Service:* No   *Networking Service:* No

Television Bureau of Advertising
http://www.tvb.org
Location: US
Job Postings: Yes   *Resume Service:* No   *Networking Service:* No

Women in Cable & Telecommunications
http://www.wict.org
Location: US
Job Postings: No   *Resume Service:* No   *Networking Service:* No

Notes

Favorite sites, useful resources

-L-

Law Enforcement

American Academy of Forensic Sciences
http://www.aafs.org
Location: US
Job Postings: Yes   *Resume Service:* No   *Networking Service:* No

American Jail Association
http://www.corrections.com/aja/
Location: US
Job Postings: Yes   *Resume Service:* No   *Networking Service:* No

International Police Association
http://www.ipa-usa.org
Location: International
Job Postings: No   *Resume Service:* No   *Networking Service:* No

International Union of Police Associations
http://www.Iupa.org
Location: International
Job Postings: No   *Resume Service:* No   *Networking Service:* No

National Sheriffs' Association
http://www.sheriffs.org
Location: US
Job Postings: No   *Resume Service:* No   *Networking Service:* No

Park Law Enforcement Association
http://www.parkranger.com
Location: US
Job Postings: No   *Resume Service:* No   *Networking Service:* Yes

Legal

Alabama State Bar
http://www.alabar.org
Location: US - Alabama
Job Postings: No   *Resume Service:* No   *Networking Service:* No

Alaska Bar Association
http://www.alaskabar.org
Location: US - Alaska
Job Postings: No   *Resume Service:* No   *Networking Service:* No

Notes
Favorite sites, useful resources

Alliance of Merger and Acquisition Advisors
http://www.advisor-alliance.com
Location: US
Job Postings: No   *Resume Service:* No   *Networking Service:* No

American Association of Law Libraries
http://www.aallnet.org
Location: US
Job Postings: Yes   *Resume Service:* No   *Networking Service:* No

American Association of Legal Nurse Consultants
http://www.aalnc.org
Location: US
Job Postings: No   *Resume Service:* No   *Networking Service:* No

American Bar Association
http://www.abanet.org
Location: US
Job Postings: Yes   *Resume Service:* No   *Networking Service:* No

American Corporate Counsel Association
http://www.acca.com
Location: US
Job Postings: Yes   *Resume Service:* No   *Networking Service:* No

American Immigration Lawyers Association
http://www.aila.org
Location: US
Job Postings: No   *Resume Service:* No   *Networking Service:* No

American Intellectual Property Law Association
http://www.aipla.org
Location: US
Job Postings: No   *Resume Service:* No   *Networking Service:* No

American Judges Association
http://www.ncsc.dni.us/aja/
Location: US
Job Postings: No   *Resume Service:* No   *Networking Service:* No

American Law and Economics Association
http://www.amlecon.org
Location: US
Job Postings: No   *Resume Service:* No   *Networking Service:* No

American Law Institute
http://www.ali-aba.org
Location: US
Job Postings: No   *Resume Service:* No   *Networking Service:* No

Notes

Favorite sites, useful resources

Arkansas State Bar Association
http://www.arkbar.com
Location: US - Arkansas
Job Postings: No   *Resume Service:* No   *Networking Service:* No

The Association of American Law Schools
http://www.aals.org
Location: US
Job Postings: No   *Resume Service:* No   *Networking Service:* No

Association for Continuing Legal Education
http://www.aclea.org
Location: US
Job Postings: No   *Resume Service:* No   *Networking Service:* No

Association of Legal Administrators
http://www.alanet.org
Location: US
Job Postings: Yes   *Resume Service:* No   *Networking Service:* No

Association of Legal Information Systems Managers
http://www.alism.org
Location: US
Job Postings: No   *Resume Service:* No   *Networking Service:* No

Association of Trial Lawyers of America
http://www.atlanet.org
Location: US
Job Postings: No   *Resume Service:* No   *Networking Service:* No

Australasian Legal Information Institute
http://austlii.law.uts.edu.au
Location: Australia
Job Postings: No   *Resume Service:* No   *Networking Service:* No

Black Entertainment & Sports Lawyers Association
http://www.besla.org
Location: US
Job Postings: No   *Resume Service:* No   *Networking Service:* No

California State Bar Association
http://www.calbar.org
Location: US - California
Job Postings: No   *Resume Service:* No   *Networking Service:* No

Canadian Bar Association
http://www.cba.org
Location: North America - Canada
Job Postings: Yes   *Resume Service:* Yes   *Networking Service:* No

Notes

Favorite sites, useful resources

Christian Legal Society
http://www.clsnet.org
Location: US
Job Postings: Yes   *Resume Service:* No   *Networking Service:* No

Colorado Bar Association
http://www.cobar.org
Location: US - Colorado
Job Postings: No   *Resume Service:* No   *Networking Service:* No

Connecticut State Bar Association
http://www.ctbar.org
Location: US - Connecticut
Job Postings: Yes   *Resume Service:* No   *Networking Service:* No

Delaware State Bar Association
http://www.dsba.org
Location: US - Delaware
Job Postings: No   *Resume Service:* No   *Networking Service:* No

District of Columbia Bar
http://www.badc.org
Location: US - District of Columbia
Job Postings: No   *Resume Service:* No   *Networking Service:* No

Education Law Association
http://www.educationlaw.org
Location: US
Job Postings: No   *Resume Service:* No   *Networking Service:* No

Florida State Bar Association
http://www.flabar.org
Location: US - Florida
Job Postings: No   *Resume Service:* No   *Networking Service:* No

Global Arbitration Mediation Association
http://www.gama.com
Location: US
Job Postings: No   *Resume Service:* No   *Networking Service:* No

Greek American Lawyers Association
http://firms.findlaw.com/gala/
Location: US
Job Postings: No   *Resume Service:* No   *Networking Service:* No

Hawaii State Bar Association
http://www.hsba.org
Location: US - Hawaii
Job Postings: No   *Resume Service:* No   *Networking Service:* No

Notes

Favorite sites, useful resources

Hispanic National Bar Association
http://www.hnba.com
Location: US
Job Postings: Yes   *Resume Service:* No   *Networking Service:* No

Idaho State Bar
http://www2.state.id.us/isb/
Location: US - Idaho
Job Postings: No   *Resume Service:* No   *Networking Service:* No

Illinois State Bar Association
http://www.illinoisbar.org
Location: US - Illinois
Job Postings: Yes   *Resume Service:* Yes   *Networking Service:* No

Indiana State Bar Association
http://www.inbar.org
Location: US - Indiana
Job Postings: No   *Resume Service:* No   *Networking Service:* No

International Association of Young Lawyers
http://www.aija.org
Location: International
Job Postings: No   *Resume Service:* No   *Networking Service:* No

Iowa State Bar Association
http://www.iowabar.org
Location: US - Iowa
Job Postings: No   *Resume Service:* No   *Networking Service:* No

Kansas State Bar Association
http://www.ksbar.org
Location: US - Kansas
Job Postings: Yes   *Resume Service:* Yes   *Networking Service:* No

Kentucky Bar Association
http://www.kybar.org
Location: US - Kentucky
Job Postings: No   *Resume Service:* No   *Networking Service:* No

Law Society of England and Wales
http://www.lawsoc.org.uk
Location: Europe - UK
Job Postings: Yes   *Resume Service:* No   *Networking Service:* No

Law Society of Singapore
http://www.lawsoc.org.sg
Location: Asia - Singapore
Job Postings: Yes   *Resume Service:* No   *Networking Service:* No

Notes

Favorite sites, useful resources

Legal Marketing Association
http://www.legalmarketing.org
Location: US
Job Postings: Yes   *Resume Service:* No   *Networking Service:* Yes

Los Angeles County Bar Association
http://www.lacba.org
Location: US - California
Job Postings: Yes   *Resume Service:* No   *Networking Service:* Yes

Louisiana State Bar Association
http://www.lsba.org
Location: US - Louisiana
Job Postings: No   *Resume Service:* No   *Networking Service:* No

Maine State Bar Association
http://www.mainebar.org
Location: US - Maine
Job Postings: Yes   *Resume Service:* Yes   *Networking Service:* No

Maryland State Bar Association
http://www.msba.org
Location: US - Maryland
Job Postings: No   *Resume Service:* No   *Networking Service:* No

Massachusetts Bar Association
http://www.massbar.org
Location: US - Massachusetts
Job Postings: Yes   *Resume Service:* No   *Networking Service:* No

Michigan State Bar Association
http://www.michbar.org
Location: US - Michigan
Job Postings: No   *Resume Service:* No   *Networking Service:* No

Minnesota State Bar Association
http://www.mnbar.org
Location: US - Minnesota
Job Postings: Yes   *Resume Service:* Yes   *Networking Service:* No

Mississippi State Bar Association
http://www.msbar.org
Location: US - Mississippi
Job Postings: No   *Resume Service:* No   *Networking Service:* No

Missouri State Bar Association
http://www.mobar.org
Location: US - Missouri
Job Postings: No   *Resume Service:* No   *Networking Service:* No

Notes
Favorite sites, useful resources

National Association of Attorneys General
http://www.naag.org
Location: US
Job Postings: Yes   *Resume Service:* No   *Networking Service:* No

National Association of College and University Attorneys
http://www.nacua.org
Location: US
Job Postings: No   *Resume Service:* No   *Networking Service:* No

National Association of Consumer Bankruptcy Attorneys
http://nacba.com
Location: US
Job Postings: No   *Resume Service:* No   *Networking Service:* No

National Association of Judiciary Interpreters and Translators
p://www.najit.org
Location: US
Job Postings: No   *Resume Service:* No   *Networking Service:* No

National Association of Legal Assistants
http://www.nala.org
Location: US
Job Postings: No   *Resume Service:* No   *Networking Service:* No

The National Association of Legal Search Consultants
http://www.nalsc.org
Location: US
Job Postings: No   *Resume Service:* No   *Networking Service:* No

National Association of Legal Secretaries
http://www.nals.org
Location: US
Job Postings: Yes   *Resume Service:* Yes   *Networking Service:* No

National Employment Lawyers Association
http://www.nela.org
Location: US
Job Postings: No   *Resume Service:* No   *Networking Service:* No

National Federation of Paralegal Associations
http://www.paralegals.org
Location: US
Job Postings: Yes   *Resume Service:* Yes   *Networking Service:* Yes

National Lawyers Association
http://www.nla.org
Location: US
Job Postings: No   *Resume Service:* No   *Networking Service:* No

Notes

Favorite sites, useful resources

National Paralegal Association
http://www.nationalparalegal.org
Location: US
Job Postings: Yes   *Resume Service:* Yes   *Networking Service:* No

Nebraska State Bar Association
http://www.nebar.com
Location: US - Nebraska
Job Postings: No   *Resume Service:* No   *Networking Service:* No

New Hampshire Bar Association
http://www.nhbar.org
Location: US - New Hampshire
Job Postings: No   *Resume Service:* No   *Networking Service:* No

New Jersey State Bar Association
http://www.njsba.com
Location: US - New Jersey
Job Postings: No   *Resume Service:* No   *Networking Service:* No

New York State Bar Association
http://www.nysba.org
Location: US - New York
Job Postings: No   *Resume Service:* No   *Networking Service:* No

North Carolina State Bar Association
http://www.barlinc.org
Location: US - North Dakota
Job Postings: No   *Resume Service:* No   *Networking Service:* No

North Dakota State Bar Association
http://www.sband.org
Location: US - North Dakota
Job Postings: No   *Resume Service:* No   *Networking Service:* No

Ohio State Bar Association
http://www.ohiobar.org
Location: US - Ohio
Job Postings: No   *Resume Service:* No   *Networking Service:* No

Oklahoma Bar Association
http://www.okbar.org
Location: US - Oklahoma
Job Postings: No   *Resume Service:* No   *Networking Service:* No

Oregon State Bar
http://www.osbar.org
Location: US - Oregon
Job Postings: No   *Resume Service:* No   *Networking Service:* No

Notes

Favorite sites, useful resources

Pennsylvania State Bar Association
http://www.pa-bar.org
Location: US - Pennsylvania
Job Postings: Yes   *Resume Service:* Yes   *Networking Service:* No

Rhode Island State Bar Association
http://www.ribar.com
Location: US - Rhode Island
Job Postings: No   *Resume Service:* No   *Networking Service:* No

South Carolina Bar
http://www.scbar.org
Location: US - South Carolina
Job Postings: No   *Resume Service:* No   *Networking Service:* No

South Dakota State Bar Association
http://www.sdbar.org
Location: US - South Dakota
Job Postings: No   *Resume Service:* No   *Networking Service:* No

State Bar of Arizona
http://www.azbar.org
Location: US - Arizona
Job Postings: No   *Resume Service:* No   *Networking Service:* No

State Bar of Georgia
http://www.gabar.org
Location: US - Georgia
Job Postings: No   *Resume Service:* No   *Networking Service:* No

State Bar of Montana
http://www.montanabar.org
Location: US - Montana
Job Postings: No   *Resume Service:* No   *Networking Service:* No

State Bar of Nevada
http://www.nvbar.org
Location: US - Nevada
Job Postings: No   *Resume Service:* No   *Networking Service:* No

State Bar of New Mexico
http://www.nmbar.org
Location: US - New Mexico
Job Postings: No   *Resume Service:* No   *Networking Service:* No

State Bar of Texas
http://www.texasbar.com
Location: US - Texas
Job Postings: No   *Resume Service:* No   *Networking Service:* No

Notes

Favorite sites, useful resources

Tennessee Bar Association
http://www.tba.org
Location: US - Tennessee
Job Postings: No   *Resume Service:* No   *Networking Service:* No

Utah State Bar
http://www.utahbar.org
Location: US - Utah
Job Postings: Yes   *Resume Service:* Yes   *Networking Service:* No

Vermont State Bar Association
http://www.vtbar.org
Location: US - Vermont
Job Postings: No   *Resume Service:* No   *Networking Service:* No

Virginia State Bar
http://www.vsb.org
Location: US - Vermont
Job Postings: No   *Resume Service:* No   *Networking Service:* No

Washington State Bar Association
http://www.wsba.org
Location: US - Washington
Job Postings: No   *Resume Service:* No   *Networking Service:* No

West Virginia State Bar Association
http://www.wvbar.org
Location: US - West Virginia
Job Postings: Yes   *Resume Service:* No   *Networking Service:* No

Wisconsin State Bar Association
http://www.wisbar.org
Location: US - Wisconsin
Job Postings: No   *Resume Service:* No   *Networking Service:* No

Wyoming State Bar
http://www.wyomingbar.org
Location: US - Wyoming
Job Postings: No   *Resume Service:* No   *Networking Service:* No

---

Looking for a new or better job?   Looking for top talent?
Use WEDDLE's publications. Visit www.weddles.com today.

- *WEDDLE's 2005/6 Guide* is the "consumer's report" of job boards.
All the site information you need to select the best job boards for you.

- *WEDDLE's 2005/6 Directory* is the "address book" of job boards.
The names and addresses of over 8,000 job boards and career portals.

Notes

Favorite sites, useful resources

Library/Information Science

American Association of Law Libraries
http://www.aallnet.org
Location: US
Job Postings: Yes   *Resume Service:* No   *Networking Service:* No

American Library Association
http://www.ala.org
Location: US
Job Postings: Yes   *Resume Service:* No   *Networking Service:* No

Art Libraries Society of North America
http://www.arlisna.org
Location: US
Job Postings: Yes   *Resume Service:* No   *Networking Service:* No

Association of College & Research Libraries
http://www.ala.org
Location: US
Job Postings: Yes   *Resume Service:* No   *Networking Service:* No

Association of Research Libraries
http://www.arl.org
Location: US
Job Postings: Yes   *Resume Service:* No   *Networking Service:* No

Computing Research Association
http://www.cra.org
Location: US
Job Postings: Yes   *Resume Service:* No   *Networking Service:* No

Urban Libraries Council
http://www.urbanlibraries.org
Location: US
Job Postings: No   *Resume Service:* No   *Networking Service:* No

Wisconsin Library Association/Wisconsin Library Association Foundation
http://www.wla.lib.wi.us
Location: US - Wisconsin
Job Postings: Yes   *Resume Service:* No   *Networking Service:* No

Linguistics/Bilingual

American Speech-Language-Hearing Association
http://www.asha.org
Location: US
Job Postings: Yes   *Resume Service:* Yes   *Networking Service:* No

Notes
Favorite sites, useful resources

The Association for Computational Linguistics
http://www.acl.org
Location: US
Job Postings: Yes   *Resume Service:* No   *Networking Service:* No

Logistics/Transportation/Operations

Advanced Transit Association
http://www.advancedtransit.org/news.aspx
Location: US
Job Postings: No   *Resume Service:* No   *Networking Service:* No

Aerospace and Electronic Systems Society
http://www.ewh.ieee.org/soc/aes/
Location: US
Job Postings: Yes   *Resume Service:* No   *Networking Service:* No

Airline Suppliers Association
http://www.airlinesuppliers.com
Location: US
Job Postings: No   *Resume Service:* No   *Networking Service:* No

Air Transport Association
http://www.air-transport.org
Location: US
Job Postings: No   *Resume Service:* No   *Networking Service:* No

American Association of State Highway and Transportation Officials
http://www.aashto.org
Location: US
Job Postings: Yes   *Resume Service:* No   *Networking Service:* No

American Concrete Pavement Association
http://www.pavement.com
Location: US
Job Postings: No   *Resume Service:* No   *Networking Service:* No

American Production and Inventory Control Society
http://www.apics.org/default.htm
Location: US
Job Postings: Yes   *Resume Service:* Yes   *Networking Service:* No

American Public Transportation Association
http://www.apta.com
Location: US
Job Postings: Yes   *Resume Service:* No   *Networking Service:* No

Notes

Favorite sites, useful resources

American Public Works Association
http://www.pubworks.org
Location: US
Job Postings: Yes   *Resume Service:* No   *Networking Service:* No

American Road and Transportation Builders Association
http://www.artba.org
Location: US
Job Postings: Yes   *Resume Service:* Yes   *Networking Service:* No

American Society for Quality
http://www.asq.org
Location: US
Job Postings: Yes   *Resume Service:* No   *Networking Service:* No

American Society of Transportation and Logistics
http://www.astl.org
Location: US
Job Postings: Yes   *Resume Service:* No   *Networking Service:* No

American Trucking Associations
http://www.trucking.org
Location: US
Job Postings: No   *Resume Service:* No   *Networking Service:* No

Association General Contractors of America
http://www.agc.org/index.ww
Location: US
Job Postings: No   *Resume Service:* No   *Networking Service:* No

Boat Owners Association of the United States
http://www.boatus.com
Location: US
Job Postings: No   *Resume Service:* No   *Networking Service:* No

Brotherhood of Locomotive Engineers and Trainmen
http://www.ble.org
Location: US
Job Postings: Yes   *Resume Service:* No   *Networking Service:* No

Brotherhood of Maintenance of Way Employees
http://www.bmwe.org/index.htm
Location: US
Job Postings: No   *Resume Service:* No   *Networking Service:* No

Community Transportation Association of America
http://www.ctaa.org
Location: US
Job Postings: Yes   *Resume Service:* No   *Networking Service:* No

Notes

Favorite sites, useful resources

Coalition for Appropriate Transportation
http://www.car-free.org
Location: US
Job Postings: No   *Resume Service:* No   *Networking Service:* No

Council of Logistics Management
http://clm1.org/Default.asp?XX=1
Location: US
Job Postings: No   *Resume Service:* No   *Networking Service:* Yes

Equipment Leasing and Finance Foundation
http://www.elaonline.com
Location: US
Job Postings: No   *Resume Service:* No   *Networking Service:* No

Equipment Leasing Association of America
http://www.elaonline.com
Location: US
Job Postings: Yes   *Resume Service:* No   *Networking Service:* No

Health Industry Distributors Association
http://www.hida.org
Location: US
Job Postings: No   *Resume Service:* No   *Networking Service:* No

Helicopter Association International
http://www.rotor.com
Location: US
Job Postings: Yes   *Resume Service:* No   *Networking Service:* No

IEEE Components, Packaging, and Manufacturing Technology Society
http://www.cpmt.org
Location: US
Job Postings: Yes   *Resume Service:* No   *Networking Service:* No

Independent Medical Distributors Association
http://www.imda.org
Location: US
Job Postings: No   *Resume Service:* No   *Networking Service:* No

Industrial Supply Association
http://www.ida-assoc.org
Location: US
Job Postings: No   *Resume Service:* No   *Networking Service:* No

Institute for Operations Research and the Management Sciences
http://www.informs.org
Location: US
Job Postings: Yes   *Resume Service:* No   *Networking Service:* No

Notes

Favorite sites, useful resources

Institute for Supply Management
http://www.napm.org
Location: US
Job Postings: Yes   *Resume Service:* Yes   *Networking Service:* No

Institute of Public Administration
http://www.theipa.org
Location: US
Job Postings: No   *Resume Service:* No   *Networking Service:* No

Institute of Transportation Engineers
http://www.ite.org/
Location: US
Job Postings: Yes   *Resume Service:* Yes   *Networking Service:* No

Intermodal Association of North America
http://www.intermodal.org/
Location: US
Job Postings: No   *Resume Service:* No   *Networking Service:* No

International Air Transport Association
http://www.iata.org
Location: International
Job Postings: No   *Resume Service:* No   *Networking Service:* No

International Association of Independent Tanker Owners
http://www.intertanko.com
Location: US
Job Postings: No   *Resume Service:* No   *Networking Service:* No

International Council on Systems Engineering
http://www.incose.org/
Location: US
Job Postings: Yes   *Resume Service:* No   *Networking Service:* No

International Parking Institute
http://www.parking.org/
Location: US
Job Postings: Yes   *Resume Service:* No   *Networking Service:* No

International Road Federation (IRF)
http://www.irfnet.org/cms/pages/en/viewpage.asp
Location: US
Job Postings: No   *Resume Service:* No   *Networking Service:* No

The International Society of Logistics (SOLE)
http://www.sole.org/default.asp
Location: US
Job Postings: Yes   *Resume Service:* Yes   *Networking Service:* No

Notes
Favorite sites, useful resources

International Transportation Safety Association
http://www.itsasafety.org/ITSA/
Location: International
Job Postings: No   *Resume Service:* No   *Networking Service:* No

The Institute of Industrial Engineers
http://www.iienet.org/
Location: US
Job Postings: Yes   *Resume Service:* Yes   *Networking Service:* No

Light Rail Transit Association
http://www.lrta.org
Location: US
Job Postings: Yes   *Resume Service:* No   *Networking Service:* No

LTD Management/LTD Shippers Association
http://www.ltdmgmt.com
Location: US
Job Postings: No   *Resume Service:* No   *Networking Service:* No

Material Handling Industry of America
http://www.mhia.org
Location: US
Job Postings: No   *Resume Service:* No   *Networking Service:* No

The Motor Bus Society
http://www.motorbussociety.org
Location: US
Job Postings: No   *Resume Service:* No   *Networking Service:* No

National Air Traffic Controllers Association
http://www.natca.org
Location: US
Job Postings: No   *Resume Service:* No   *Networking Service:* No

National Air Transportation Association
http://www.nata-online.org
Location: US
Job Postings: No   *Resume Service:* No   *Networking Service:* No

National Asphalt Pavement Association
http://www.hotmix.org
Location: US
Job Postings: No   *Resume Service:* No   *Networking Service:* No

National Association of Air Traffic Specialists
http://www.naats.org
Location: US
Job Postings: No   *Resume Service:* No   *Networking Service:* No

Notes

Favorite sites, useful resources

National Broadcast Pilots Association
http://www.nbpa.rotor.com
Location: US
Job Postings: No   *Resume Service:* No   *Networking Service:* No

National Contract Management Association
http://www.ncmahq.org
Location: US
Job Postings: No   *Resume Service:* No   *Networking Service:* No

National Defense Industrial Association
http://www.adpa.org
Location: US
Job Postings: No   *Resume Service:* No   *Networking Service:* No

National Electronic Distributors Association
http://www.nedassoc.org
Location: US
Job Postings: Yes   *Resume Service:* Yes   *Networking Service:* No

National Vehicle Leasing Association
http://www.nva.org
Location: US
Job Postings: No   *Resume Service:* No   *Networking Service:* No

Professional Retail Store Maintenance
http://www.prsm.com
Location: US
Job Postings: No   *Resume Service:* No   *Networking Service:* No

Society for Maintenance and Reliability Professionals
http://www.smrp.org/index.php
Location: US
Job Postings: Yes   *Resume Service:* No   *Networking Service:* No

Society of Logistics Engineers
http://www.sole.org
Location: US
Job Postings: No   *Resume Service:* No   *Networking Service:* No

Society of Reliability Engineers
http://www.enre.umd.edu/sre.htm
Location: US
Job Postings: No   *Resume Service:* No   *Networking Service:* No

Toy Shippers Association
http://www.toysa.com
Location: US
Job Postings: No   *Resume Service:* No   *Networking Service:* No

Notes

Favorite sites, useful resources

Transport Workers Union of America
http://www.twu.org
Location: US
Job Postings: No   *Resume Service:* No   *Networking Service:* No

United Auto Workers
http://www.uaw.org/index2.cfm
Location: US
Job Postings: No   *Resume Service:* No   *Networking Service:* No

United Transportation Union
http://www.utu.org
Location: US
Job Postings: No   *Resume Service:* No   *Networking Service:* No

-M-

Military Personnel

Air Force Association
http://www.afa.org
Location: US
Job Postings: No   *Resume Service:* No   *Networking Service:* No

American Society of Military Comptrollers
http://www.asmconline.org
Location: US
Job Postings: Yes   *Resume Service:* No   *Networking Service:* No

American Society of Naval Engineers
http://www.navalengineers.org
Location: US
Job Postings: Yes   *Resume Service:* No   *Networking Service:* No

Association of VA Psychologist Leaders
http://www.avapl.org
Location: US
Job Postings: No   *Resume Service:* No   *Networking Service:* No

Association of the United States Army
http://www.ausa.org
Location: US
Job Postings: No   *Resume Service:* No   *Networking Service:* No

---

Looking for a new or better job?   Looking for top talent?
Use WEDDLE's publications. Visit www.weddles.com today.

Notes
Favorite sites, useful resources

Joint Service Academies Jobs Electronically (JSAJE)
http://www.jsaje.com
Location: US
Job Postings: Yes   *Resume Service:* Yes   *Networking Service:* No

Military Officers Association of America
http://www.moaa.org
Location: US
Job Postings: Yes   *Resume Service:* Yes   *Networking Service:* Yes

Noncommissioned Officers Association of America
http://www.ncoausa.org
Location: US
Job Postings: Yes   *Resume Service:* Yes   *Networking Service:* No

Music

American Federation of Musicians
http://www.afm.org
Location: US
Job Postings: Yes   *Resume Service:* No   *Networking Service:* No

Audio Publishers Association
http://www.audiopub.org
Location: US
Job Postings: No   *Resume Service:* No   *Networking Service:* No

International Music Products Association
http://www.namm.com
Location: International
Job Postings: No   *Resume Service:* No   *Networking Service:* No

The National Association of Composers
http://www.music-usa.org
Location: US
Job Postings: No   *Resume Service:* No   *Networking Service:* No

National Music Publishers Association
http://www.nmpa.org
Location: US
Job Postings: No   *Resume Service:* No   *Networking Service:* No

---

Looking for a new or better job?   Looking for top talent?
Use WEDDLE's publications. Visit www.weddles.com today.
- **WEDDLE's 2005/6 Guide is the "consumer's report" of job boards.**
- **WEDDLE's 2005/6 Directory is the "address book" of job boards.**

Notes

Favorite sites, useful resources

-N-

Non-Profit

American Society of Association Executives
http://www.asaenet.org
Location: US
Job Postings: Yes   *Resume Service:* Yes   *Networking Service:* No

Association for the Study of the Grants Economy
http://www.gratseconomics.org
Location: US
Job Postings: No   *Resume Service:* No   *Networking Service:* No

Association of Fundraising Professionals
http://www.afpnet.org
Location: US
Job Postings: Yes   *Resume Service:* Yes   *Networking Service:* Yes

National Society of Fund Raising Executives
http://www.nsfre.org
Location: US
Job Postings: Yes   *Resume Service:* No   *Networking Service:* No

The Management Assistance Program for Nonprofits
http://www.mapnp.org
Location: US
Job Postings: No   *Resume Service:* No   *Networking Service:* No

-P-

Packaging

Glass Packaging Institute
http://www.gpi.org
Location: US
Job Postings: No   *Resume Service:* No   *Networking Service:* No

IEEE Components, Packaging, and Manufacturing Technology Society
http://www.cpmt.org
Location: US
Job Postings: Yes   *Resume Service:* No   *Networking Service:* No

Retail Packaging Manufacturer's Association
http://www.rpma.org
Location: US
Job Postings: No   *Resume Service:* No   *Networking Service:* No

Notes

Favorite sites, useful resources

Women in Packaging
http://www.womeninpackaging.org
Location: US
Job Postings: Yes   *Resume Service:* No   *Networking Service:* No

Pharmaceutical

American Academy of Pharmaceutical Physicians
http://www.aapp.org
Location: US
Job Postings: Yes   *Resume Service:* No   *Networking Service:* No

American Association of Pharmaceutical Scientists
http://www.aapspharmaceutica.com
Location: US
Job Postings: Yes   *Resume Service:* Yes   *Networking Service:* No

American Pharmacists Association
http://www.aphanet.org
Location: US
Job Postings: Yes   *Resume Service:* Yes   *Networking Service:* No

American Society of Consultant Pharmacists
http://www.ascp.com
Location: US
Job Postings: No   *Resume Service:* No   *Networking Service:* No

American Society of Health-System Pharmacists
http://www.ashp.org
Location: US
Job Postings: Yes   *Resume Service:* No   *Networking Service:* No

American Society of Pharmacognosy
http://www.phcog.org
Location: US
Job Postings: Yes   *Resume Service:* No   *Networking Service:* No

Association of Pharmacy Technicians
http://www.pharmacytechnician.com
Location: Europe - France
Job Postings: No   *Resume Service:* No   *Networking Service:* No

Beauty and Barber Supply Institute
http://www.bbsi.org
Location: US
Job Postings: No   *Resume Service:* No   *Networking Service:* No

Notes
Favorite sites, useful resources

California Korean Pharmacists Association
http://www.kpha.com
Location: US - California
Job Postings: Yes   *Resume Service:* No   *Networking Service:* No

California Pharmacists Association
http://www.cpha.com
Location: US - California
Job Postings: Yes   *Resume Service:* No   *Networking Service:* No

Canadian Society of Pharmaceutical Sciences
http://www.ualberta.ca/%7Ecsps/
Location: North America - Canada
Job Postings: Yes   *Resume Service:* No   *Networking Service:* No

ChemPharma
http://www.chempharma.org/
Location: US - New Jersey
Job Postings: Yes   *Resume Service:* Yes   *Networking Service:* No

Drug Information Association
http://www.diahome.org
Location: US
Job Postings: Yes   *Resume Service:* No   *Networking Service:* No

European Society of Clinical Pharmacy
http://www.escp.nl
Location: Europe
Job Postings: No   *Resume Service:* No   *Networking Service:* No

French Society of Pharmacology
http://www.pharmacol-fr.org
Location: Europe - France
Job Postings: No   *Resume Service:* No   *Networking Service:* No

Georgia Pharmacy Association
http://www.gpha.org
Location: US - Georgia
Job Postings: Yes   *Resume Service:* No   *Networking Service:* No

An International Association for Pharmaceutical Science & Technology (PDA)
http://www.pda.org
Location: US
Job Postings: Yes   *Resume Service:* Yes   *Networking Service:* Yes

International Pharmaceutical Federation
http://www.pharmweb.net
Location: International
Job Postings: Yes   *Resume Service:* No   *Networking Service:* No

Notes

Favorite sites, useful resources

International Society for Pharmacoepidemiology
http://www.pharmacoepi.org
Location: International
Job Postings: Yes   *Resume Service:* No   *Networking Service:* No

International Society for Pharmaceutical Engineering
http://www.ispe.org
Location: US - Florida
Job Postings: Yes   *Resume Service:* No   *Networking Service:* No

National Association of Chain Drug Stores
http://www.nacds.org
Location: US
Job Postings: No   *Resume Service:* No   *Networking Service:* No

National Community Pharmacists Association
http://www.ncpanet.org
Location: US
Job Postings: Yes   *Resume Service:* No   *Networking Service:* No

National Pharmaceutical Association
http://www.npa.co.uk
Location: Europe - UK
Job Postings: No   *Resume Service:* No   *Networking Service:* No

National Wholesale Druggists' Association
http://www.nwda.org
Location: US
Job Postings: No   *Resume Service:* No   *Networking Service:* No

New York State Society of Health-Systems Pharmacists
http://www.nyschp.org
Location: US - New York
Job Postings: Yes   *Resume Service:* No   *Networking Service:* No

Ohio Pharmacists Association
http://www.ohiopharmacists.org
Location: US - Ohio
Job Postings: Yes   *Resume Service:* No   *Networking Service:* No

Pediatric Pharmacy Advocacy Group
http://www.ppag.org
Location: US
Job Postings: Yes   *Resume Service:* No   *Networking Service:* No

Royal Pharmaceutical Society of Great Britain
http://www.rpsgb.org.uk
Location: Europe - UK
Job Postings: Yes   *Resume Service:* No   *Networking Service:* No

Notes

Favorite sites, useful resources

Society of Hospital Pharmacists of Australia
http://www.shpa.org.au
Location: Australia
Job Postings: Yes   *Resume Service:* No   *Networking Service:* No

South African Association of Hospital & Institutional Pharmacists
http://www.saahip.org.za
Location: Africa
Job Postings: No   *Resume Service:* No   *Networking Service:* No

United States Pharmacopoeia
http://www.usp.org
Location: US
Job Postings: Yes   *Resume Service:* Yes   *Networking Service:* No

Utah Pharmaceutical Association
http://www.upha.com
Location: US - Utah
Job Postings: No   *Resume Service:* No   *Networking Service:* No

Virginia Pharmacists Association
http://pharmacy.su.edu/vpha/
Location: US - Virginia
Job Postings: No   *Resume Service:* No   *Networking Service:* No

West Virginia Society of Health-Systems Pharmacists
http://www.wvshp.org
Location: US - West Virginia
Job Postings: Yes   *Resume Service:* No   *Networking Service:* No

Physics

American Institute of Physics
http://www.aip.org
Location: US
Job Postings: Yes   *Resume Service:* Yes   *Networking Service:* No

American Physical Society
http://www.aps.org
Location: US
Job Postings: Yes   *Resume Service:* Yes   *Networking Service:* Yes

---

Looking for a new or better job?   Looking for top talent?
Use WEDDLE's publications. Visit www.weddles.com today.
- **WEDDLE's 2005/6 Guide** is the "consumer's report" of job boards.
- **WEDDLE's 2005/6 Directory** is the "address book" of job boards.

Notes

Favorite sites, useful resources

Printing/Bookbinding

Association for Suppliers of Printing, Publishing and Converting Technologies
http://www.npes.org
Location: US
Job Postings: No *Resume Service:* No *Networking Service:* No

Digital Printing & Imaging Association
http://www.dpia.org
Location: US
Job Postings: Yes *Resume Service:* Yes *Networking Service:* No

Printing and Imaging Association
http://www.piatexas.org
Location: US
Job Postings: Yes *Resume Service:* No *Networking Service:* No

Psychology/Neuroscience

Academy of Counseling Psychology
http://www.aacop.net
Location: US
Job Postings: No *Resume Service:* No *Networking Service:* No

American Academy of Child and Adolescent Psychiatry
http://www.aacap.org
Location: US
Job Postings: Yes *Resume Service:* No *Networking Service:* No

American Academy of Clinical Psychiatrists
http://www.aacp.com
Location: US
Job Postings: No *Resume Service:* No *Networking Service:* No

American Academy of Experts in Traumatic Stress
http://www.aaets.org
Location: US
Job Postings: No *Resume Service:* No *Networking Service:* No

American Academy of Psychotherapists
http://www.aapweb.com
Location: US
Job Postings: No *Resume Service:* No *Networking Service:* No

American Association of Anger Management Providers
http://www.angermanagementproviders.com
Location: US
Job Postings: No *Resume Service:* No *Networking Service:* No

Notes

Favorite sites, useful resources

American Association for Geriatric Psychiatry
http://www.aagpgpa.org
Location: US
Job Postings: Yes   *Resume Service:* No   *Networking Service:* No

American Association for Marriage and Family Therapy
http://www.aamft.org/index_nm.asp
Location: US
Job Postings: Yes   *Resume Service:* Yes   *Networking Service:* No

American Association of Psychotherapists
http://www.angelfire.com/realm2/hypnosis
Location: US
Job Postings: No   *Resume Service:* No   *Networking Service:* No

American Board of Psychiatry and Neurology
http://www.abpn.com
Location: US
Job Postings: No   *Resume Service:* No   *Networking Service:* No

American College of Mental Health Administration
http://www.acmha.org
Location: US
Job Postings: No   *Resume Service:* No   *Networking Service:* No

American Counseling Association
http://www.counseling.org
Location: US
Job Postings: Yes   *Resume Service:* No   *Networking Service:* No

American Mental Health Counselor Association
http://www.amhca.org
Location: US
Job Postings: No   *Resume Service:* No   *Networking Service:* No

American Orthopsychiatric Association
http://www.amerortho.org
Location: US
Job Postings: No   *Resume Service:* No   *Networking Service:* No

American Psychiatric Association
http://www.psych.org
Location: US
Job Postings: Yes   *Resume Service:* No   *Networking Service:* No

American Psychiatric Nurses Association
http://www.apna.org
Location: US
Job Postings: Yes   *Resume Service:* No   *Networking Service:* No

Notes

Favorite sites, useful resources

American Psychological Society
http://www.psychologicalscience.org
Location: US
Job Postings: Yes   *Resume Service:* No   *Networking Service:* No

American Psychotherapy and Medical Hypnosis Association
http://apmha.com
Location: US
Job Postings: No   *Resume Service:* No   *Networking Service:* No

American Psychotherapy Association
http://www.americanpsychotherapy.com/index.php
Location: US
Job Postings: No   *Resume Service:* No   *Networking Service:* No

American School Counselor Association
http://www.schoolcounselor.org
Location: US
Job Postings: No   *Resume Service:* No   *Networking Service:* No

Association for Birth Psychology
http://birthpsychology.org/index.html
Location: US
Job Postings: No   *Resume Service:* No   *Networking Service:* No

Canadian Counseling Association
http://www.ccacc.ca
Location: North America - Canada
Job Postings: No   *Resume Service:* No   *Networking Service:* No

Cognitive Neuroscience Society
http://www.cogneurosociety.org
Location: US
Job Postings: No   *Resume Service:* No   *Networking Service:* No

Cognitive Science Society
http://www.cognitivesciencesociety.org
Location: US
Job Postings: Yes   *Resume Service:* No   *Networking Service:* No

Council for Children with Behavioral Disorders
http://www.ccbd.net
Location: US
Job Postings: No   *Resume Service:* No   *Networking Service:* No

Division 42 online: Psychologists in Independent Practice
http://www.division42.org
Location: US
Job Postings: No   *Resume Service:* No   *Networking Service:* No

Notes

Favorite sites, useful resources

EMDR International Association
http://www.emdria.org
Location: US
Job Postings: No   *Resume Service:* No   *Networking Service:* No

Institute of Psychology and Markets
http://www.psychologyandmarkets.org
Location: US
Job Postings: No   *Resume Service:* No   *Networking Service:* No

International Association of Anxiety Management
http://www.anxman.org
Location: US
Job Postings: No   *Resume Service:* No   *Networking Service:* No

International Association of Eating Disorders Professionals
http://www.iaedp.com
Location: US
Job Postings: Yes   *Resume Service:* Yes   *Networking Service:* No

International Association for Regression Research and Therapies, Inc
http://www.iarrt.org
Location: US
Job Postings: No   *Resume Service:* No   *Networking Service:* No

The International Society for Behaviorology
http://ww2.lafayette.edu/~allanr/behavior.html
Location: US
Job Postings: No   *Resume Service:* No   *Networking Service:* No

National Association of Alcoholism and Drug Abuse Counselors
http://www.naadac.org
Location: US
Job Postings: Yes   *Resume Service:* No   *Networking Service:* No

National Association of Cognitive-Behavioral Therapists
http://www.nacbt.org
Location: US
Job Postings: No   *Resume Service:* No   *Networking Service:* No

The National Association of School Psychologists
http://www.naspcareercenter.org
Location: US
Job Postings: Yes   *Resume Service:* Yes   *Networking Service:* No

The National Mental Health Association
http://www.nmha.org
Location: US
Job Postings: No   *Resume Service:* No   *Networking Service:* No

Notes

Favorite sites, useful resources

Society for Advancement of Behavior Analysis
http://www.abainternational.org/saba/
Location: US
Job Postings: No   *Resume Service:* No   *Networking Service:* No

Society for Industrial & Organizational Psychology
http://www.siop.org
Location: US
Job Postings: Yes   *Resume Service:* No   *Networking Service:* No

Society for Quantitative Analyses of Behavior
http://sqab.psychology.org
Location: US
Job Postings: No   *Resume Service:* No   *Networking Service:* No

The Therapeutic Milieu
http://www.therapeuticmilieu.org
Location: US
Job Postings: No   *Resume Service:* No   *Networking Service:* No

United States Association for Body Psychotherapy
http://www.usabp.org
Location: US
Job Postings: Yes   *Resume Service:* No   *Networking Service:* No

Publishing

American Booksellers Association
http://www.bookweb.org
Location: US
Job Postings: No   *Resume Service:* No   *Networking Service:* Yes

American Jewish Press Association
http://www.ajpa.org
Location: US
Job Postings: Yes   *Resume Service:* Yes   *Networking Service:* No

Association of American Publishers
http://www.publishers.org
Location: US
Job Postings: Yes   *Resume Service:* No   *Networking Service:* No

Association of Graphic Solutions Providers (IPA)
http://www.ipa.org
Location: International
Job Postings: No   *Resume Service:* No   *Networking Service:* No

Notes

Favorite sites, useful resources

Association for Suppliers of Printing, Publishing and Converting Technologies
http://www.npes.org
Location: US
Job Postings: No   *Resume Service:* No   *Networking Service:* No

Audio Publishers Association
http://www.audiopub.org
Location: US
Job Postings: No   *Resume Service:* No   *Networking Service:* No

Editorial Freelancers Association
http://www.the-efa.org
Location: US
Job Postings: Yes   *Resume Service:* No   *Networking Service:* No

Electronic Publishing Association
http://www.epaonline.com
Location: International
Job Postings: No   *Resume Service:* No   *Networking Service:* No

Independent Press Association
http://www.indypress.org
Location: US
Job Postings: Yes   *Resume Service:* No   *Networking Service:* No

International Association of Scholarly Publishers
http://lcweb.loc.gov/loc/cfbook/coborg/iasp.html
Location: International
Job Postings: No   *Resume Service:* No   *Networking Service:* No

International Newspaper Marketing Association
http://www.inma.org
Location: International
Job Postings: Yes   *Resume Service:* No   *Networking Service:* No

The National Association of Independent Publishers
http://lcweb.loc.gov/loc/cfbook/coborg/nai.html
Location: US
Job Postings: No   *Resume Service:* No   *Networking Service:* No

National Association of Real Estate Publishers
http://www.narep.com
Location: US
Job Postings: No   *Resume Service:* No   *Networking Service:* No

National Music Publishers Association
http://www.nmpa.org
Location: US
Job Postings: No   *Resume Service:* No   *Networking Service:* No

Notes

Favorite sites, useful resources

National Writer's Union
http://www.nwu.org
Location: US
Job Postings: Yes *Resume Service:* No *Networking Service:* No

Publishers Marketing Association
http://www.pma-online.org
Location: US
Job Postings: No *Resume Service:* No *Networking Service:* No

Small Publishers Association of North America
http://www.spannet.org
Location: US
Job Postings: No *Resume Service:* No *Networking Service:* No

University Research Magazine Association
http://www.urma.org
Location: US
Job Postings: No *Resume Service:* No *Networking Service:* Yes

Purchasing

Institute for Supply Management
http://www.ism.ws
Location: US
Job Postings: Yes *Resume Service:* No *Networking Service:* No

National Association of Governmental Purchasing
www.nigp.org
Location: US
Job Postings: No *Resume Service:* No *Networking Service:* No

Purchasing Management Association of Boston
http://www.pmaboston.org
Location: US - Massachusetts
Job Postings: No *Resume Service:* No *Networking Service:* No

The National Institute of Governmental Purchasing
http://www.nigp.org
Location: US
Job Postings: No *Resume Service:* No *Networking Service:* No

---

Looking for a new or better job? Looking for top talent?
Use WEDDLE's publications. Visit www.weddles.com today.
- *WEDDLE's 2005/6 Guide* is the "consumer's report" of job boards.
- *WEDDLE's 2005/6 Directory* is the "address book" of job boards.

Notes
Favorite sites, useful resources

-Q-

Quality Assurance

American National Standards Institute
http://www.ansi.org
Location: US
Job Postings: Yes   *Resume Service:* No   *Networking Service:* No

American Society for Quality
http://www.asq.org
Location: US
Job Postings: Yes   *Resume Service:* No   *Networking Service:* No

Association for Retail Technology Standards
http://www.nrf-arts.org
Location: US
Job Postings: No   *Resume Service:* No   *Networking Service:* Yes

Certified Financial Planner Board of Standards
http://www.CFP-Board.org
Location: US
Job Postings: No   *Resume Service:* No   *Networking Service:* No

Financial Accounting Standards Board
http://www.fasb.org
Location: US
Job Postings: Yes   *Resume Service:* No   *Networking Service:* No

Governmental Accounting Standards Board
http://www.gasb.org
Location: US
Job Postings: No   *Resume Service:* No   *Networking Service:* No

International Society for Performance Improvement
http://www.ispi.org
Location: International
Job Postings: Yes   *Resume Service:* No   *Networking Service:* No

National Association for Healthcare Quality
http://www.nahq.org
Location: US
Job Postings: Yes   *Resume Service:* No   *Networking Service:* No

Society for Maintenance and Reliability Professionals
http://www.smrp.org/index.php
Location: US
Job Postings: Yes   *Resume Service:* No   *Networking Service:* No

Notes

Favorite sites, useful resources

Society for Software Quality
http://www.ssq.org
Location: US
Job Postings: No   *Resume Service:* No   *Networking Service:* No

-R-

Recruitment

American Staffing Association
http://www.staffingtoday.net
Location: US
Job Postings: No   *Resume Service:* No   *Networking Service:* No

Association of Canadian Search Employment and Staffing Services
http://www.acsess.org
Location: North America - Canada
Job Postings: No   *Resume Service:* No   *Networking Service:* No

The Association of Executive Search Consultants
http://www.aesc.org
Location: US
Job Postings: No   *Resume Service:* No   *Networking Service:* No

Association for Internet Recruiting
http://www.recruitersnetwork.com
Location: US
Job Postings: Yes   *Resume Service:* No   *Networking Service:* Yes

International Association of Corporate and Professional Recruitment
http://www.iacpr.org
Location: International
Job Postings: No   *Resume Service:* No   *Networking Service:* No

The National Association for Alternative Staffing
http://www.naas-net.org
Location: US
Job Postings: No   *Resume Service:* No   *Networking Service:* No

The National Association for Health Care Recruitment
http://www.nahcr.com
Location: US
Job Postings: No   *Resume Service:* No   *Networking Service:* No

---

**Looking for a new or better job?   Looking for top talent?
Use WEDDLE's publications. Visit www.weddles.com today.**

Notes

Favorite sites, useful resources

The National Association of Legal Search Consultants
http://www.nalsc.org
Location: US
Job Postings: No   *Resume Service:* No   *Networking Service:* No

National Association of Medical Staff Services
http://www.namss.org
Location: US
Job Postings: Yes   *Resume Service:* No   *Networking Service:* No

National Association of Executive Recruiters
http://www.naer.org
Location: US
Job Postings: No   *Resume Service:* No   *Networking Service:* No

National Association of Personnel Services
http://www.napsweb.org
Location: US
Job Postings: No   *Resume Service:* No   *Networking Service:* No

National Insurance Recruiters Association
http://www.nirassn.com
Location: US
Job Postings: No   *Resume Service:* No   *Networking Service:* No

National Personnel Associates
http://www.npainc.com
Location: US
Job Postings: No   *Resume Service:* No   *Networking Service:* No

New Jersey Staffing Association
http://www.njsa.com
Location: US - New Jersey
Job Postings: Yes   *Resume Service:* No   *Networking Service:* No

South Carolina Association of Personnel Services
http://www.scaps.org
Location: US - South Carolina
Job Postings: No   *Resume Service:* No   *Networking Service:* No

Regional—USA

Alabama

Alabama State Bar
http://www.alabar.org
Job Postings: No   *Resume Service:* No   *Networking Service:* No

Notes

Favorite sites, useful resources

Alaska

Alaska Bar Association
http://www.alaskabar.org
Job Postings: No   *Resume Service:* No   *Networking Service:* No

Arizona

St. Augustine and St. Johns County Board of Realtors
http://www.bor.com
Job Postings: No   *Resume Service:* No   *Networking Service:* No

State Bar of Arizona
http://www.azbar.org
Job Postings: No   *Resume Service:* No   *Networking Service:* No

Arkansas

Arkansas State Bar Association
http://www.arkbar.com
Job Postings: No   *Resume Service:* No   *Networking Service:* No

California

California Association of Employers
http://www.employers.org
Job Postings: No   *Resume Service:* No   *Networking Service:* No

California Association of Orthodontists
http://www.caortho.org
Job Postings: No   *Resume Service:* No   *Networking Service:* No

California Association of Realtors
http://www.car.org
Job Postings: No   *Resume Service:* No   *Networking Service:* No

California Dental Association
http://www.cda.org
Job Postings: No   *Resume Service:* No   *Networking Service:* No

California Korean Pharmacists Association
http://www.kpha.com
Job Postings: Yes   *Resume Service:* No   *Networking Service:* No

Notes

Favorite sites, useful resources

California Pharmacists Association
http://www.cpha.com
Job Postings: Yes   *Resume Service:* No   *Networking Service:*No

California State Bar Association
http://www.calbar.org
Job Postings: No   *Resume Service:* No   *Networking Service:*No

Los Angeles County Bar Association
http://www.lacba.org
Job Postings: Yes   *Resume Service:* No   *Networking Service:*Yes

Los Angeles Dental Society
http://www.ladentalsociety.com
Job Postings: No   *Resume Service:* No   *Networking Service:*No

Northern California Human Resources Association
http://www.nchra.org
Job Postings: Yes   *Resume Service:* No   *Networking Service:*No

Colorado

Colorado Bar Association
http://www.cobar.org
Job Postings: No   *Resume Service:* No   *Networking Service:*No

Colorado Dental Association
http://www.cdaonline.org
Job Postings: No   *Resume Service:* No   *Networking Service:*No

Connecticut

Connecticut State Bar Association
http://www.ctbar.org
Job Postings: Yes   *Resume Service:* No   *Networking Service:*No

Delaware

Delaware State Bar Association
http://www.dsba.org
Job Postings: No   *Resume Service:* No   *Networking Service:*No

---

Looking for a new or better job?   Looking for top talent?
Use WEDDLE's publications. Visit www.weddles.com today.

Notes

Favorite sites, useful resources

District of Columbia

DC Science Writers Association
http://www.dcswa.org
Job Postings: Yes   *Resume Service:* No   *Networking Service:* No

District of Columbia Bar
http://www.badc.org
Job Postings: No   *Resume Service:* No   *Networking Service:* No

Human Resource Association of the National Capital Area
http://www.hra-nca.org
Job Postings: No   *Resume Service:* No   *Networking Service:* No

Florida

Florida Dental Association
http://www.floridadental.org
Job Postings: No   *Resume Service:* No   *Networking Service:* No

Florida State Bar Association
http://www.flabar.org
Job Postings: No   *Resume Service:* No   *Networking Service:* No

Georgia

Georgia Department of Human Resources
http://www.dhrjobs.com
Job Postings: Yes   *Resume Service:* No   *Networking Service:* No

Georgia Pharmacy Association
http://www.gpha.org
Job Postings: Yes   *Resume Service:* No   *Networking Service:* No

State Bar of Georgia
http://www.gabar.org
Job Postings: No   *Resume Service:* No   *Networking Service:* No

Hawaii

Hawaii State Bar Association
http://www.hsba.org
Job Postings: No   *Resume Service:* No   *Networking Service:* No

Notes

Favorite sites, useful resources

Idaho

Idaho State Bar
http://www2.state.id.us/isb/
Job Postings: No   *Resume Service:* No   *Networking Service:* No

Illinois

Chicago Medical Society
http://www.cmsdocs.org
Job Postings: Yes   *Resume Service:* Yes   *Networking Service:* No

Chicago Software Association
http://www.csa.org/
Job Postings: Yes   *Resume Service:* Yes   *Networking Service:* No

Chicagoland Chapter American Society of Training and Development
http://www.ccastd.org
Job Postings: Yes   *Resume Service:* No   *Networking Service:* No

Human Resources Management Association of Chicago
http://www.hrmac.org
Job Postings: Yes   *Resume Service:* No   *Networking Service:* No

Illinois State Bar Association
http://www.illinoisbar.org
Job Postings: Yes   *Resume Service:* Yes   *Networking Service:* No

Illinois State Dental Society
http://www.isds.org
Job Postings: No   *Resume Service:* No   *Networking Service:* No

Indiana

Indiana State Bar Association
http://www.inbar.org
Job Postings: No   *Resume Service:* No   *Networking Service:* No

Iowa

Iowa State Bar Association
http://www.iowabar.org
Job Postings: No   *Resume Service:* No   *Networking Service:* No

Notes

Favorite sites, useful resources

Kansas

Kansas State Bar Association
http://www.ksbar.org

Job Postings: Yes	*Resume Service:* Yes	*Networking Service:* No

Kentucky

Kentucky Bar Association
http://www.kybar.org

Job Postings: No	*Resume Service:* No	*Networking Service:* No

Kentucky Dental Association
http://www.kyda.org

Job Postings: No	*Resume Service:* No	*Networking Service:* No

Louisiana

Louisiana State Bar Association
http://www.lsba.org

Job Postings: No	*Resume Service:* No	*Networking Service:* No

Maine

Maine State Bar Association
http://www.mainebar.org

Job Postings: Yes	*Resume Service:* Yes	*Networking Service:* No

Maryland

Maryland State Bar Association
http://www.msba.org

Job Postings: No	*Resume Service:* No	*Networking Service:* No

Maryland State Dental Association
http://www.msda.com

Job Postings: No	*Resume Service:* No	*Networking Service:* No

Massachusetts

Massachusetts Bar Association
http://www.massbar.org

Job Postings: Yes	*Resume Service:* No	*Networking Service:* No

Notes

Favorite sites, useful resources

Massachusetts Council of Human Service Providers
http://www.providers.org
Job Postings: Yes   *Resume Service:* No   *Networking Service:*No

Massachusetts Dental Society
http://www.massdental.org
Job Postings: Yes   *Resume Service:* No   *Networking Service:*No

New England Human Resources Association
http://www.nehra.com
Job Postings: Yes   *Resume Service:* Yes   *Networking Service:*No

Purchasing Management Association of Boston
http://www.pmaboston.org
Job Postings: No   *Resume Service:* No   *Networking Service:*No

Michigan

Human Resource Management Association of Mid Michigan
http://www.hrmamm.com
Job Postings: Yes   *Resume Service:* No   *Networking Service:*No

Michigan Dental Association
http://www.michigandental.org
Job Postings: Yes   *Resume Service:* No   *Networking Service:*No

Michigan State Bar Association
http://www.michbar.org
Job Postings: No   *Resume Service:* No   *Networking Service:*No

Minnesota

Minnesota State Bar Association
http://www.mnbar.org
Job Postings: Yes   *Resume Service:* Yes   *Networking Service:*No

Mississippi

Mississippi State Bar Association
http://www.msbar.org
Job Postings: No   *Resume Service:* No   *Networking Service:*No

---

Looking for a new or better job?   Looking for top talent?
Jse WEDDLE's publications. Visit www.weddles.com today.

Notes

Favorite sites, useful resources

Missouri

Missouri Dental Association
http://www.modental.org
Job Postings: Yes   *Resume Service:* No   *Networking Service:* No

Missouri State Bar Association
http://www.mobar.org
Job Postings: No   *Resume Service:* No   *Networking Service:* No

Montana

State Bar of Montana
http://www.montanabar.org
Job Postings: No   *Resume Service:* No   *Networking Service:* No

Nebraska

Nebraska State Bar Association
http://www.nebar.com
Job Postings: No   *Resume Service:* No   *Networking Service:* No

Nevada

Nevada Dental Association
http://www.nvda.org
Job Postings: No   *Resume Service:* No   *Networking Service:* No

State Bar of Nevada
http://www.nvbar.org
Job Postings: No   *Resume Service:* No   *Networking Service:* No

New Hampshire

New Hampshire Bar Association
http://www.nhbar.org
Job Postings: No   *Resume Service:* No   *Networking Service:* No

New Jersey

New Jersey Dental Association
http://www.njda.org
Job Postings: No   *Resume Service:* No   *Networking Service:* No

Notes

Favorite sites, useful resources

New Jersey Staffing Association
http://www.njsa.com
Job Postings: Yes   *Resume Service:* No   *Networking Service:* No

New Jersey State Bar Association
http://www.njsba.com
Job Postings: No   *Resume Service:* No   *Networking Service:* No

New Jersey Metro EMA
http://www.njmetroema.org
Job Postings: No   *Resume Service:* No   *Networking Service:* No

New Mexico

State Bar of New Mexico
http://www.nmbar.org
Job Postings: No   *Resume Service:* No   *Networking Service:* No

New York

Dental Lab Association of the State of New York
http://www.dlany.org
Job Postings: Yes   *Resume Service:* No   *Networking Service:* No

Greater Rochester Association of Realtors
http://www.homesteadnet.com
Job Postings: No   *Resume Service:* No   *Networking Service:* No

New York New Media Association
http://www.nynma.org
Job Postings: Yes   *Resume Service:* Yes   *Networking Service:* No

New York Society of Security Analysts, Inc.
http://www.nyssa.org
Job Postings: No   *Resume Service:* No   *Networking Service:* No

New York State Bar Association
http://www.nysba.org
Job Postings: No   *Resume Service:* No   *Networking Service:* No

New York State Dental Association
http://www.nysdental.org
Job Postings: No   *Resume Service:* No   *Networking Service:* No

Notes

Favorite sites, useful resources

New York State Society of Health-Systems Pharmacists
http://www.nyschp.org
Job Postings: Yes   *Resume Service:* No   *Networking Service:* No

Specialty Advertising Association of Greater New York
http://www.saagny.org
Job Postings: No   *Resume Service:* No   *Networking Service:* No

North Carolina

North Carolina Dental Society
http://www.ncdental.org
Job Postings: Yes   *Resume Service:* Yes   *Networking Service:* No

North Carolina State Bar Association
http://www.barlinc.org
Job Postings: No   *Resume Service:* No   *Networking Service:* No

North Dakota

North Dakota Dental Association
http://www.nddental.com
Job Postings: Yes   *Resume Service:* No   *Networking Service:* No

North Dakota State Bar Association
http://www.sband.org
Job Postings: No   *Resume Service:* No   *Networking Service:* No

Ohio

Greater Cleveland Dental Society
http://www.gcds.org
Job Postings: Yes   *Resume Service:* No   *Networking Service:* No

Ohio Dental Association
http://www.oda.org
Job Postings: No   *Resume Service:* No   *Networking Service:* No

Ohio Pharmacists Association
http://www.ohiopharmacists.org
Job Postings: Yes   *Resume Service:* No   *Networking Service:* No

Ohio State Bar Association
http://www.ohiobar.org
Job Postings: No   *Resume Service:* No   *Networking Service:* No

Notes

Favorite sites, useful resources

Oklahoma

Oklahoma Bankers Association
http://www.oba.com
Job Postings: Yes   *Resume Service:* Yes   *Networking Service:* No

Oklahoma Bar Association
http://www.okbar.org
Job Postings: No   *Resume Service:* No   *Networking Service:* No

Oklahoma Public Employees Association
http://www.opea.org
Job Postings: No   *Resume Service:* No   *Networking Service:* No

Tulsa Area Human Resources Association
http://www.tahra.org
Job Postings: Yes   *Resume Service:* No   *Networking Service:* No

Oregon

Oregon Dental Association
http://www.oregondental.org
Job Postings: No   *Resume Service:* No   *Networking Service:* No

Oregon State Bar
http://www.osbar.org
Job Postings: No   *Resume Service:* No   *Networking Service:* No

Pennsylvania

Pennsylvania Dental Association
http://www.padental.org
Job Postings: Yes   *Resume Service:* No   *Networking Service:* No

Pennsylvania Institute of Certified Public Accountants
http://www.picpa.com
Job Postings: Yes   *Resume Service:* Yes   *Networking Service:* Yes

Pennsylvania State Bar Association
http://www.pa-bar.org
Job Postings: Yes   *Resume Service:* Yes   *Networking Service:* No

---

Looking for a new or better job?   Looking for top talent?
se WEDDLE's publications. Visit www.weddles.com today.

Notes

Favorite sites, useful resources

Rhode Island

Rhode Island Dental Association
http://www.ridental.com
Job Postings: Yes   *Resume Service:* No   *Networking Service:* No

Rhode Island State Bar Association
http://www.ribar.com
Job Postings: No   *Resume Service:* No   *Networking Service:* No

South Carolina

South Carolina Association of Personnel Services
http://www.scaps.org
Job Postings: No   *Resume Service:* No   *Networking Service:* No

South Carolina Bar
http://www.scbar.org
Job Postings: No   *Resume Service:* No   *Networking Service:* No

South Carolina Dental Association
http://www.scda.org
Job Postings: Yes   *Resume Service:* No   *Networking Service:* No

South Dakota

South Dakota Bankers Association
http://www.sdba.com
Job Postings: No   *Resume Service:* No   *Networking Service:* No

South Dakota State Bar Association
http://www.sdbar.org
Job Postings: No   *Resume Service:* No   *Networking Service:* No

Tennessee

Tennessee Bar Association
http://www.tba.org
Job Postings: No   *Resume Service:* No   *Networking Service:* No

---

Looking for a new or better job?   Looking for top talent?
Use WEDDLE's publications. Visit www.weddles.com today.

- *WEDDLE's 2005/6 Guide* is the "consumer's report" of job boards.
- *WEDDLE's 2005/6 Directory* is the "address book" of job boards.

Notes

Favorite sites, useful resources

Texas

Dallas Building Owners & Managers Association
http://www.bomadallas.org
Job Postings: No   *Resume Service:* No   *Networking Service:* No

Dallas Human Resource Management Association
http://www.dallashr.org
Job Postings: Yes   *Resume Service:* Yes   *Networking Service:* No

State Bar of Texas
http://www.texasbar.com
Job Postings: No   *Resume Service:* No   *Networking Service:* No

Utah

Utah Association of CPAs
http://www.uacpa.org
Job Postings: Yes   *Resume Service:* No   *Networking Service:* No

Utah Pharmaceutical Association
http://www.upha.com
Job Postings: No   *Resume Service:* No   *Networking Service:* No

Utah State Bar
http://www.utahbar.org
Job Postings: Yes   *Resume Service:* Yes   *Networking Service:* No

Vermont

Vermont State Bar Association
http://www.vtbar.org
Job Postings: No   *Resume Service:* No   *Networking Service:* No

Virginia

Virginia State Bar
http://www.vsb.org
Job Postings: No   *Resume Service:* No   *Networking Service:* No

Virginia Dental Association
http://www.vadental.org
Job Postings: No   *Resume Service:* No   *Networking Service:* No

Notes

Favorite sites, useful resources

Virginia Pharmacists Association
http://pharmacy.su.edu/vpha/
Job Postings: No   *Resume Service:* No   *Networking Service:*No

Washington

Washington Biotechnology Biomedical Association
http://www.wabio.com
Job Postings: No   *Resume Service:* No   *Networking Service:*No

Washington State Bar Association
http://www.wsba.org
Job Postings: No   *Resume Service:* No   *Networking Service:*No

Washington State Dental Association
http://www.wsda.org
Job Postings: No   *Resume Service:* No   *Networking Service:*No

West Virginia

West Virginia Society of Health-Systems Pharmacists
http://www.wvshp.org
Job Postings: Yes   *Resume Service:* No   *Networking Service:*No

West Virginia State Bar Association
http://www.wvbar.org
Job Postings: Yes   *Resume Service:* No   *Networking Service:*No

Wisconsin

Wisconsin Dental Association
http://www.wisconsindental.com
Job Postings: No   *Resume Service:* No   *Networking Service:*No

Wisconsin Library Association/Wisconsin Library Association Foundation
http://www.wla.lib.wi.us
Job Postings: Yes   *Resume Service:* No   *Networking Service:*No

Wisconsin Medical Society
http://www.wisconsinmedicalsociety.org
Job Postings: Yes   *Resume Service:* Yes   *Networking Service:*No

Wisconsin Realtors Association
http://www.wra.org
Job Postings: No   *Resume Service:* No   *Networking Service:*No

Notes

Favorite sites, useful resources

Wisconsin State Bar Association
http://www.wisbar.org
Job Postings: No   *Resume Service:* No   *Networking Service:*No

Wyoming

Wyoming State Bar
http://www.wyomingbar.org
Job Postings: No   *Resume Service:* No   *Networking Service:*No

Puerto Rico

Puerto Rico Manufacturers Association
http://www.prma.com
Job Postings: No   *Resume Service:* No   *Networking Service:*No

Religion

American Academy of Religion
http://www.aarweb.org
Location: US
Job Postings: Yes   *Resume Service:* No   *Networking Service:* No

Central Conference of American Rabbis
http://www.ccarnet.org
Location: US
Job Postings: No   *Resume Service:* No   *Networking Service:* No

Christian Brothers Services
http://www.cbservices.org
Location: US
Job Postings: No   *Resume Service:* No   *Networking Service:* No

Christian Legal Society
http://www.clsnet.org
Location: US
Job Postings: Yes   *Resume Service:* No   *Networking Service:* No

International Association of Jewish Vocational Services
http://www.jvsnj.org/iajvs.html
Location: US
Job Postings: Yes   *Resume Service:* No   *Networking Service:* No

---

Looking for a new or better job?   Looking for top talent?
Jse WEDDLE's publications. Visit www.weddles.com today.

Notes

Favorite sites, useful resources

National Association of Church Business Administration
http://www.nacba.net
Location: US
Job Postings: Yes   *Resume Service:* No   *Networking Service:* No

National Association of Church Personnel Administrators
http://www.nacpa.org
Location: US
Job Postings: No   *Resume Service:* No   *Networking Service:* No

National Association of Temple Educators
http://www.rj.org/nate/
Location: US
Job Postings: No   *Resume Service:* No   *Networking Service:* No

National Church of Goods Association
http://www.ncgaweb.com
Location: US
Job Postings: No   *Resume Service:* No   *Networking Service:* No

National Religious Broadcasters Association
http://www.nrb.org
Location: US
Job Postings: Yes   *Resume Service:* No   *Networking Service:* No

Retail/Wholesale

American Booksellers Association
http://www.bookweb.org
Location: US
Job Postings: No   *Resume Service:* No   *Networking Service:* Yes

Association for Retail Technology Standards
http://www.nrf-arts.org
Location: US
Job Postings: No   *Resume Service:* No   *Networking Service:* Yes

Bureau of Wholesale Sales Representatives
http://www.bwsr.com
Location: US
Job Postings: Yes   *Resume Service:* Yes   *Networking Service:* No

Consumer Electronics Manufacturers Association
http://www.cemacity.org
Location: US
Job Postings: No   *Resume Service:* No   *Networking Service:* No

Notes

Favorite sites, useful resources

Electronics Representatives Association
http://www.era.org
Location: US
Job Postings: Yes   *Resume Service:* Yes   *Networking Service:* No

Footware Distributors and Retailers of America
http://www.fdra.org
Location: US
Job Postings: No   *Resume Service:* No   *Networking Service:* No

Fresh Produce and Floral Council
http://www.fpfc.org
Location: US
Job Postings: No   *Resume Service:* No   *Networking Service:* No

FTD Association
http://www.ftdassociation.org
Location: US
Job Postings: No   *Resume Service:* No   *Networking Service:* No

Home Furnishings International Association
http://www.hfia.com
Location: US
Job Postings: No   *Resume Service:* No   *Networking Service:* No

International Association of Department Stores
http://www.iads.org
Location: US
Job Postings: No   *Resume Service:* No   *Networking Service:* No

International Mass Retail Association
http://www.imra.org
Location: US
Job Postings: No   *Resume Service:* No   *Networking Service:* No

National Association of Chain Drug Stores
http://www.nacds.org
Location: US
Job Postings: No   *Resume Service:* No   *Networking Service:* No

National Association of Convenience Stores
http://www.cstorecentral.com
Location: US
Job Postings: No   *Resume Service:* No   *Networking Service:* No

National Automatic Merchandising Association
http://www.vending.org
Location: US
Job Postings: Yes   *Resume Service:* Yes   *Networking Service:* No

Notes

Favorite sites, useful resources

National Housewares Manufacturers Association
http://www.housewares.org
Location: US
Job Postings: Yes   *Resume Service:* Yes   *Networking Service:* No

National Mail Order Association
http://www.nmoa.org
Location: US
Job Postings: Yes   *Resume Service:* No   *Networking Service:* No

National Retail Federation
http://www.nrf.com
Location: US
Job Postings: Yes   *Resume Service:* Yes   *Networking Service:* No

National Retail Hardware Association and Home Center Institute
http://www.nrha.org
Location: US
Job Postings: No   *Resume Service:* No   *Networking Service:* No

North American Retail Dealers Association
http://www.narda.com
Location: US
Job Postings: No   *Resume Service:* No   *Networking Service:* No

Professional Apparel Association
http://www.proapparel.com
Location: US
Job Postings: No   *Resume Service:* No   *Networking Service:* No

Professional Retail Store Maintenance
http://www.prsm.com
Location: US
Job Postings: No   *Resume Service:* No   *Networking Service:* No

Retail Packaging Manufacturer's Association
http://www.rpma.org
Location: US
Job Postings: No   *Resume Service:* No   *Networking Service:* No

Society of American Florists
http://www.safnow.org
Location: US
Job Postings: No   *Resume Service:* No   *Networking Service:* No

Sporting Goods Manufacturers Association
http://www.sportlink.com
Location: US
Job Postings: Yes   *Resume Service:* No   *Networking Service:* No

Notes

Favorite sites, useful resources

The Business and Institutional Furniture Manufacturer's Association
http://www.bifma.com
Location: US
Job Postings: No   *Resume Service:* No   *Networking Service:* No

The National Bicycle Dealers Association
http://www.nbda.com
Location: US
Job Postings: No   *Resume Service:* No   *Networking Service:* No

The National Ice Cream and Yogurt Retailers Association
http://www.nicyra.org
Location: US
Job Postings: No   *Resume Service:* No   *Networking Service:* No

Warehouse Club Focus
http://www.warehouseclubfocus.com
Location: US
Job Postings: No   *Resume Service:* No   *Networking Service:* No

-S-

Sales/Marketing

Academy of Management
http://www.aomonline.org
Location: US
Job Postings: Yes   *Resume Service:* No   *Networking Service:* No

Academy of Marketing Science
http://www.ams-web.org
Location: US
Job Postings: No   *Resume Service:* No   *Networking Service:* No

Advertising Education Forum
http://www.aeforum.org
Location: Europe - UK
Job Postings: No   *Resume Service:* No   *Networking Service:* No

Advertising Research Foundation
http://www.arfsite.org
Location: US
Job Postings: No   *Resume Service:* No   *Networking Service:* No

---

Notes
Favorite sites, useful resources

American Academy of Advertising
http://advertising.utexas.edu/AAA/
Location: US
Job Postings: Yes   *Resume Service:* No   *Networking Service:* No

American Advertising Federation
http://www.aaf.org
Location: US
Job Postings: Yes   *Resume Service:* Yes   *Networking Service:* No

American Association of Advertising Agencies
http://www.aaaa.org
Location: US
Job Postings: No   *Resume Service:* No   *Networking Service:* No

American Association for Public Opinion Research
http://www.aapor.org
Location: US
Job Postings: No   *Resume Service:* No   *Networking Service:* No

American Marketing Association
http://www.marketingpower.com
Location: US
Job Postings: Yes   *Resume Service:* Yes   *Networking Service:* Yes

American Society for Public Administration (ASPA)
http://www.aspanet.org/scriptcontent/index.cfm
Location: US
Job Postings: Yes   *Resume Service:* Yes   *Networking Service:* No

American Telemarketing Association
http://www.ataconnect.org
Location: US
Job Postings: No   *Resume Service:* No   *Networking Service:* No

American Teleservices Association
http://www.ataconnect.org
Location: US
Job Postings: No   *Resume Service:* No   *Networking Service:* No

Association for the Advancement of Relationship Marketing
http://www.aarm.org
Location: US
Job Postings: Yes   *Resume Service:* No   *Networking Service:* No

Association for Corporate Growth
http://www.acg.org
Location: US
Job Postings: Yes   *Resume Service:* No   *Networking Service:* No

Notes
Favorite sites, useful resources

Association of Direct Marketing Agencies
http://www.the-dma.org
Location: US
Job Postings: Yes   *Resume Service:* Yes   *Networking Service:* No

Association of International Product Marketing Managers
http://www.aipmm.com
Location: International
Job Postings: Yes   *Resume Service:* Yes   *Networking Service:* No

Association of Investment Management Sales Executives
http://www.aimse.com
Location: US
Job Postings: No   *Resume Service:* No   *Networking Service:* No

Bank Marketing Association
http://www.bmanet.org
Location: US
Job Postings: No   *Resume Service:* No   *Networking Service:* No

Broker Management Council
http://www.bmsales.com
Location: US
Job Postings: No   *Resume Service:* No   *Networking Service:* No

Bureau of Wholesale Sales Representatives
http://www.bwsr.com
Location: US
Job Postings: Yes   *Resume Service:* Yes   *Networking Service:* No

Business Marketing Association
http://www.marketing.org
Location: US
Job Postings: Yes   *Resume Service:* Yes   *Networking Service:* No

Canadian Professional Sales Association
http://www.cpsa.com
Location: North America - Canada
Job Postings: Yes   *Resume Service:* Yes   *Networking Service:* No

CMO Council
http://www.cmocouncil.org
Location: US
Job Postings: No   *Resume Service:* No   *Networking Service:* No

Commercial Development and Marketing Association
http://cdmaonline.org/home.html
Location: US
Job Postings: Yes   *Resume Service:* No   *Networking Service:* No

Notes

Favorite sites, useful resources

Construction Marketing Research Council
http://www.cmrc.net
Location: US
Job Postings: No   *Resume Service:* No   *Networking Service:* No

Coupon Professionals
http://www.couponpros.org
Location: US
Job Postings: Yes   *Resume Service:* No   *Networking Service:* No

The Direct Marketing Association
http://www.the-dma.org
Location: US
Job Postings: Yes   *Resume Service:* Yes   *Networking Service:* No

Direct Selling Association
http://www.dsa.org
Location: US
Job Postings: No   *Resume Service:* No   *Networking Service:* No

Electronics Representatives Association
http://www.era.org
Location: US
Job Postings: Yes   *Resume Service:* Yes   *Networking Service:* No

eMarketing Association
http://www.emarketingassociation.com
Location: US
Job Postings: Yes   *Resume Service:* Yes   *Networking Service:* No

Emissions Marketing Association
http://www.emissions.org/
Location: US
Job Postings: No   *Resume Service:* No   *Networking Service:* No

Food Marketing Institute
http://www.fmi.org
Location: US
Job Postings: No   *Resume Service:* No   *Networking Service:* No

Glass Packaging Institute
http://www.gpi.org
Location: US
Job Postings: No   *Resume Service:* No   *Networking Service:* No

Health Industry Distributors Association
http://www.hida.org
Location: US
Job Postings: No   *Resume Service:* No   *Networking Service:* No

Notes

Favorite sites, useful resources

High-Tech Marketing Alliance
http://64.45.51.38/
Location: US
Job Postings: Yes   *Resume Service:* No   *Networking Service:* No

Hong Kong Institute of Marketing
http://www.hkim.org.hk
Location: Asia - Hong Kong
Job Postings: Yes   *Resume Service:* No   *Networking Service:* No

Hospitality Sales & Marketing Association International
http://www.hsmai.org
Location: International
Job Postings: No   *Resume Service:* No   *Networking Service:* No

Imperial Polk Advertising Federation
http://www.polkadfed.com
Location: US
Job Postings: Yes   *Resume Service:* No   *Networking Service:* No

Independent Film & Television Alliance
http://www.ifta-online.org
Location: US
Job Postings: No   *Resume Service:* No   *Networking Service:* No

Independent Medical Distributors Association
http://www.imda.org
Location: US
Job Postings: No   *Resume Service:* No   *Networking Service:* No

Information Technology Services Marketing Association
http://www.itsma.com
Location: US
Job Postings: No   *Resume Service:* No   *Networking Service:* No

Institute for Public Relations
http://www.instituteforpr.com
Location: US
Job Postings: No   *Resume Service:* No   *Networking Service:* No

International Advertising Association
http://www.iaaglobal.org
Location: International
Job Postings: Yes   *Resume Service:* No   *Networking Service:* No

International Customer Service Association
http://www.icsa.com
Location: International
Job Postings: Yes   *Resume Service:* Yes   *Networking Service:* No

Notes

Favorite sites, useful resources

International Newspaper Marketing Association
http://www.inma.org
Location: International
Job Postings: Yes   *Resume Service:* No   *Networking Service:* No

Internet Advertising Bureau
http://www.itsma.com
Location: US
Job Postings: No   *Resume Service:* No   *Networking Service:* No

Internet Marketing and Advertising Association
http://www.imaa.org
Location: US
Job Postings: No   *Resume Service:* No   *Networking Service:* No

Internet Marketing Association
http://www.imanetwork.org
Location: US
Job Postings: No   *Resume Service:* No   *Networking Service:* No

Legal Marketing Association
http://www.legalmarketing.org
Location: US
Job Postings: Yes   *Resume Service:* Yes   *Networking Service:* No

Mail Advertising Service Association
http://www.masa.org
Location: US
Job Postings: No   *Resume Service:* No   *Networking Service:* No

Manufacturers' Agents National Association
http://www.manaonline.org
Location: US
Job Postings: No   *Resume Service:* No   *Networking Service:* No

Marketing Institute of Ireland
http://www.mii.ie
Location: Europe - Ireland
Job Postings: No   *Resume Service:* No   *Networking Service:* No

Marketing Management Association
http://www.mmaglobal.org
Location: US
Job Postings: No   *Resume Service:* No   *Networking Service:* No

Marketing Research Association
http://www.mra-net.org
Location: US
Job Postings: No   *Resume Service:* No   *Networking Service:* No

Notes
Favorite sites, useful resources

Marketing Science Institute
http://www.msi.org
Location: US
Job Postings: Yes   *Resume Service:* No   *Networking Service:* No

National Agri-Marketing Association
http://www.nama.org
Location: US
Job Postings: No   *Resume Service:* No   *Networking Service:* No

National Association for Promotional and Advertising Allowances
http://www.napaa.org
Location: US
Job Postings: No   *Resume Service:* No   *Networking Service:* No

National Association of Commissioned Travel Agents
http://www.nacta.com
Location: US
Job Postings: No   *Resume Service:* No   *Networking Service:* No

National Association of General Merchandise Representatives
http://www.nagmr.org
Location: US
Job Postings: No   *Resume Service:* No   *Networking Service:* No

National Association of Sales Professionals
http://www.nasp.com
Location: US
Job Postings: Yes   *Resume Service:* Yes   *Networking Service:* No

National Association of Wholesalers
http://www.naw.org
Location: US
Job Postings: No   *Resume Service:* No   *Networking Service:* No

National Field Selling Association
http://www.nfsa.com
Location: US
Job Postings: Yes   *Resume Service:* No   *Networking Service:* No

National Mail Order Association
http://www.nmoa.org
Location: US
Job Postings: No   *Resume Service:* No   *Networking Service:* No

National Sports Marketing Network
http://www.sportsmarketingnetwork.com/
Location: US
Job Postings: Yes   *Resume Service:* No   *Networking Service:* No

Notes

Favorite sites, useful resources

Pi Sigma Epsilon
http://www.pisigmaepsilon.org
Location: US
Job Postings: No   *Resume Service:* No   *Networking Service:* No

Point-of-Purchase Advertising Institute
http://www.popai.com
Location: International
Job Postings: No   *Resume Service:* No   *Networking Service:* No

Produce Marketing Association
http://www.pma.com
Location: US
Job Postings: Yes   *Resume Service:* No   *Networking Service:* No

Product Development and Management Association
http://www.pdma.org
Location: US
Job Postings: Yes   *Resume Service:* Yes   *Networking Service:* No

Professional Society for Sales and Marketing Training
http://www.smt.org
Location: US
Job Postings: Yes   *Resume Service:* Yes   *Networking Service:* No

Promotion Marketing Association
http://www.pmalink.org
Location: US
Job Postings: Yes   *Resume Service:* Yes   *Networking Service:* No

Public Relations Society of America
http://www.prsa.org
Location: US
Job Postings: Yes   *Resume Service:* Yes   *Networking Service:* No

Publishers Marketing Association
http://www.pma-online.org
Location: US
Job Postings: No   *Resume Service:* No   *Networking Service:* No

Qualitative Research Consultants Association
http://www.qrca.org
Location: US
Job Postings: Yes   *Resume Service:* No   *Networking Service:* No

Sales & Marketing Executives International
http://www.smei.org
Location: US
Job Postings: Yes   *Resume Service:* No   *Networking Service:* No

Notes
Favorite sites, useful resources

Sales Professionals USA
http://www.salesprofessionals-usa.com
Location: US
Job Postings: No   *Resume Service:* No   *Networking Service:* No

Sales Special Interest Group
http://mkt.cba.cmich.edu
Location: US
Job Postings: Yes   *Resume Service:* No   *Networking Service:* No

Salesup.com
http://www.salesup.com
Location: US
Job Postings: No   *Resume Service:* No   *Networking Service:* No

Society for Consumer Psychology
http://fisher.osu.edu/marketing/scp/
Location: US
Job Postings: No   *Resume Service:* No   *Networking Service:* No

Society for Marketing Advances
http://mkt.cba.cmich.edu/sma/
Location: US
Job Postings: No   *Resume Service:* No   *Networking Service:* No

Society for Marketing Professional Services
http://www.smps.org
Location: US
Job Postings: Yes   *Resume Service:* Yes   *Networking Service:* No

Society of Professional Consultants
http://www.spconsultants.org
Location: US
Job Postings: No   *Resume Service:* No   *Networking Service:* No

Strategic Account Management Association
http://www.nams.org
Location: US
Job Postings: Yes   *Resume Service:* No   *Networking Service:* No

Strategic Management Society
http://www.smsweb.org
Location: US
Job Postings: Yes   *Resume Service:* No   *Networking Service:* No

---

Looking for a new or better job?   Looking for top talent?
Jse WEDDLE's publications. Visit www.weddles.com today.

Notes

Favorite sites, useful resources

The Arthur Page Society
http://www.awpagesociety.com
Location: US
Job Postings: Yes   *Resume Service:* No   *Networking Service:* No

Trade Show Exhibitors Association
http://www.tsea.org
Location: US
Job Postings: No   *Resume Service:* No   *Networking Service:* No

United Professional Sales Association
http://www.upsa.ws
Location: US
Job Postings: No   *Resume Service:* No   *Networking Service:* No

United Professional Sales Association International
http://www.upsa-intl.org
Location: International
Job Postings: Yes   *Resume Service:* No   *Networking Service:* No

The Utility Marketing Association
http://www.umaonline.com
Location: US
Job Postings: Yes   *Resume Service:* No   *Networking Service:* No

World Federation of Direct Selling Associations
http://www.wfdsa.org
Location: US
Job Postings: No   *Resume Service:* No   *Networking Service:* No

Science

Adhesion Society
http://www.adhesionsociety.org
Location: US
Job Postings: No   *Resume Service:* No   *Networking Service:* No

American Academy of Forensic Sciences
http://www.aafs.org
Location: US
Job Postings: Yes   *Resume Service:* No   *Networking Service:* No

American Anthropological Association
http://www.aaanet.org
Location: US
Job Postings: Yes   *Resume Service:* Yes   *Networking Service:* No

Notes

Favorite sites, useful resources

American Association for the Advancement of Science
http://www.aaas.org
Location: US
Job Postings: Yes   *Resume Service:* Yes   *Networking Service:* No

American Association for Artificial Intelligence
http://www.aaai.org
Location: US
Job Postings: No   *Resume Service:* No   *Networking Service:* No

American Association for Clinical Chemistry
http://www.aacc.org/
Location: US
Job Postings: Yes   *Resume Service:* Yes   *Networking Service:* No

American Astronomical Society
http://www.aas.org
Location: US
Job Postings: Yes   *Resume Service:* No   *Networking Service:* No

American Chemical Society
http://www.acs.org
Location: US
Job Postings: Yes   *Resume Service:* Yes   *Networking Service:* No

American Institute of Biological Sciences
http://www.aibs.org
Location: US
Job Postings: Yes   *Resume Service:* No   *Networking Service:* No

American Institute of Chemical Engineers
http://www.aiche.org
Location: US
Job Postings: Yes   *Resume Service:* Yes   *Networking Service:* No

American Institute of Chemists
http://www.theaic.org/
Location: US
Job Postings: No   *Resume Service:* No   *Networking Service:* No

American Institute of Physics
http://www.aip.org
Location: US
Job Postings: Yes   *Resume Service:* Yes   *Networking Service:* No

American Meteor Society
http://www.amsmeteors.org
Location: US
Job Postings: No   *Resume Service:* No   *Networking Service:* No

Notes

Favorite sites, useful resources

American Physical Society
http://www.aps.org
Location: US
Job Postings: Yes   *Resume Service:* Yes   *Networking Service:* Yes

American Society of Agronomy
http://www.agronomy.org
Location: US
Job Postings: No   *Resume Service:* No   *Networking Service:* No

American Society of Animal Science
http://www.asas.org
Location: US
Job Postings: Yes   *Resume Service:* Yes   *Networking Service:* No

American Society for Gravitational and Space Biology
http://asgsb.indstate.edu
Location: US
Job Postings: Yes   *Resume Service:* No   *Networking Service:* No

American Society for Information Science
http://www.asi.org
Location: US
Job Postings: No   *Resume Service:* No   *Networking Service:* No

American Society for Microbiology
http://www.asm.org
Location: US
Job Postings: Yes   *Resume Service:* Yes   *Networking Service:* No

American Society of Plant Physiologists
http://www.aspb.org
Location: US
Job Postings: Yes   *Resume Service:* No   *Networking Service:* No

Analytical and Life Science Systems Association
http://www.alssa.org
Location: US
Job Postings: No   *Resume Service:* No   *Networking Service:* No

Association for Women in Science
http://www.awis.org/
Location: US
Job Postings: Yes   *Resume Service:* No   *Networking Service:* No

Association of American State Geologists
http://www.kgs.ukans.edu/AASG/
Location: US
Job Postings: No   *Resume Service:* No   *Networking Service:* No

Notes
Favorite sites, useful resources

Association of Consulting Chemists and Chemical Engineers
http://www.chemconsult.org
Location: US
Job Postings: No   *Resume Service:* No   *Networking Service:* No

The Association of Formulation Chemists
http://www.afc-us.org
Location: US
Job Postings: No   *Resume Service:* No   *Networking Service:* Yes

Association of Official Analytical Chemists
http://www.aoac.org
Location: US
Job Postings: No   *Resume Service:* No   *Networking Service:* No

Canadian Astronomical Society
http://www.casca.ca
Location: North America - Canada
Job Postings: No   *Resume Service:* No   *Networking Service:* No

Canadian Society of Pharmaceutical Sciences
http://www.ualberta.ca/%7Ecsps/
Location: North America - Canada
Job Postings: Yes   *Resume Service:* No   *Networking Service:* No

Chemical Heritage Association
http://www.chemheritage.org
Location: US
Job Postings: No   *Resume Service:* No   *Networking Service:* No

ChemPharma
http://www.chempharma.org/
Location: US - New Jersey
Job Postings: Yes   *Resume Service:* Yes   *Networking Service:* No

Council for Agricultural Science and Technology
http://www.cast-science.org
Location: US
Job Postings: No   *Resume Service:* No   *Networking Service:* No

Council of Science Editors
http://www.amwa.org
Location: US
Job Postings: Yes   *Resume Service:* No   *Networking Service:* No

DC Science Writers Association
http://www.dcswa.org
Location: US - District of Columbia
Job Postings: Yes   *Resume Service:* No   *Networking Service:* No

Notes

Favorite sites, useful resources

Decision Sciences Institute
http://www.decisionsciences.org
Location: US
Job Postings: Yes   *Resume Service:* No   *Networking Service:* No

Division of Organic Chemistry
http://www.organicdivision.org
Location: US
Job Postings: No   *Resume Service:* No   *Networking Service:* No

Electrochemical Society
http://www.electrochem.org
Location: US
Job Postings: Yes   *Resume Service:* No   *Networking Service:* No

Energy Science and Technology Software Center
http://www.osti.gov/estsc
Location: US
Job Postings: No   *Resume Service:* No   *Networking Service:* No

European Association for Astronomy Education
http://www.algonet.se/~sirius/eaae.htm
Location: Europe
Job Postings: No   *Resume Service:* No   *Networking Service:* No

Federation of American Scientists
http://www.fas.org/main/home.jsp
Location: US
Job Postings: No   *Resume Service:* No   *Networking Service:* No

Federation of American Societies for Experimental Biology
http://www.faseb.org
Location: US
Job Postings: Yes   *Resume Service:* No   *Networking Service:* No

Geochemical Society
http://gs.wustl.edu
Location: US
Job Postings: No   *Resume Service:* No   *Networking Service:* No

Institute of Food Science & Technology
http://www.ifst.org
Location: US
Job Postings: Yes   *Resume Service:* No   *Networking Service:* No

International Society for Genetic and Evolutionary Computation
http://www.isgec.org
Location: US
Job Postings: No   *Resume Service:* No   *Networking Service:* No

Notes

Favorite sites, useful resources

International Society of Heterocyclic Chemistry
http://euch6f.chem.emory.edu/ishc.html
Location: US
Job Postings: No   *Resume Service:* No   *Networking Service:* No

International Union of Pure and Applied Chemistry
http://www.iupac.org
Location: US
Job Postings: No   *Resume Service:* No   *Networking Service:* No

The Manufacturing, Science and Finance Union
http://www.amicustheunion.org
Location: Europe - UK
Job Postings: Yes   *Resume Service:* No   *Networking Service:* No

National Academy of Sciences
http://www.nationalacademies.org
Location: US
Job Postings: No   *Resume Service:* No   *Networking Service:* No

National Association of Biology Teachers
http://www.nabt.org
Location: US
Job Postings: No   *Resume Service:* No   *Networking Service:* No

National Association of Science Writers
http://www.nasw.org
Location: US
Job Postings: No   *Resume Service:* No   *Networking Service:* No

National Science Teachers Association
http://www.nsta.org/
Location: US
Job Postings: Yes   *Resume Service:* Yes   *Networking Service:* No

The Oxygen Society
http://www.oxygensociety.org
Location: US
Job Postings: No   *Resume Service:* No   *Networking Service:* No

The Planetary Society
http://planetary.org
Location: US
Job Postings: No   *Resume Service:* No   *Networking Service:* No

Society for College Science Teachers
http://www.scst.suu.edu/
Location: US
Job Postings: No   *Resume Service:* No   *Networking Service:* No

Notes

Favorite sites, useful resources

Society for Economic Botany
http://www.econbot.org/
Location: US
Job Postings: No   *Resume Service:* No   *Networking Service:* No

Society of Economic Geologists
http://www.segweb.org/
Location: US
Job Postings: No   *Resume Service:* No   *Networking Service:* No

Society for Experimental Biology and Medicine
http://www.sebm.org
Location: US
Job Postings: No   *Resume Service:* No   *Networking Service:* No

Students for the Exploration and Development of Space
http://www.seds.org
Location: US
Job Postings: No   *Resume Service:* No   *Networking Service:* No

University Research Magazine Association
http://www.urma.org
Location: US
Job Postings: No   *Resume Service:* No   *Networking Service:* Yes

Washington Biotechnology Biomedical Association
http://www.wabio.com
Location: US - Washington
Job Postings: No   *Resume Service:* No   *Networking Service:* No

Social Service/Individual & Community

Academy of Counseling Psychology
http://www.aacop.net
Location: US
Job Postings: No   *Resume Service:* No   *Networking Service:* No

American Academy of Child and Adolescent Psychiatry
http://www.aacap.org
Location: US
Job Postings: Yes   *Resume Service:* Yes   *Networking Service:* No

American Academy of Experts in Traumatic Stress
http://www.aaets.org
Location: US
Job Postings: No   *Resume Service:* No   *Networking Service:* No

Notes

Favorite sites, useful resources

American Academy of Psychotherapists
http://www.aapweb.com
Location: US
Job Postings: No   *Resume Service:* No   *Networking Service:* No

American Association of Anger Management Providers
http://www.angermanagementproviders.com
Location: US
Job Postings: No   *Resume Service:* No   *Networking Service:* No

American Association of Family and Consumer Sciences
http://www.aafcs.org
Location: US
Job Postings: Yes   *Resume Service:* Yes   *Networking Service:* No

American Association for Geriatric Psychiatry
http://www.aagpgpa.org
Location: US
Job Postings: Yes   *Resume Service:* No   *Networking Service:* No

American Association for Marriage and Family Therapy
http://www.aamft.org/index_nm.asp
Location: US
Job Postings: Yes   *Resume Service:* Yes   *Networking Service:* No

American Association of Professional Hypnotherapists
http://aaph.org
Location: US
Job Postings: No   *Resume Service:* No   *Networking Service:* No

American Association of Psychotherapists
http://www.angelfire.com/realm2/hypnosis
Location: US
Job Postings: No   *Resume Service:* No   *Networking Service:* No

American Board of Examiners in Clinical Social Work
http://www.abecsw.org
Location: US
Job Postings: Yes   *Resume Service:* No   *Networking Service:* No

American College of Mental Health Administration
http://www.acmha.org
Location: US
Job Postings: No   *Resume Service:* No   *Networking Service:* No

American Counseling Association
www.counseling.org//AM//Template.cfm?Section=Home
Location: US
Job Postings: Yes   *Resume Service:* Yes   *Networking Service:* No

Notes
Favorite sites, useful resources

American Hypnosis Association
http://www.hypnosis.edu/aha
Location: US
Job Postings: No   *Resume Service:* No   *Networking Service:* No

American Mental Health Counselor Association
http://www.amhca.org
Location: US
Job Postings: No   *Resume Service:* No   *Networking Service:* No

American Orthopsychiatric Association
http://www.amerortho.org
Location: US
Job Postings: No   *Resume Service:* No   *Networking Service:* No

American Planning Association
http://www.planning.org
Location: US
Job Postings: Yes   *Resume Service:* Yes   *Networking Service:* No

American Psychiatric Association
http://www.psych.org
Location: US
Job Postings: Yes   *Resume Service:* No   *Networking Service:* No

American Psychotherapy Association
http://www.americanpsychotherapy.com/index.php
Location: US
Job Postings: No   *Resume Service:* No   *Networking Service:* No

American Psychotherapy and Medical Hypnosis Association
http://apmha.com
Location: US
Job Postings: No   *Resume Service:* No   *Networking Service:* No

American Society of Clinical Hypnosis
http://www.asch.net
Location: US
Job Postings: No   *Resume Service:* No   *Networking Service:* No

American Society of Criminology
http://www.asc41.com
Location: US
Job Postings: Yes   *Resume Service:* No   *Networking Service:* No

American Society for Public Administration (ASPA)
http://www.aspanet.org/scriptcontent/index.cfm
Location: US
Job Postings: Yes   *Resume Service:* Yes   *Networking Service:* No

Notes

Favorite sites, useful resources

American Sociological Association
http://www.asanet.org
Location: US
Job Postings: Yes   *Resume Service:* Yes   *Networking Service:* No

Anabaptist Sociology and Anthropology Association
www.hillsdale.edu/AcademicAssociations/Sociology/a
Location: US
Job Postings: No   *Resume Service:* No   *Networking Service:* No

Association for Applied and Therapeutic Humor
http://aath.org
Location: US
Job Postings: No   *Resume Service:* No   *Networking Service:* No

Association for Behavioral Analysis
http://www.abainternational.org
Location: US
Job Postings: Yes   *Resume Service:* Yes   *Networking Service:* No

Association for Birth Psychology
http://birthpsychology.org/index.html
Location: US
Job Postings: No   *Resume Service:* No   *Networking Service:* No

Association of Black Sociologists
http://www.blacksociologists.org
Location: US
Job Postings: No   *Resume Service:* No   *Networking Service:* Yes

Association for Direct Instruction
http://www.adihome.org/phpshop/bin/
Location: US
Job Postings: No   *Resume Service:* No   *Networking Service:* No

Association of Ethical and Professional Hypnotherapists
http://www.hypnotherapy-training.info/aeph.htm
Location: US
Job Postings: No   *Resume Service:* No   *Networking Service:* No

Association of Mormon Counselors and Psychotherapists
http://www.amcap.net
Location: US
Job Postings: No   *Resume Service:* No   *Networking Service:* No

Association of Qualified Curative Hypnotherapists
http://www.aqch.org
Location: US
Job Postings: No   *Resume Service:* No   *Networking Service:* No

Notes
Favorite sites, useful resources

Association of VA Psychologist Leaders
http://www.avapl.org/
Location: US
Job Postings: No   *Resume Service:* No   *Networking Service:* No

Behaviorists for Social Responsibility
http://www.bfsr.org
Location: US
Job Postings: No   *Resume Service:* No   *Networking Service:* No

Center for Social Services Research
http://cssr.berkeley.edu
Location: US
Job Postings: Yes   *Resume Service:* No   *Networking Service:* No

Christian Brothers Services
http://www.cbservices.org
Location: US
Job Postings: No   *Resume Service:* No   *Networking Service:* No

Cognitive Neuroscience Society
http://www.cogneurosociety.org
Location: US
Job Postings: No   *Resume Service:* No   *Networking Service:* No

Cognitive Science Society
http://www.cognitivesciencesociety.org
Location: US
Job Postings: Yes   *Resume Service:* No   *Networking Service:* No

Council for Children with Behavioral Disorders
http://www.ccbd.net
Location: US
Job Postings: No   *Resume Service:* No   *Networking Service:* No

Division 42 online: Psychologists in Independent Practice
http://www.division42.org
Location: US
Job Postings: No   *Resume Service:* No   *Networking Service:* No

EMDR International Association
http://www.emdria.org
Location: International
Job Postings: No   *Resume Service:* No   *Networking Service:* No

Georgia Department of Human Resources
http://www.dhrjobs.com
Location: US - Georgia
Job Postings: Yes   *Resume Service:* No   *Networking Service:* No

Notes

Favorite sites, useful resources

International Association of Anxiety Management
http://www.anxman.org
Location: International
Job Postings: No   *Resume Service:* No   *Networking Service:* No

International Association of Eating Disorders Professionals
http://www.iaedp.com
Location: International
Job Postings: Yes   *Resume Service:* Yes   *Networking Service:* No

International Association for Regression Research and Therapies, Inc
http://www.iarrt.org
Location: International
Job Postings: No   *Resume Service:* No   *Networking Service:* No

International Medical and Dental Hypnotherapy Association
http://www.infinityinst.com/imdha_about.html
Location: International
Job Postings: No   *Resume Service:* No   *Networking Service:* No

The International Network on Personal Relationships
http://www.inpr.org
Location: US
Job Postings: No   *Resume Service:* No   *Networking Service:* No

The International Society for Behaviorology
http://ww2.lafayette.edu/~allanr/behavior.html
Location: US
Job Postings: No   *Resume Service:* No   *Networking Service:* No

National Association of Alcoholism and Drug Abuse Counselors
http://www.naadac.org
Location: US
Job Postings: Yes   *Resume Service:* No   *Networking Service:* No

National Association of Cognitive-Behavioral Therapists
http://www.nacbt.org
Location: US
Job Postings: No   *Resume Service:* No   *Networking Service:* No

National Association of Social Workers
http://www.naswdc.org
Location: US
Job Postings: Yes   *Resume Service:* No   *Networking Service:* No

National Board for Certified Clinical Hypnotherapists, Inc
http://www.natboard.com
Location: US
Job Postings: No   *Resume Service:* No   *Networking Service:* No

Notes

Favorite sites, useful resources

National Career Development Association
http://www.ncda.org
Location: US
Job Postings: No   *Resume Service:* No   *Networking Service:* No

National Guild of Hypnotists, Inc
http://www.ngh.net
Location: US
Job Postings: No   *Resume Service:* No   *Networking Service:* No

North American Association of Christian Social Workers
http://www.nacsw.org
Location: US
Job Postings: Yes   *Resume Service:* Yes   *Networking Service:* No

Planners Network
http://www.plannersnetwork.org/pnetwork/www/
Location: US
Job Postings: Yes   *Resume Service:* No   *Networking Service:* No

Society for Advancement of Behavior Analysis
http://www.abainternational.org/saba/
Location: US
Job Postings: No   *Resume Service:* No   *Networking Service:* No

Society for Applied Sociology
http://www.appliedsoc.org
Location: US
Job Postings: Yes   *Resume Service:* No   *Networking Service:* No

Society for Quantitative Analyses of Behavior
http://sqab.psychology.org
Location: US
Job Postings: No   *Resume Service:* No   *Networking Service:* No

The Society for the Scientific Study of Sexuality
http://www.sexscience.org
Location: US
Job Postings: Yes   *Resume Service:* No   *Networking Service:* No

Society for Social Work and Research
http://www.sswr.org
Location: US
Job Postings: Yes   *Resume Service:* No   *Networking Service:* No

Standard Celeration Society
http://www.celeration.org
Location: US
Job Postings: No   *Resume Service:* No   *Networking Service:* No

Notes

Favorite sites, useful resources

The Therapeutic Milieu
http://www.therapeuticmilieu.org
Location: US
Job Postings: No   *Resume Service:* No   *Networking Service:* No

United States Association for Body Psychotherapy
http://www.usabp.org
Location: US
Job Postings: Yes   *Resume Service:* No   *Networking Service:* No

World Association for Sexology
http://www.tc.umn.edu/~colem001/was/wasindex.htm
Location: International
Job Postings: No   *Resume Service:* No   *Networking Service:* No

Sports/Recreation

Black Entertainment & Sports Lawyers Association
http://www.besla.org
Location: US
Job Postings: No   *Resume Service:* No   *Networking Service:* No

Golf Course Builders Association of America
http://www.gcbaa.org
Location: US
Job Postings: No   *Resume Service:* No   *Networking Service:* No

Golf Course Superintendents Association of America
http://www.gcsaa.org
Location: US
Job Postings: Yes   *Resume Service:* No   *Networking Service:* No

International Coach Federation
http://www.coachfederation.org
Location: International
Job Postings: No   *Resume Service:* No   *Networking Service:* No

International Fitness Association
http://www.ifafitness.com
Location: International
Job Postings: No   *Resume Service:* No   *Networking Service:* No

International Health, Racquet & Sportsclub Association
http://www.ihrsa.org
Location: International
Job Postings: No   *Resume Service:* No   *Networking Service:* No

Notes

Favorite sites, useful resources

National Athletic Trainers' Association
http://www.nata.org
Location: US
Job Postings: Yes   *Resume Service:* No   *Networking Service:* No

The National Bicycle Dealers Association
http://www.nbda.com
Location: US
Job Postings: No   *Resume Service:* No   *Networking Service:* No

National Recreation and Park Association
http://www.nrpa.org
Location: US
Job Postings: No   *Resume Service:* No   *Networking Service:* No

National Sports Marketing Network
http://www.sportsmarketingnetwork.com/
Location: US
Job Postings: Yes   *Resume Service:* No   *Networking Service:* No

Outdoor Advertising Association of America
http://www.oaaa.org
Location: US
Job Postings: No   *Resume Service:* No   *Networking Service:* No

Professional Golf Teachers Association of America
http://www.pgtaa.com
Location: US
Job Postings: No   *Resume Service:* No   *Networking Service:* No

Statistics/Mathematics

American Mathematical Society
http://www.ams.org
Location: US
Job Postings: No   *Resume Service:* No   *Networking Service:* No

American Statistical Association
http://www.amstat.org
Location: US
Job Postings: Yes   *Resume Service:* No   *Networking Service:* No

Society for Industrial and Applied Mathematics
http://www.siam.org
Location: US
Job Postings: Yes   *Resume Service:* No   *Networking Service:* No

Notes

Favorite sites, useful resources

-T-

Telecommunications

Association for Educational Communications and Technology
http://www.aect.org
Location: US
Job Postings: Yes   *Resume Service:* No   *Networking Service:* No

Association for Local Telecommunications Services
http://www.alts.org
Location: US
Job Postings: No   *Resume Service:* No   *Networking Service:* No

Competitive Telecommunications Association
http://www.comptel.org
Location: US
Job Postings: No   *Resume Service:* No   *Networking Service:* No

Computer and Communications Industry Associations
http://www.ccianet.org
Location: US
Job Postings: No   *Resume Service:* No   *Networking Service:* No

Computer Science and Telecommunications Board
http://www.nationalacademies.org/cstb/
Location: US
Job Postings: No   *Resume Service:* No   *Networking Service:* No

European Competitive Telecommunications Association
http://www.ectaweb.org
Location: Europe
Job Postings: No   *Resume Service:* No   *Networking Service:* No

Information Technology & Telecommunications Association
http://www.tca.org
Location: US
Job Postings: No   *Resume Service:* No   *Networking Service:* No

International Communications Association
http://icanet.com
Location: International
Job Postings: No   *Resume Service:* No   *Networking Service:* No

Multi-Media Telecommunications Association
http://www.mmta.org
Location: US
Job Postings: No   *Resume Service:* No   *Networking Service:* No

Notes
Favorite sites, useful resources

The National Association of Black Telecommunications Professionals
http://www.nabtp.org
Location: US
Job Postings: No   *Resume Service:* No   *Networking Service:* No

The National Association of Radio and Telecommunications Engineers
http://www.narte.org
Location: US
Job Postings: Yes   *Resume Service:* No   *Networking Service:* No

National Association of Telecommunications Officers and Advisors
http://www.natoa.org
Location: US
Job Postings: No   *Resume Service:* No   *Networking Service:* No

Telecommunications and Technology Professionals Serving State Government
http://www.nastd.org
Location: US
Job Postings: No   *Resume Service:* No   *Networking Service:* No

United States Telephone Association
http://www.usta.org
Location: US
Job Postings: No   *Resume Service:* No   *Networking Service:* No

Women in Cable & Telecommunications
http://www.wict.org
Location: US
Job Postings: No   *Resume Service:* No   *Networking Service:* No

Trade Organizations

American Society of Association Executives
http://www.asaenet.org
Location: US
Job Postings: Yes   *Resume Service:* Yes   *Networking Service:* No

Federation of International Trade Associations
http://www.fita.org
Location: US
Job Postings: No   *Resume Service:* No   *Networking Service:* No

International Association of Association Management Companies
http://www.iaamc.org
Location: International
Job Postings: No   *Resume Service:* No   *Networking Service:* No

Notes
Favorite sites, useful resources

Training

American Society for Training & Development
http://www.astd.org
Location: US
Job Postings: Yes   *Resume Service:* Yes   *Networking Service:* Yes

American Training & Seminar Association
http://www.AmericanTSA.com
Location: US
Job Postings: No   *Resume Service:* No   *Networking Service:* No

Association of Macintosh Trainers
http://www.mactrainers.com
Location: US
Job Postings: No   *Resume Service:* No   *Networking Service:* No

Chicagoland Chapter American Society of Training and Development
http://www.ccastd.org
Location: US - Illinois
Job Postings: Yes   *Resume Service:* No   *Networking Service:* No

Council for Advancement & Support of Education
http://www.case.org
Location: US
Job Postings: Yes   *Resume Service:* No   *Networking Service:* No

National Association of Gender Diversity Training
http://www.gendertraining.com
Location: US
Job Postings: No   *Resume Service:* No   *Networking Service:* No

Professional Society for Sales and Marketing Training
http://www.smt.org
Location: US
Job Postings: Yes   *Resume Service:* Yes   *Networking Service:* No

Transportation/Commercial & Public

Advanced Transit Association
http://www.advancedtransit.org/news.aspx
Location: US
Job Postings: No   *Resume Service:* No   *Networking Service:* No

Air Transport Association
http://www.air-transport.org
Location: US
Job Postings: No   *Resume Service:* No   *Networking Service:* No

Notes
Favorite sites, useful resources

American Association of Port Authorities
http://www.aapa-ports.org
Location: US
Job Postings: Yes   *Resume Service:* No   *Networking Service:* No

American Association of State Highway and Transportation Officials
http://www.aashto.org
Location: US
Job Postings: Yes   *Resume Service:* No   *Networking Service:* No

American Public Transportation Association
http://www.apta.com
Location: US
Job Postings: Yes   *Resume Service:* No   *Networking Service:* No

American Society of Transportation and Logistics
http://www.astl.org
Location: US
Job Postings: Yes   *Resume Service:* No   *Networking Service:* No

American Trucking Association
http://www.truckline.com
Location: US
Job Postings: Yes   *Resume Service:* Yes   *Networking Service:* No

Brotherhood of Locomotive Engineers and Trainmen
http://www.ble.org
Location: US
Job Postings: Yes   *Resume Service:* No   *Networking Service:* No

Brotherhood of Maintenance of Way Employees
http://www.bmwe.org/index.htm
Location: US
Job Postings: No   *Resume Service:* No   *Networking Service:* No

Community Transportation Association of America
http://www.ctaa.org
Location: US
Job Postings: Yes   *Resume Service:* No   *Networking Service:* No

Helicopter Association International
http://www.rotor.com
Location: US
Job Postings: No   *Resume Service:* No   *Networking Service:* No

International Council of Aircraft Owner and Pilot Associations
http://www.iaopa.org
Location: International
Job Postings: No   *Resume Service:* No   *Networking Service:* No

Notes

Favorite sites, useful resources

International Transportation Safety Administration
http://www.itsasafety.org/ITSA/
Location: International
Job Postings: No   *Resume Service:* No   *Networking Service:* No

Light Rail Transit Association
http://www.lrta.org
Location: US
Job Postings: Yes   *Resume Service:* No   *Networking Service:* No

The Motor Bus Society
http://www.motorbussociety.org
Location: US
Job Postings: No   *Resume Service:* No   *Networking Service:* No

National Air Traffic Controllers Association
http://www.natca.org
Location: US
Job Postings: No   *Resume Service:* No   *Networking Service:* No

National Air Transportation Association
http://www.nata-online.org
Location: US
Job Postings: No   *Resume Service:* No   *Networking Service:* No

National Association of Air Traffic Specialists
http://www.naats.org
Location: US
Job Postings: No   *Resume Service:* No   *Networking Service:* No

Society of Automotive Engineers
http://www.sae.org
Location: US
Job Postings: Yes   *Resume Service:* Yes   *Networking Service:* No

Transport Workers Union of America
http://www.twu.org
Location: US
Job Postings: No   *Resume Service:* No   *Networking Service:* No

United Transportation Union
http://www.utu.org
Location: US
Job Postings: No   *Resume Service:* No   *Networking Service:* No

---

Looking for a new or better job?   Looking for top talent?

se WEDDLE's publications. Visit www.weddles.com today.

Notes

Favorite sites, useful resources

Travel

American Society of Travel Agents
http://www.astanet.com
Location: US
Job Postings: No   *Resume Service:* No   *Networking Service:* No

Association of British Travel Agents
http://www.abtanet.com
Location: Europe - UK
Job Postings: No   *Resume Service:* No   *Networking Service:* No

Association of Corporate Travel Executives
http://www.acte.org
Location: US
Job Postings: No   *Resume Service:* No   *Networking Service:* No

International Association of Air Travel Couriers
http://www.courier.org
Location: US
Job Postings: No   *Resume Service:* No   *Networking Service:* No

International Association of Conventions and Visitors Bureaus
http://www.iacvb.org
Location: International
Job Postings: Yes   *Resume Service:* No   *Networking Service:* No

National Association for Independent Contractors in Travel
http://www.ossn.com
Location: US
Job Postings: No   *Resume Service:* No   *Networking Service:* No

National Association of Commissioned Travel Agents
http://www.nacta.com
Location: US
Job Postings: No   *Resume Service:* No   *Networking Service:* No

National Business Travel Association
http://www.nbta.org
Location: US
Job Postings: Yes   *Resume Service:* No   *Networking Service:* No

Notes
Favorite sites, useful resources

Looking for a new or better job?   Looking for top talent?
Use WEDDLE's publications.
Visit www.weddles.com today.

- *WEDDLE's 2005/6 Guide* **is the "consumer's report" of job boards.**

We've selected 350 of the best job boards and career portals across a broad array of career fields and industries. These sites are then described with a full page of information about their features, services and fees so that you can "comparison shop" them to find the best sites for you.

- *WEDDLE's 2005/6 Directory* **is the "address book" of job boards.**

We list over 8,000 job boards and career portals and organize them by the career field, industry and/or location on which they focus. Each site is listed by its name and address on the Internet so that you can identify and visit the sites that are most likely to work for you.